# THE KING'S Beast

1

## STORY & ART BY

## Rei Toma

# THE KING'S *Beast*

## 1

## CONTENTS

# Chapter 1

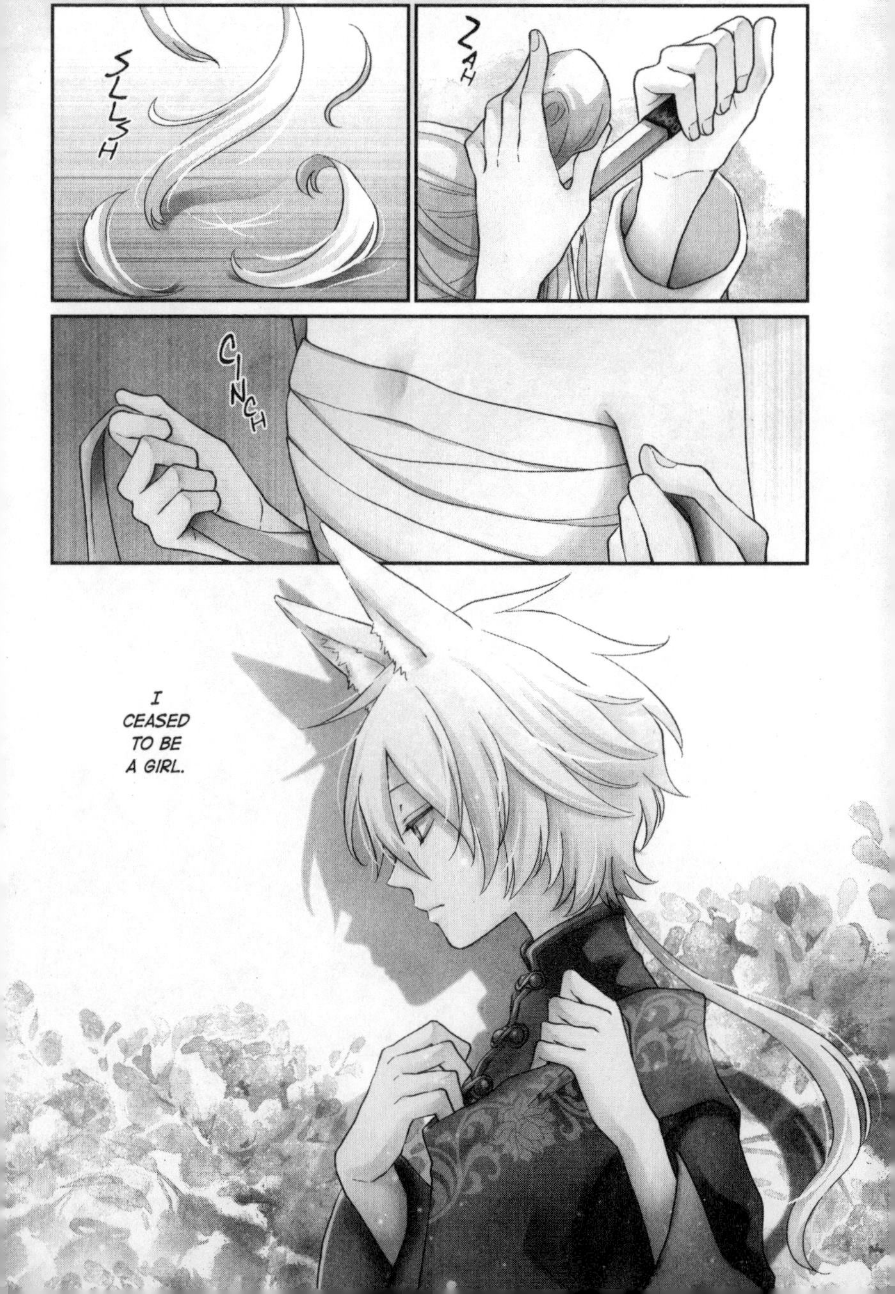
ZAH
SLLSH
CINCH
I CEASED TO BE A GIRL.

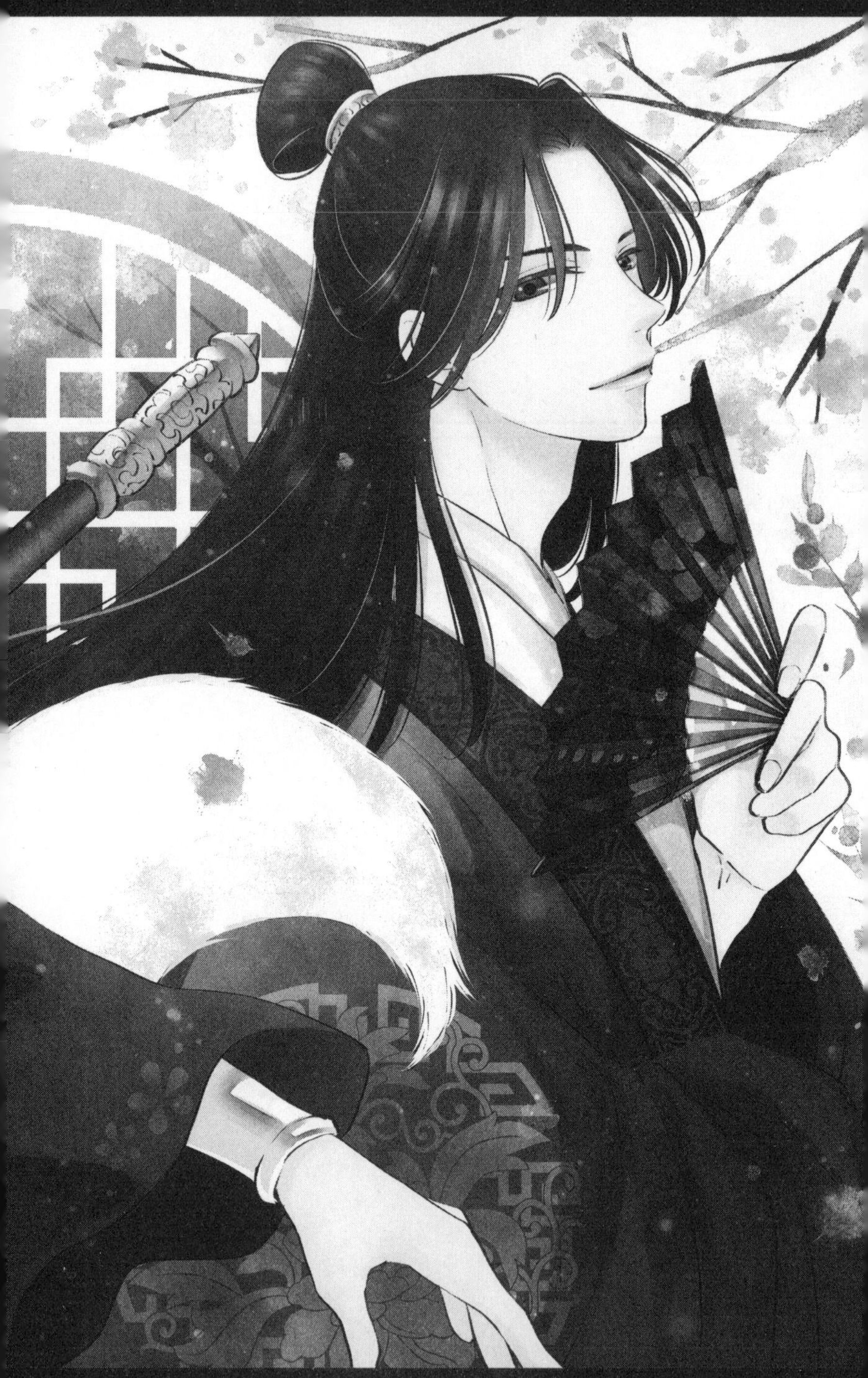

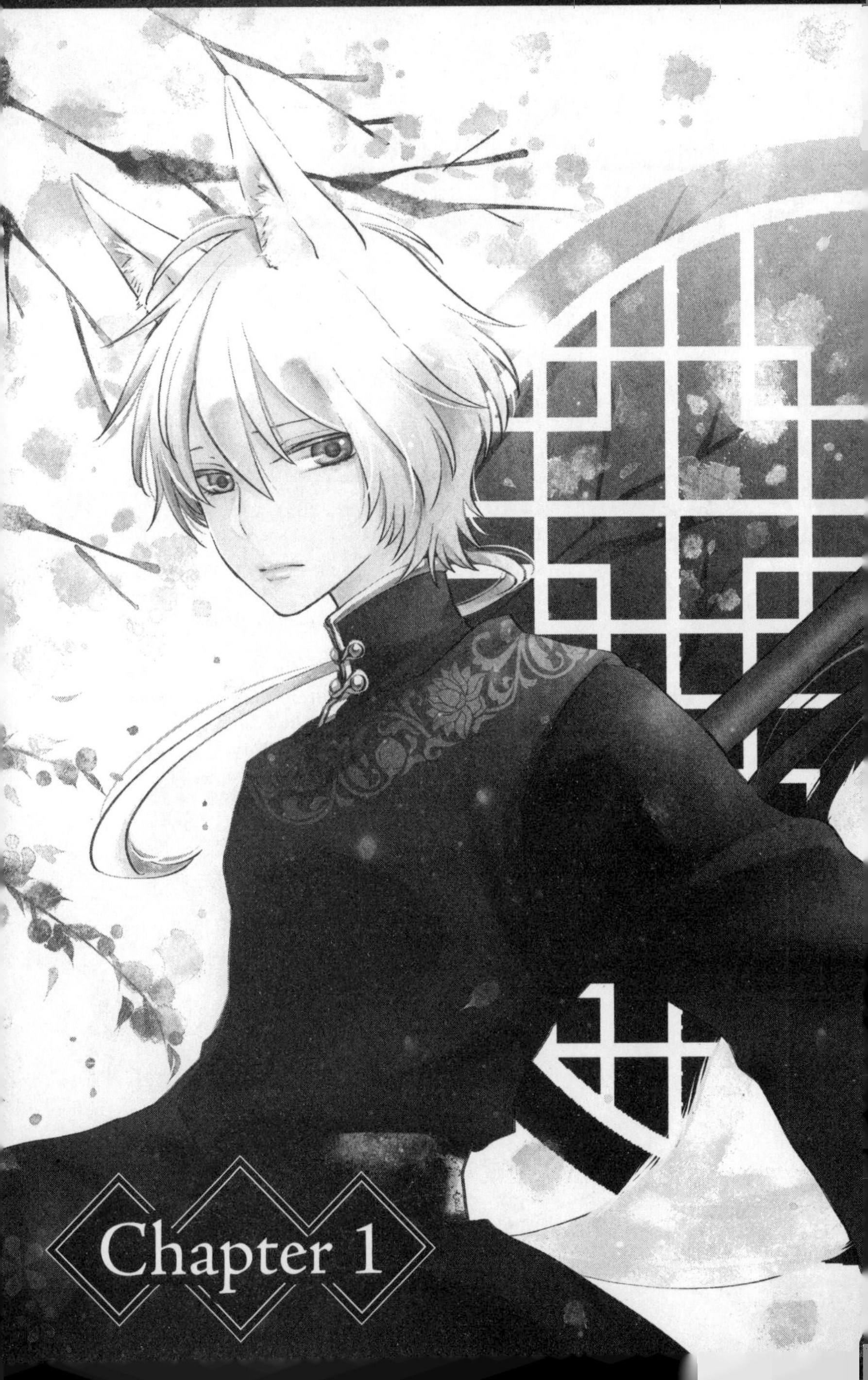

# Chapter 1

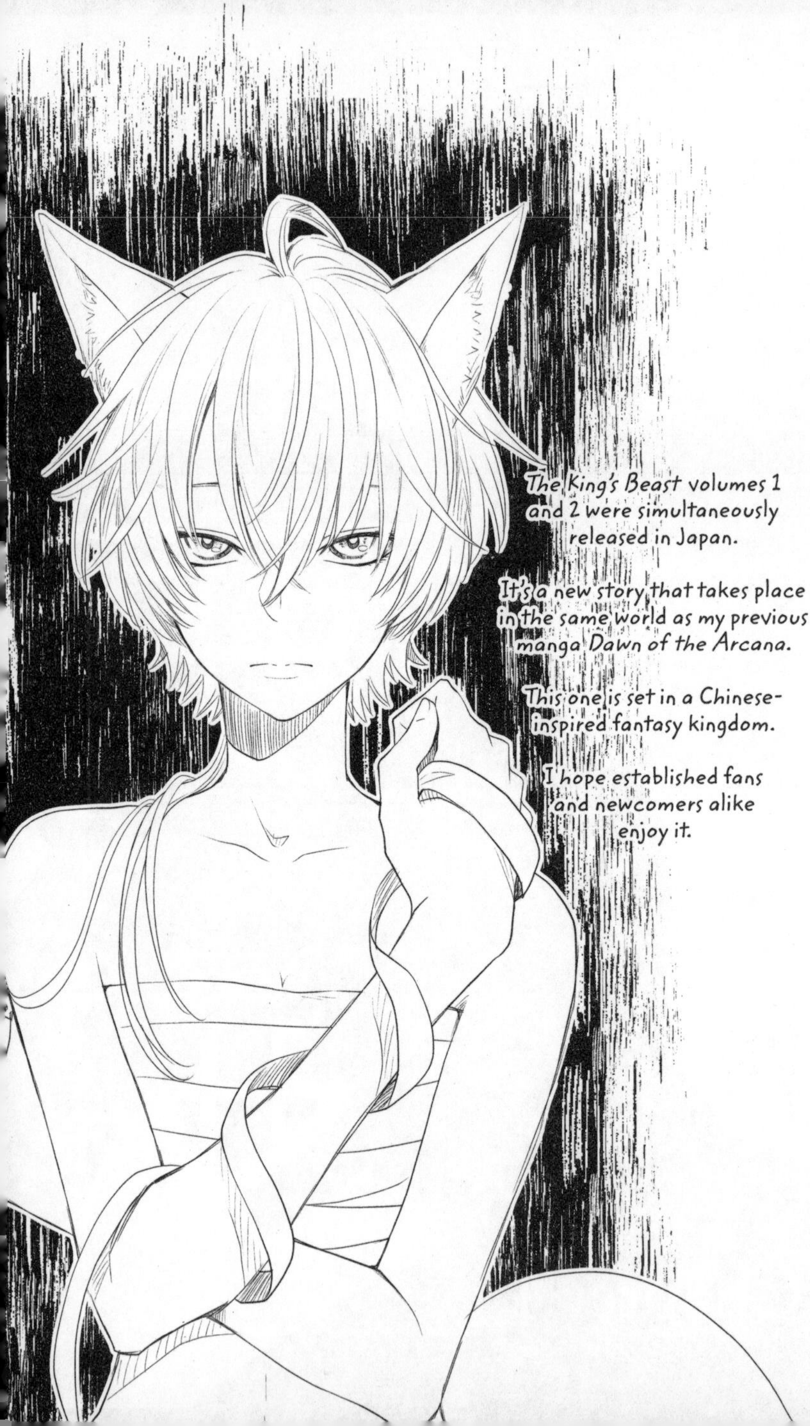
*The King's Beast* volumes 1 and 2 were simultaneously released in Japan.
It's a new story that takes place in the same world as my previous manga *Dawn of the Arcana*.
This one is set in a Chinese-inspired fantasy kingdom.
I hope established fans and newcomers alike enjoy it.

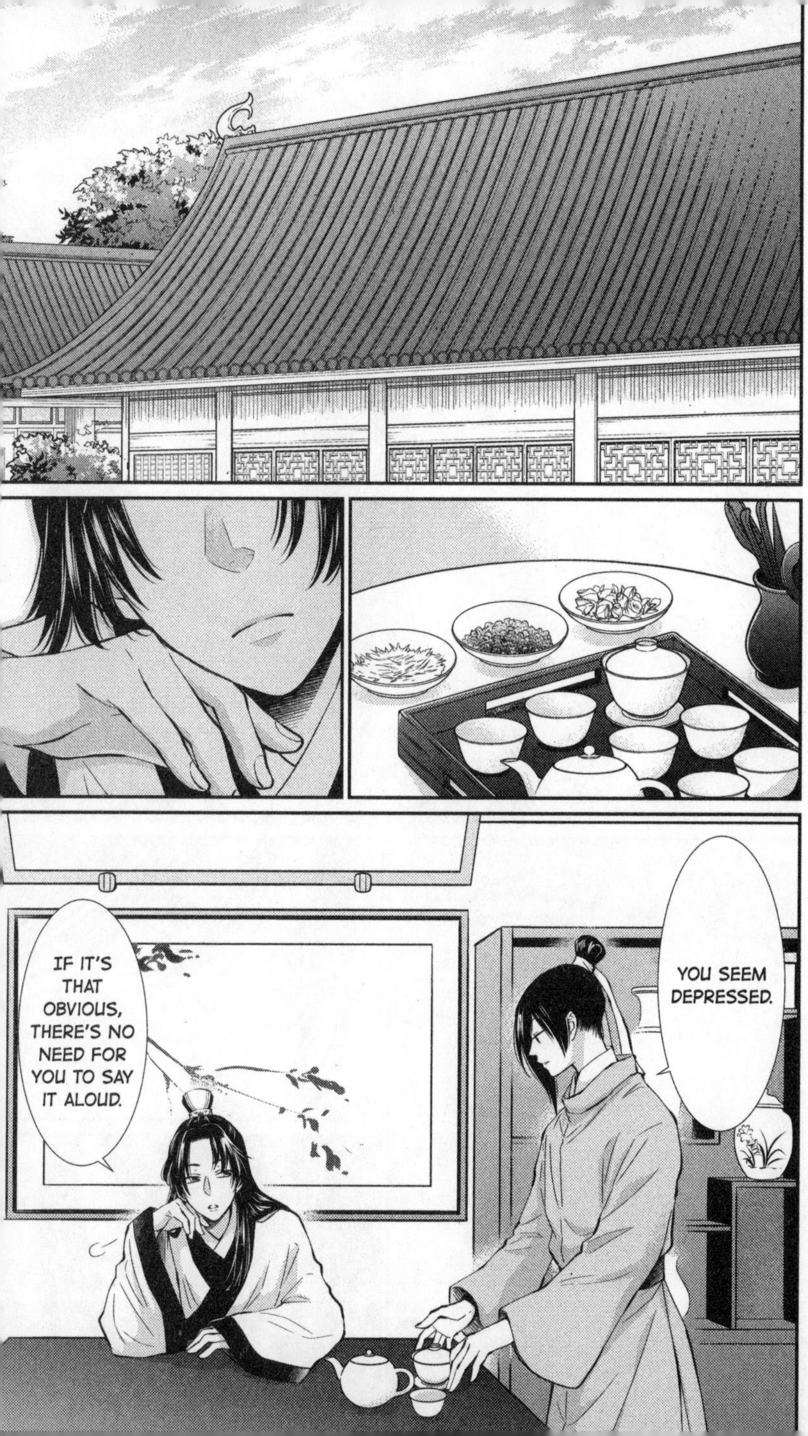
YOU SEEM DEPRESSED.
IF IT'S THAT OBVIOUS, THERE'S NO NEED FOR YOU TO SAY IT ALOUD.

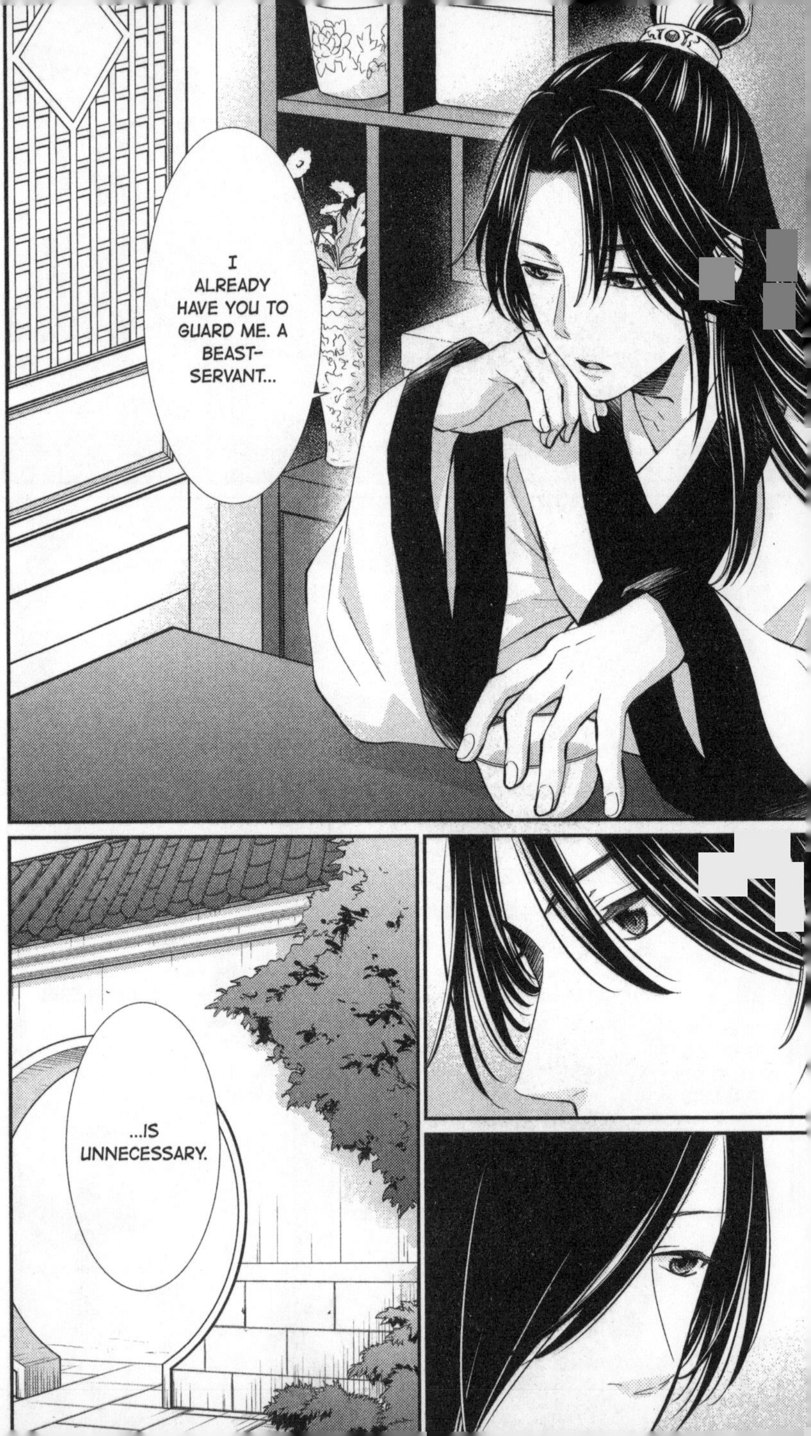
I ALREADY HAVE YOU TO GUARD ME. A BEAST-SERVANT...
...IS UNNECESSARY.

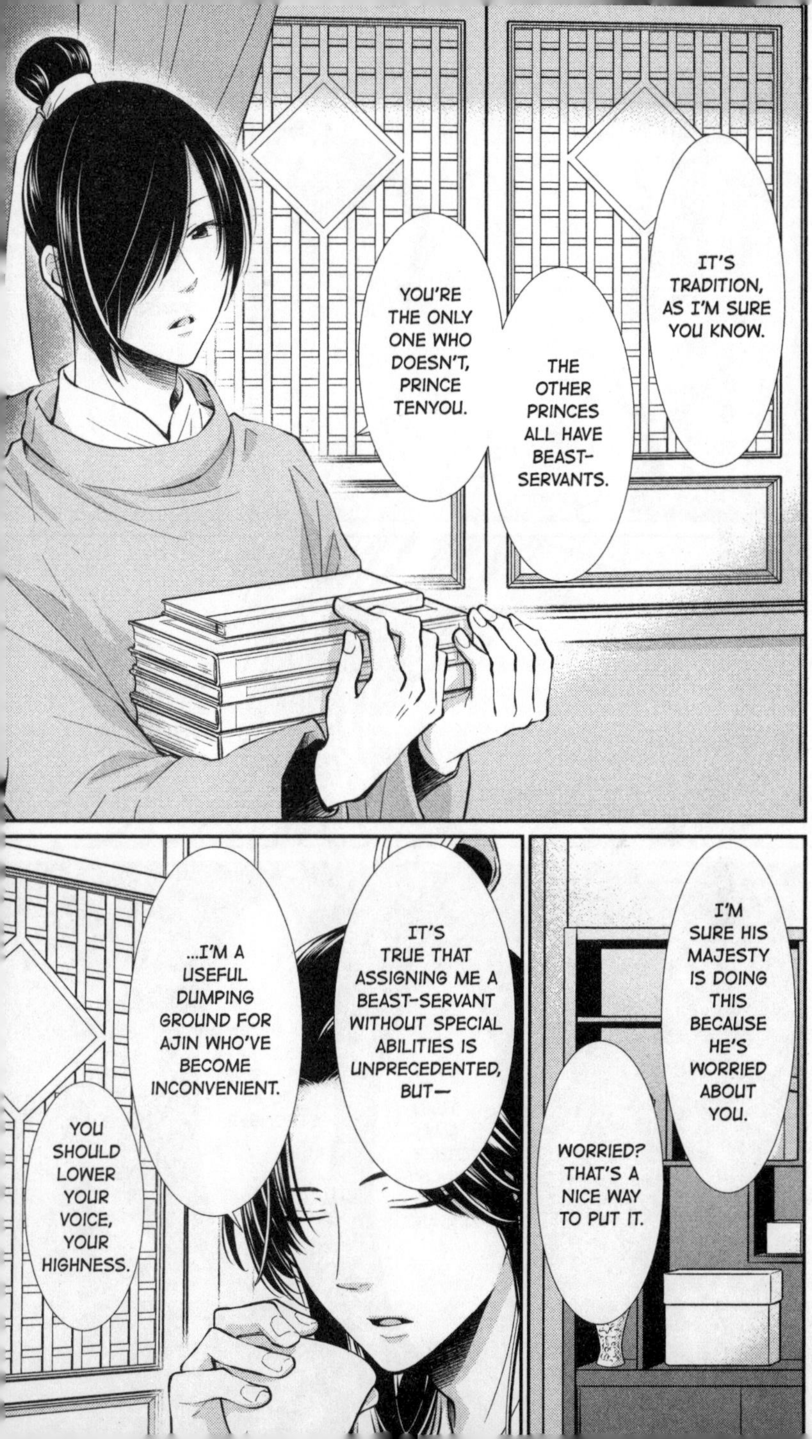
IT'S TRADITION, AS I'M SURE YOU KNOW.
THE OTHER PRINCES ALL HAVE BEAST-SERVANTS.
YOU'RE THE ONLY ONE WHO DOESN'T, PRINCE TENYOU.
I'M SURE HIS MAJESTY IS DOING THIS BECAUSE HE'S WORRIED ABOUT YOU.
WORRIED? THAT'S A NICE WAY TO PUT IT.
IT'S TRUE THAT ASSIGNING ME A BEAST-SERVANT WITHOUT SPECIAL ABILITIES IS UNPRECEDENTED, BUT—
...I'M A USEFUL DUMPING GROUND FOR AJIN WHO'VE BECOME INCONVENIENT.
YOU SHOULD LOWER YOUR VOICE, YOUR HIGHNESS.

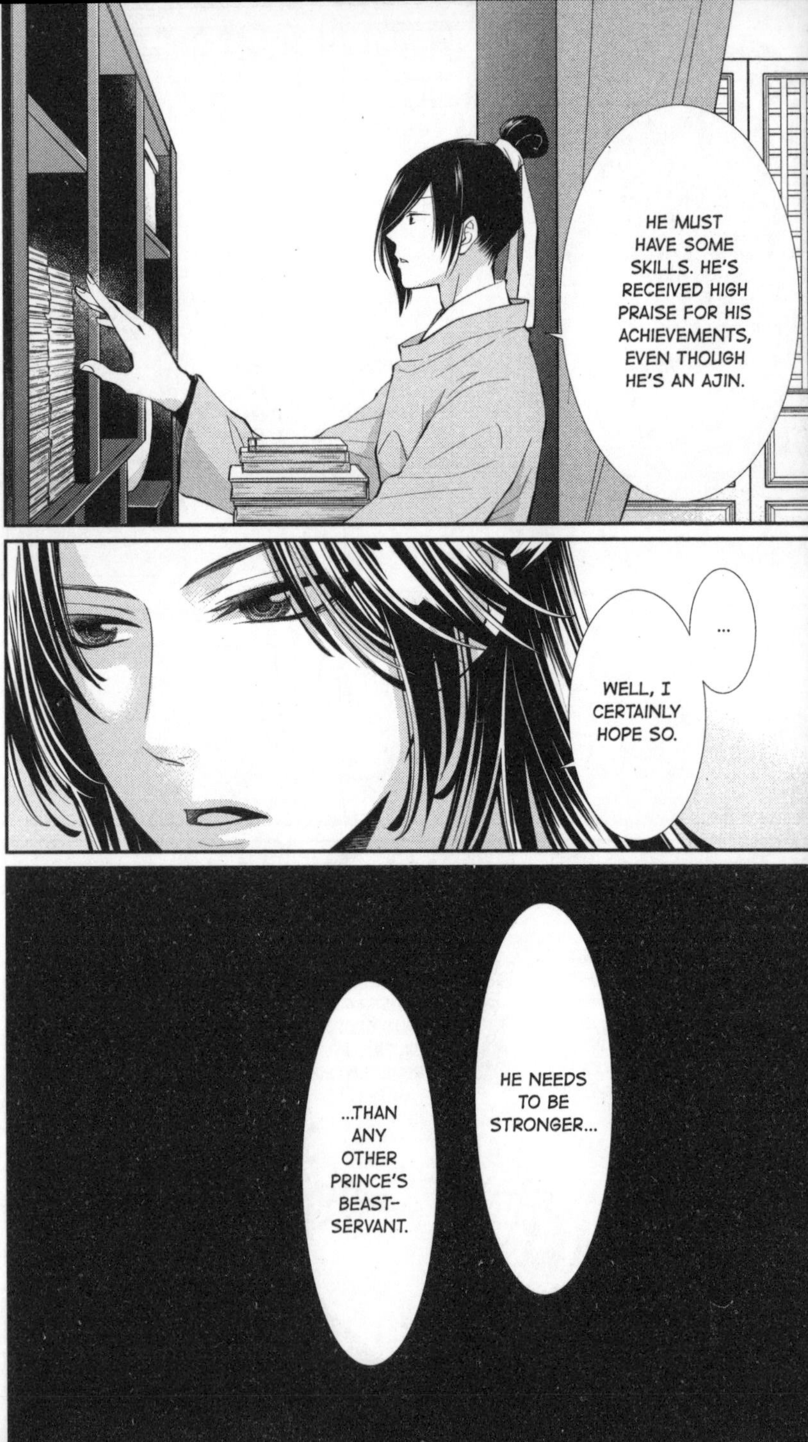
HE MUST HAVE SOME SKILLS. HE'S RECEIVED HIGH PRAISE FOR HIS ACHIEVEMENTS, EVEN THOUGH HE'S AN AJIN.
...
WELL, I CERTAINLY HOPE SO.
HE NEEDS TO BE STRONGER...
...THAN ANY OTHER PRINCE'S BEAST-SERVANT.

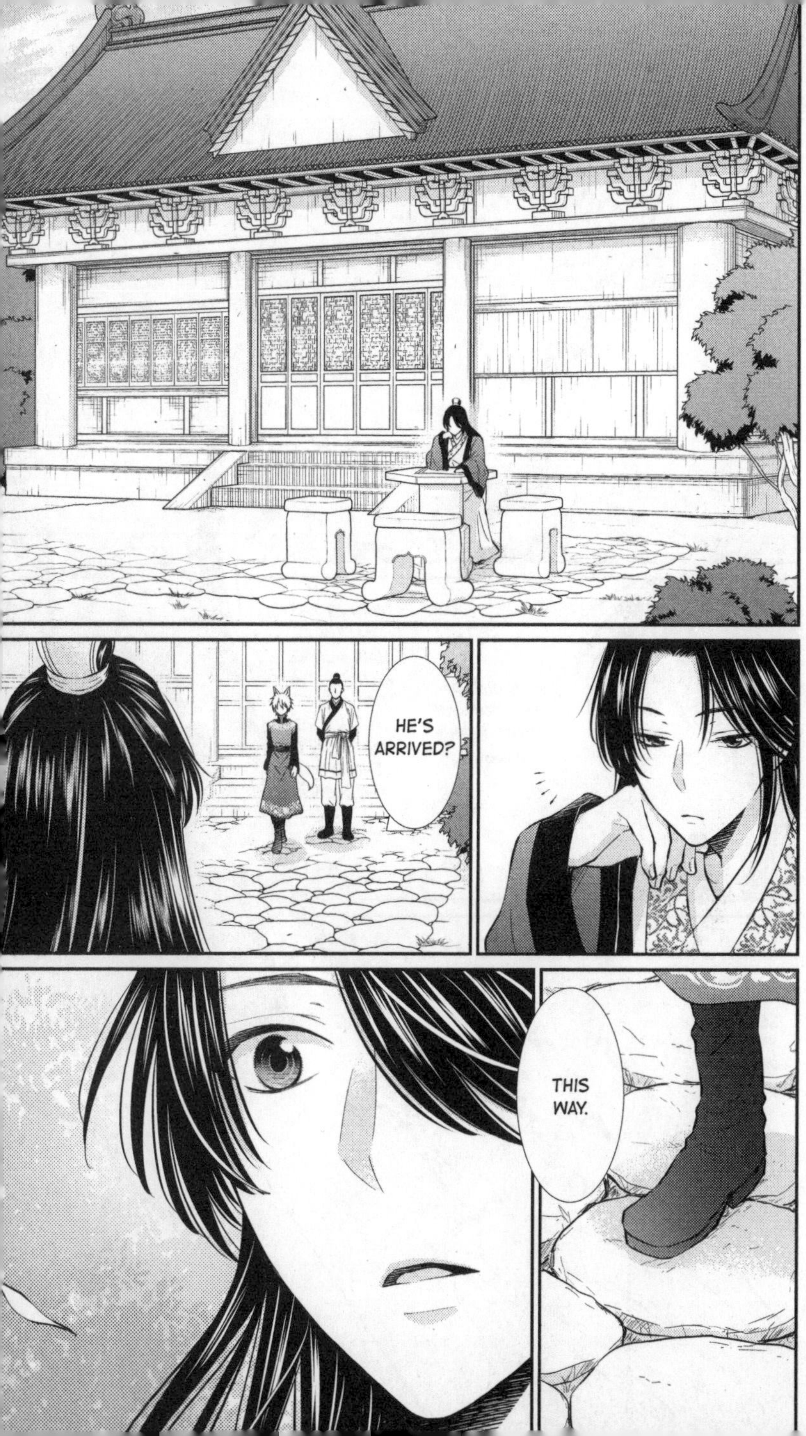
HE'S ARRIVED?
THIS WAY.

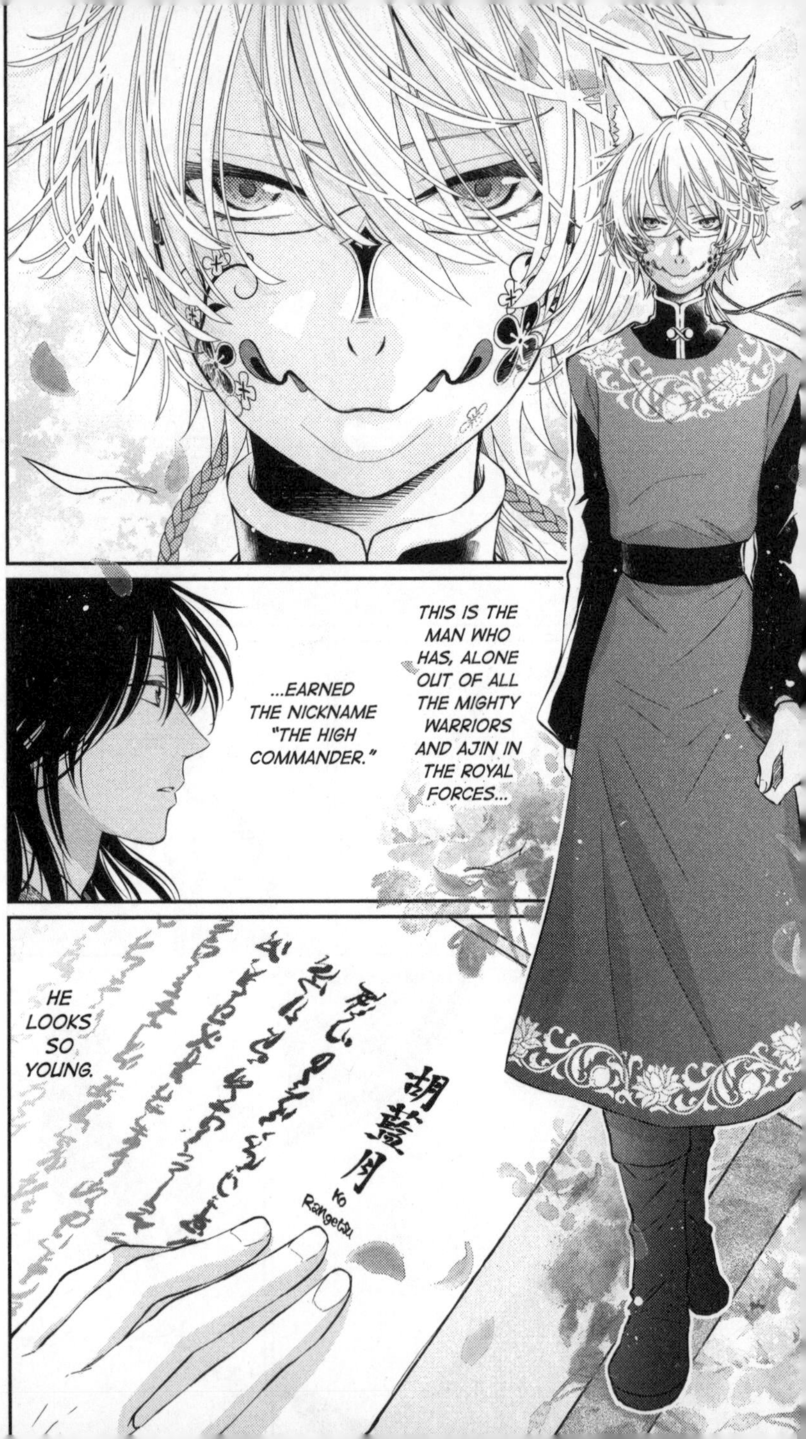
THIS IS THE MAN WHO HAS, ALONE OUT OF ALL THE MIGHTY WARRIORS AND AJIN IN THE ROYAL FORCES...
...EARNED THE NICKNAME "THE HIGH COMMANDER."
胡藍月
Ko Rangetsu
HE LOOKS SO YOUNG.

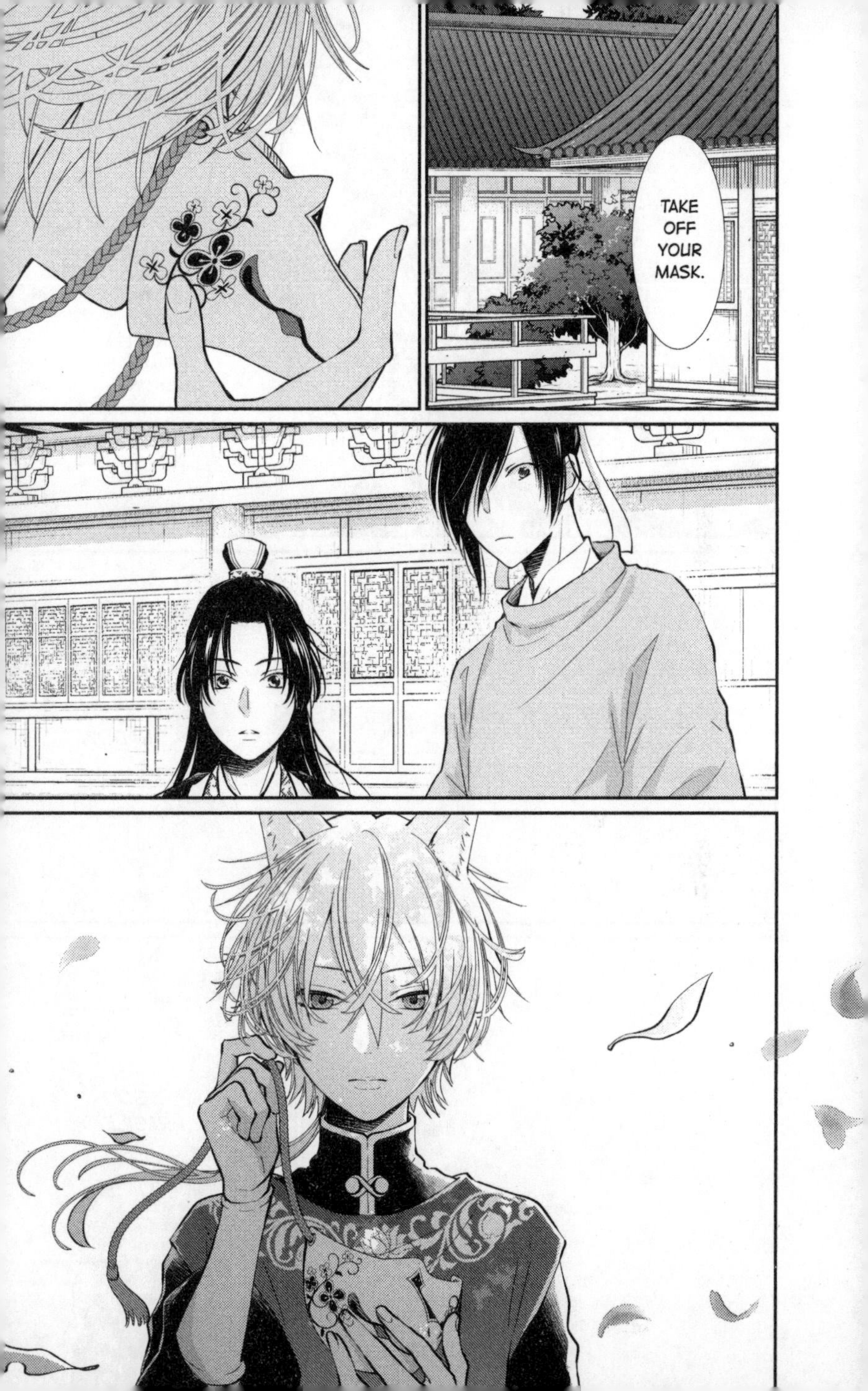
TAKE OFF YOUR MASK.

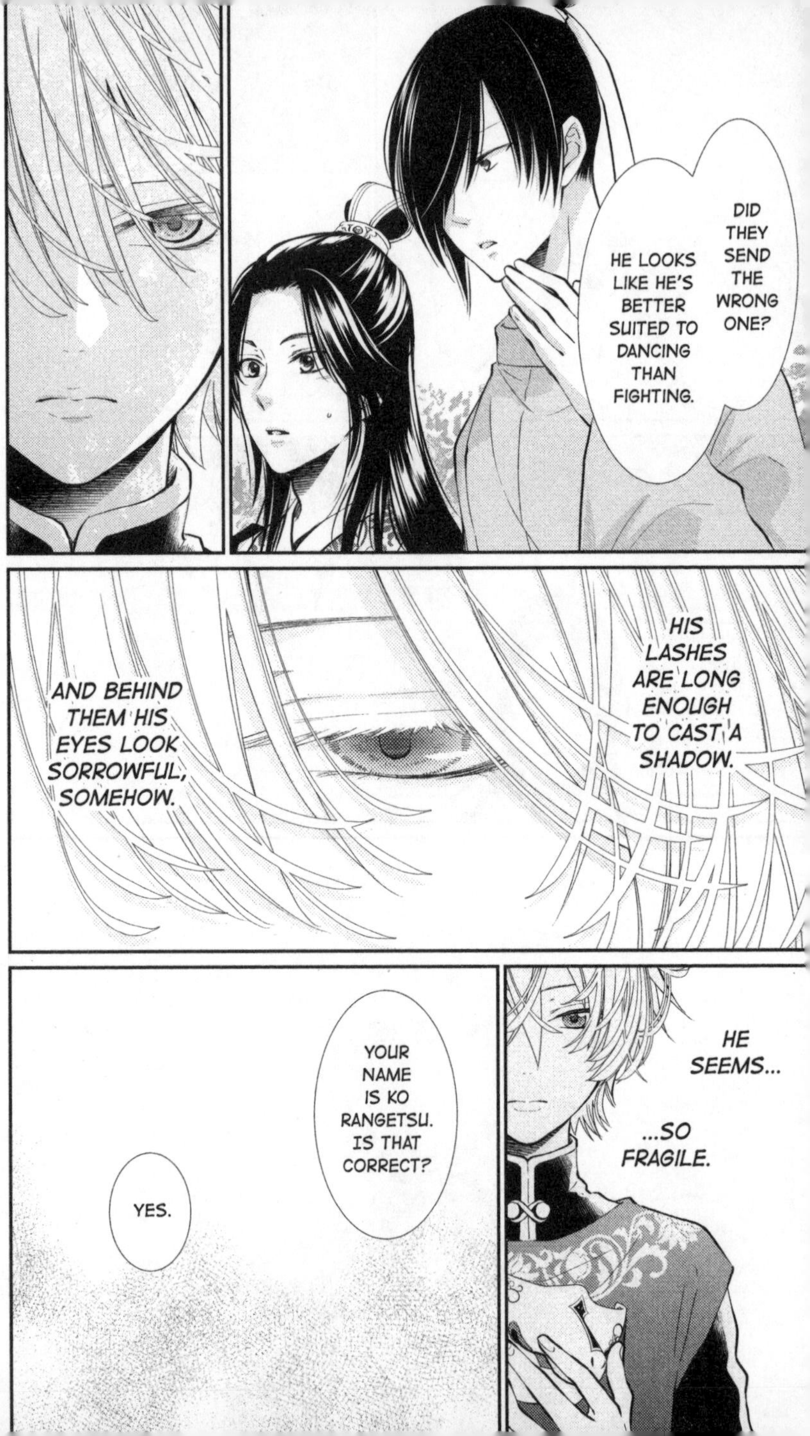
DID THEY SEND THE WRONG ONE?
HE LOOKS LIKE HE'S BETTER SUITED TO DANCING THAN FIGHTING.
HIS LASHES ARE LONG ENOUGH TO CAST A SHADOW.
AND BEHIND THEM HIS EYES LOOK SORROWFUL, SOMEHOW.
HE SEEMS...
...SO FRAGILE.
YOUR NAME IS KO RANGETSU. IS THAT CORRECT?
YES.

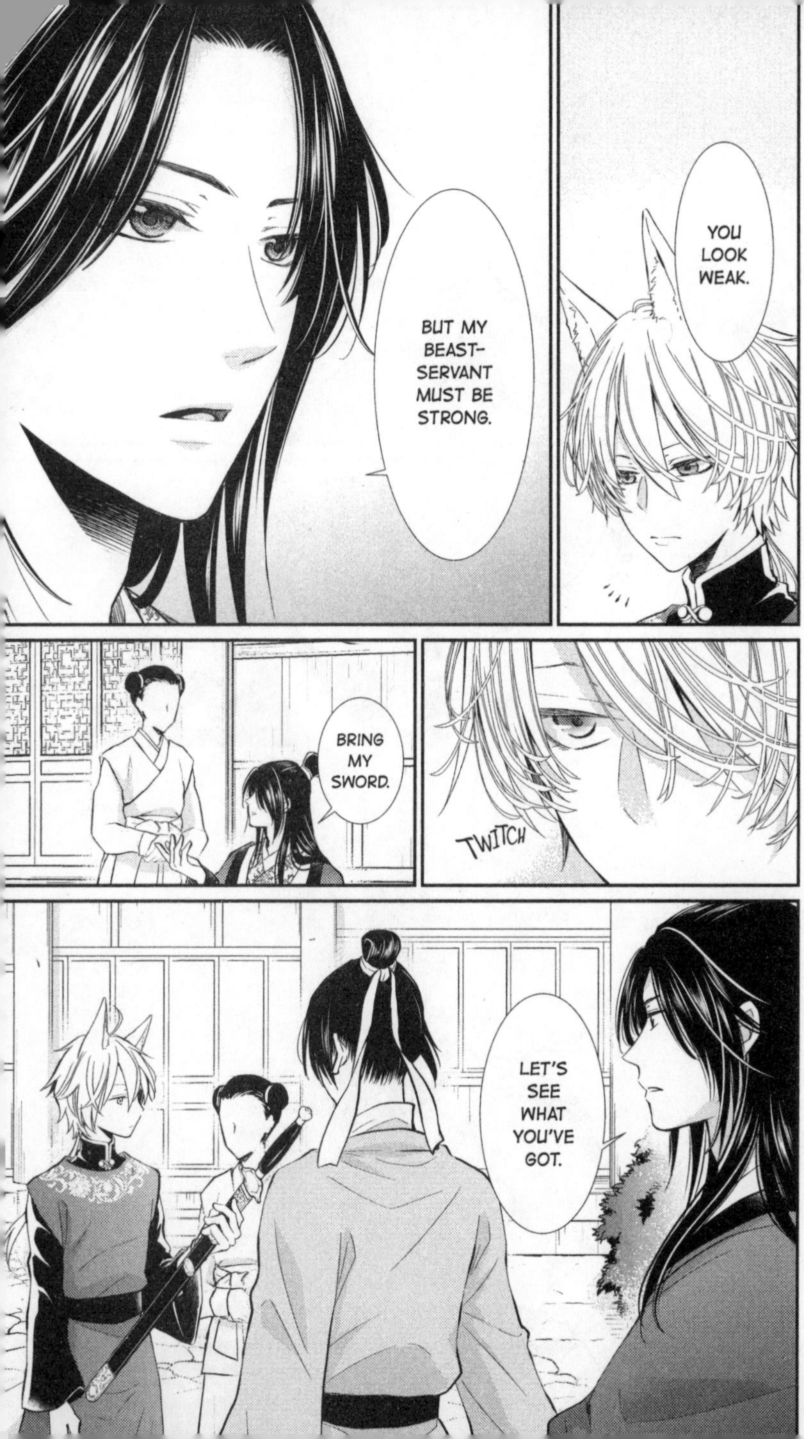
YOU LOOK WEAK.
BUT MY BEAST-SERVANT MUST BE STRONG.
TWITCH
BRING MY SWORD.
LET'S SEE WHAT YOU'VE GOT.

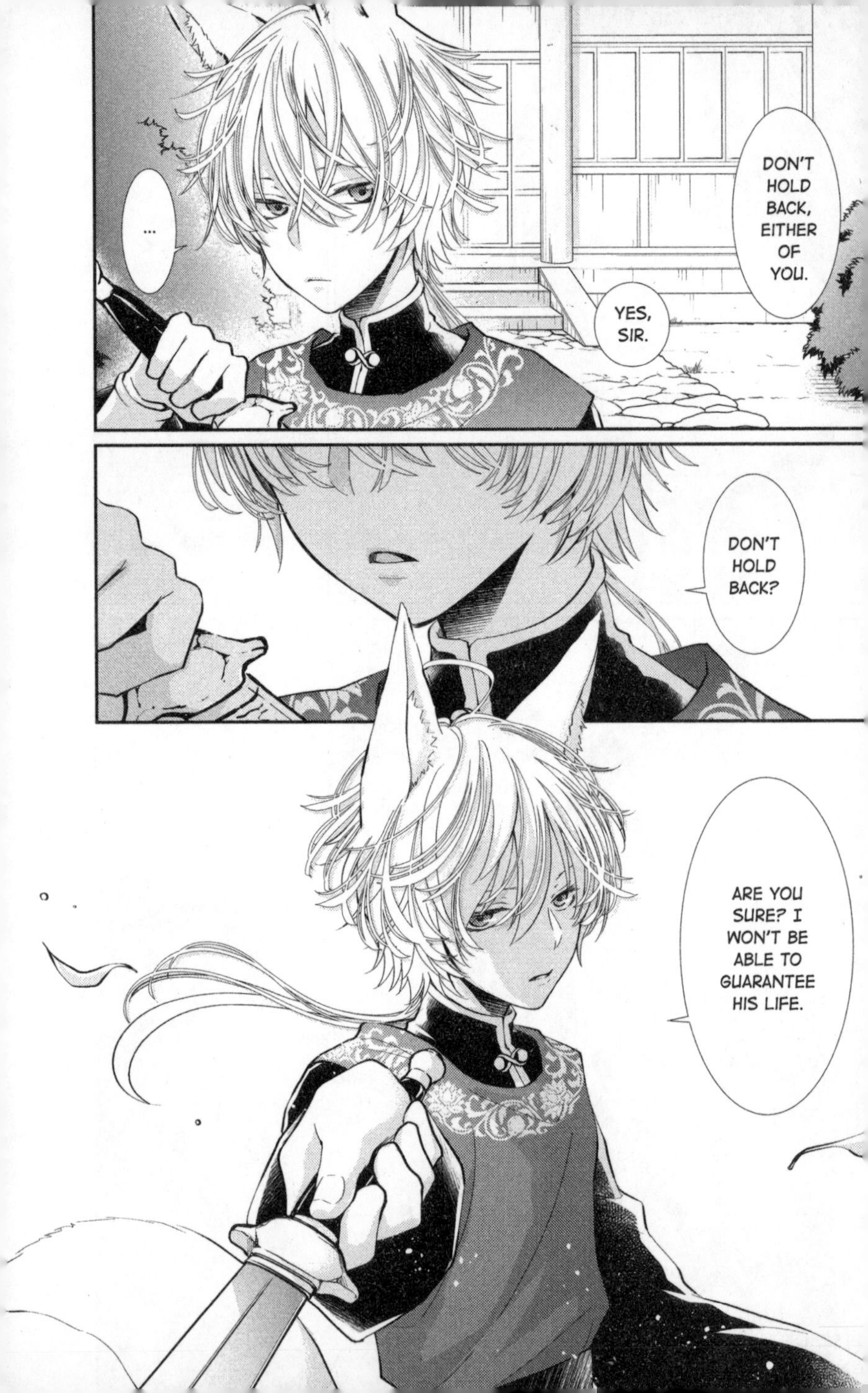
DON'T HOLD BACK, EITHER OF YOU.
YES, SIR.
...
DON'T HOLD BACK?
ARE YOU SURE? I WON'T BE ABLE TO GUARANTEE HIS LIFE.

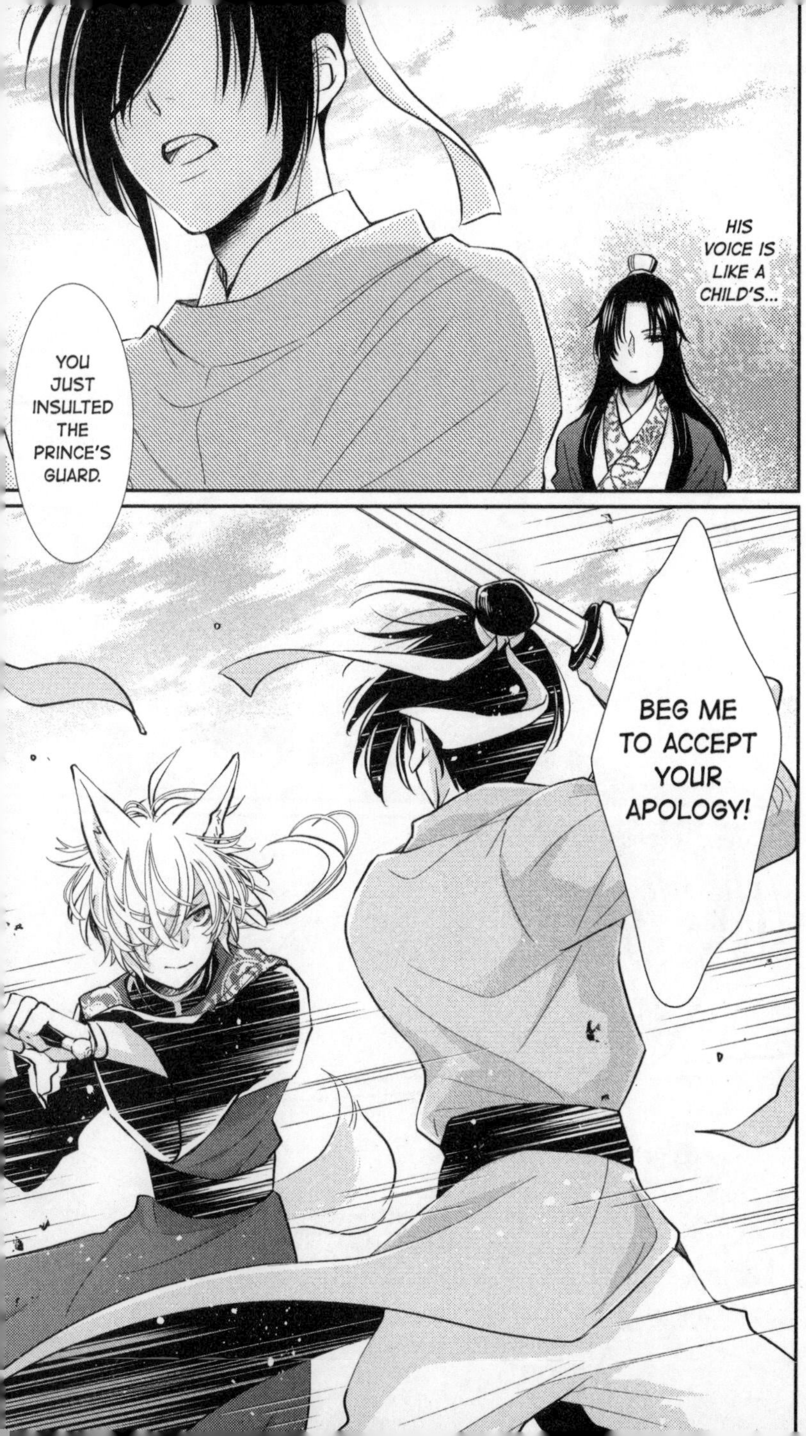
HIS VOICE IS LIKE A CHILD'S...
YOU JUST INSULTED THE PRINCE'S GUARD.
BEG ME TO ACCEPT YOUR APOLOGY!

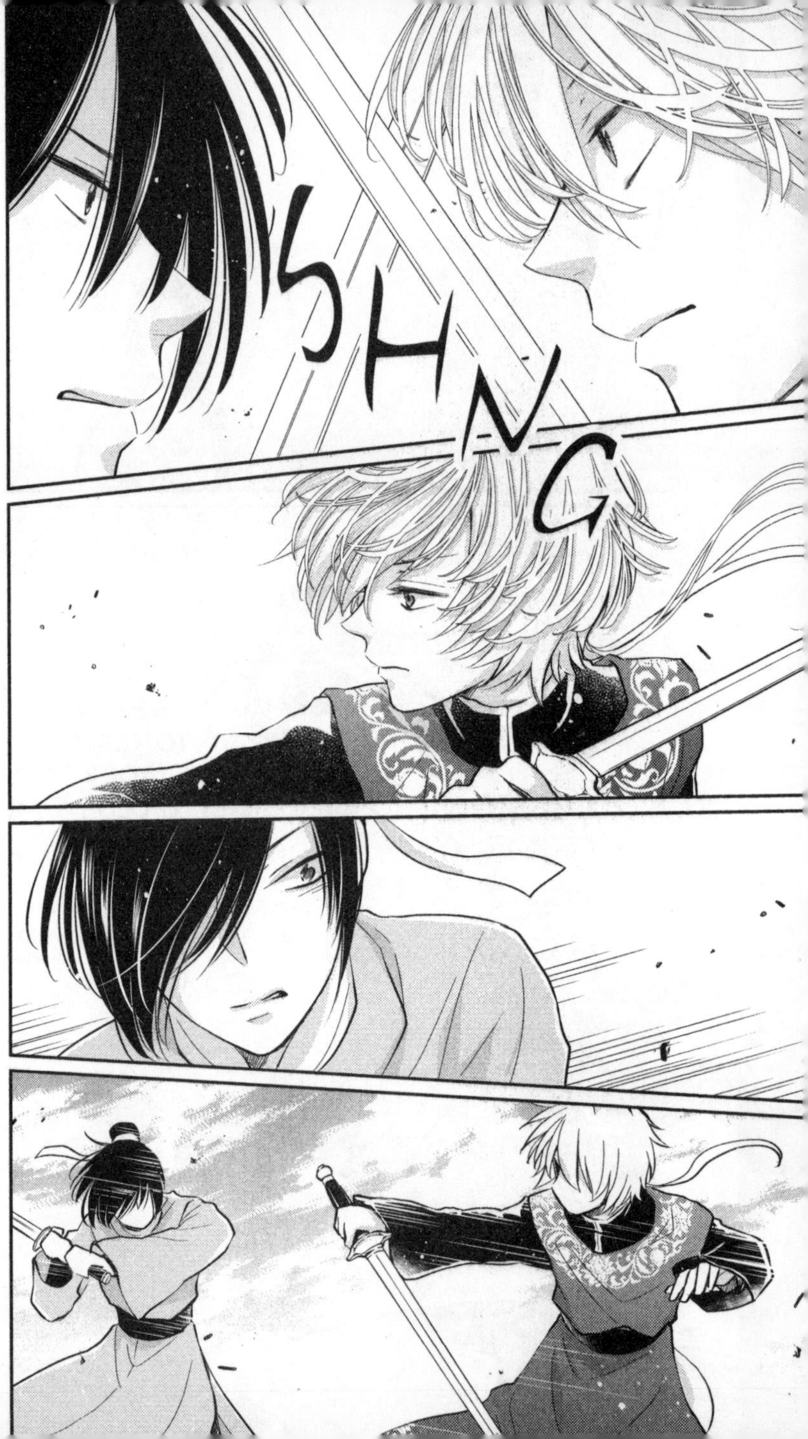
SHNG

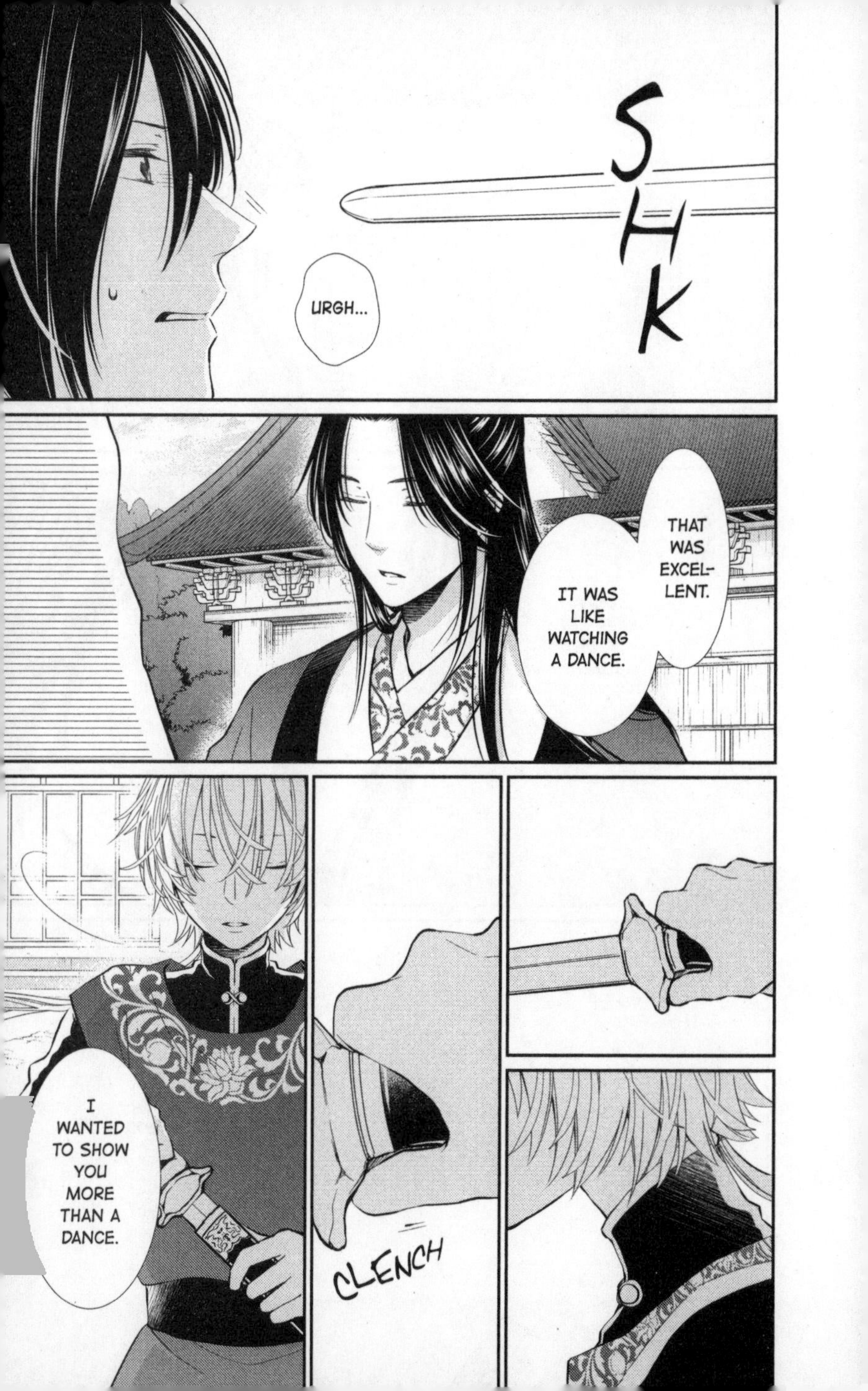
SHK
URGH...
THAT WAS EXCEL-LENT.
IT WAS LIKE WATCHING A DANCE.
CLENCH
I WANTED TO SHOW YOU MORE THAN A DANCE.

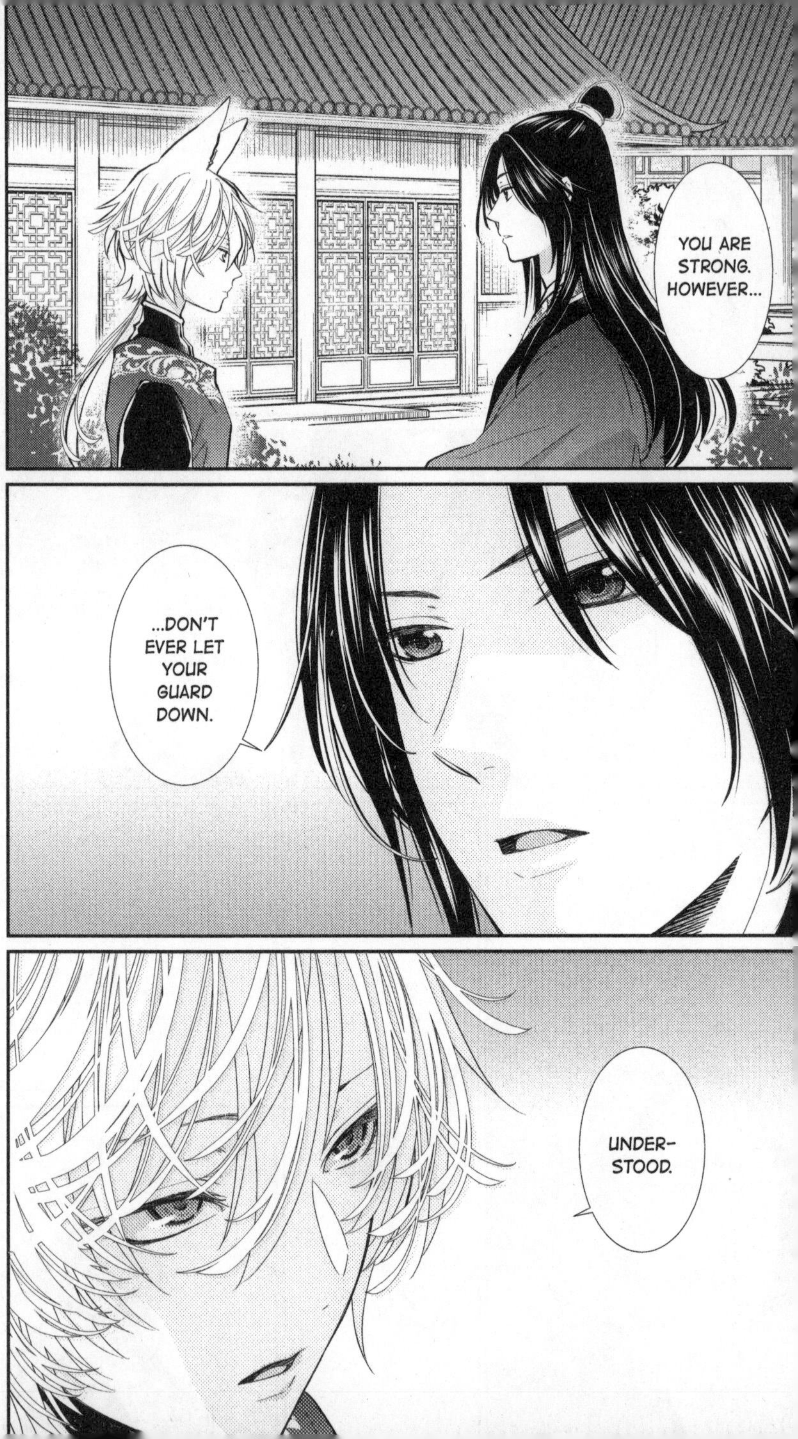
YOU ARE STRONG. HOWEVER...
...DON'T EVER LET YOUR GUARD DOWN.
UNDER-STOOD.

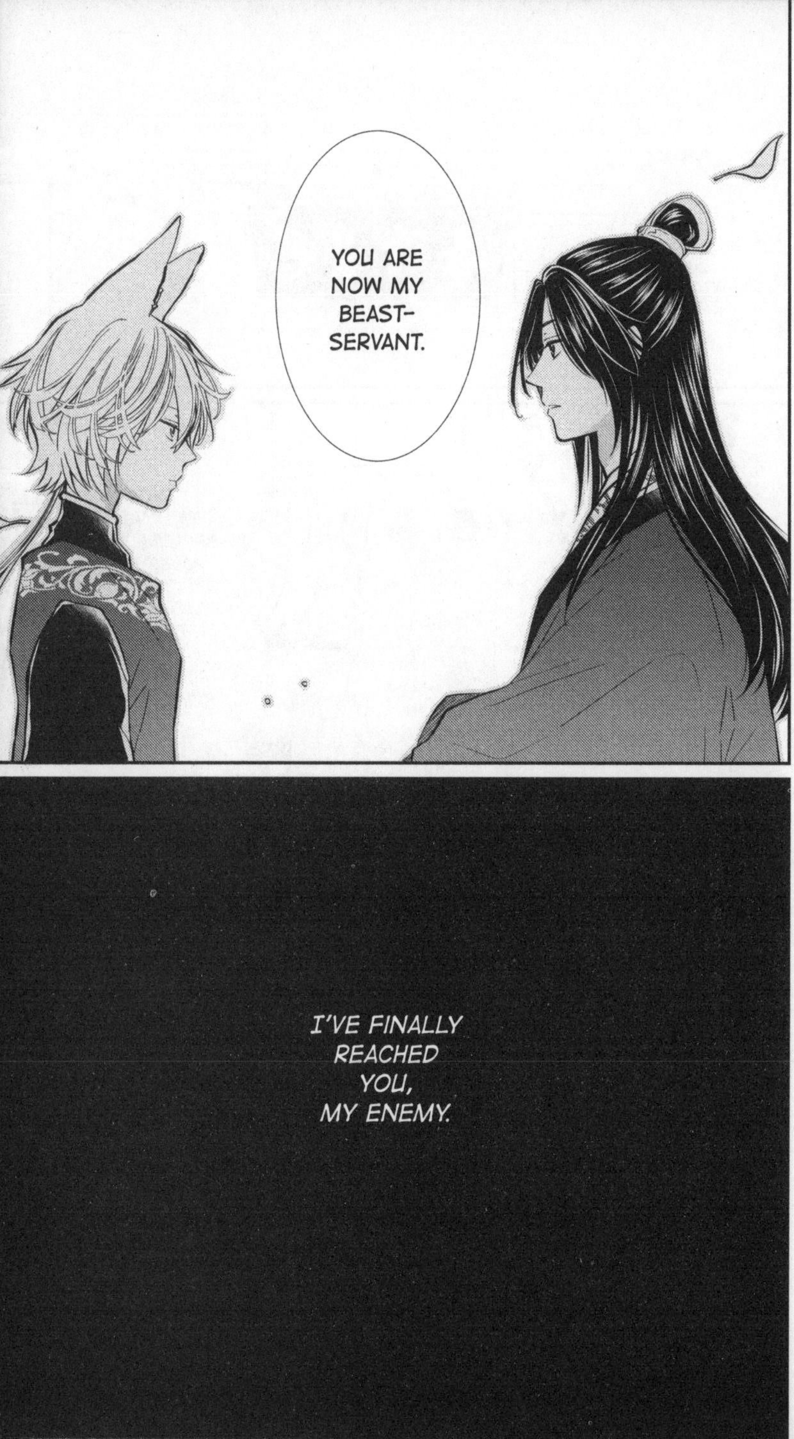
YOU ARE NOW MY BEAST-SERVANT.
I'VE FINALLY REACHED YOU, MY ENEMY.

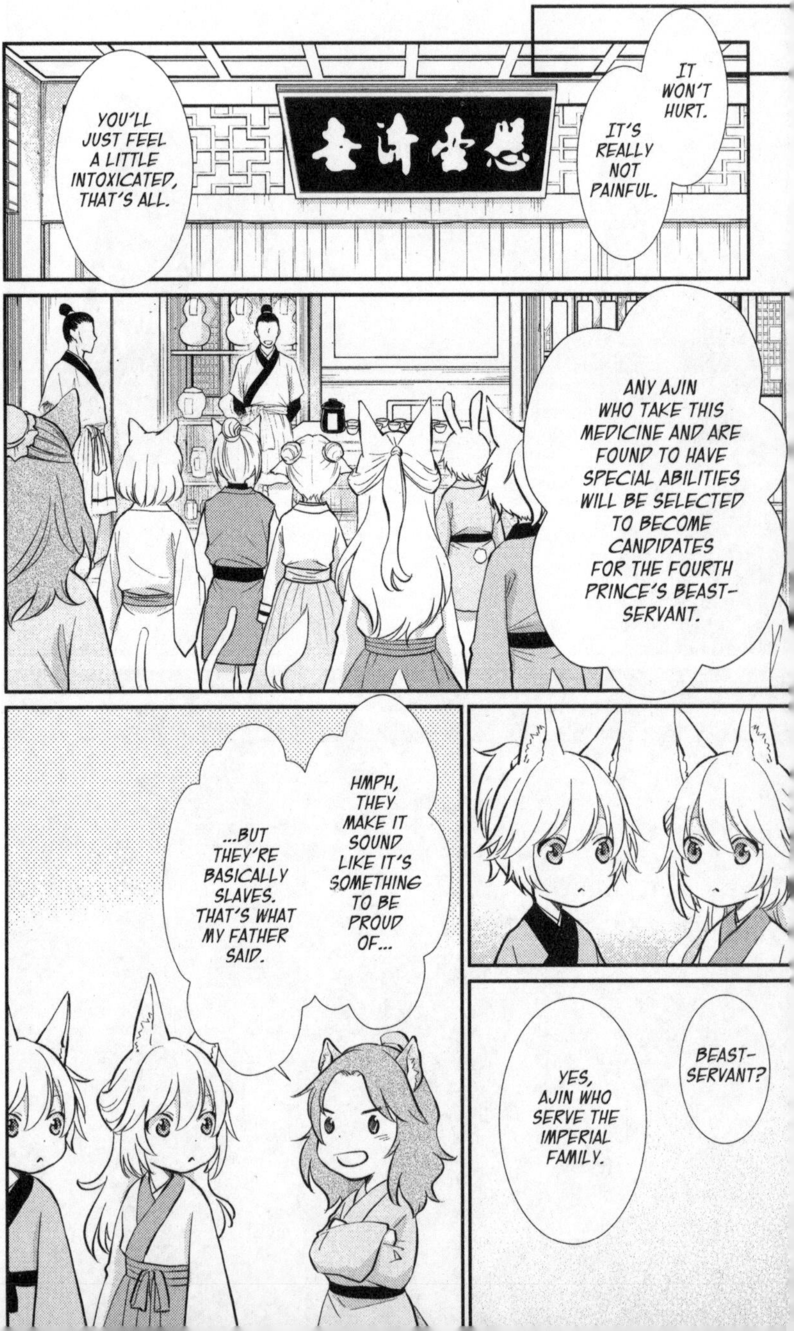
IT WON'T HURT.
IT'S REALLY NOT PAINFUL.
YOU'LL JUST FEEL A LITTLE INTOXICATED, THAT'S ALL.
ANY AJIN WHO TAKE THIS MEDICINE AND ARE FOUND TO HAVE SPECIAL ABILITIES WILL BE SELECTED TO BECOME CANDIDATES FOR THE FOURTH PRINCE'S BEAST-SERVANT.
BEAST-SERVANT?
YES, AJIN WHO SERVE THE IMPERIAL FAMILY.
HMPH, THEY MAKE IT SOUND LIKE IT'S SOMETHING TO BE PROUD OF...
...BUT THEY'RE BASICALLY SLAVES. THAT'S WHAT MY FATHER SAID.

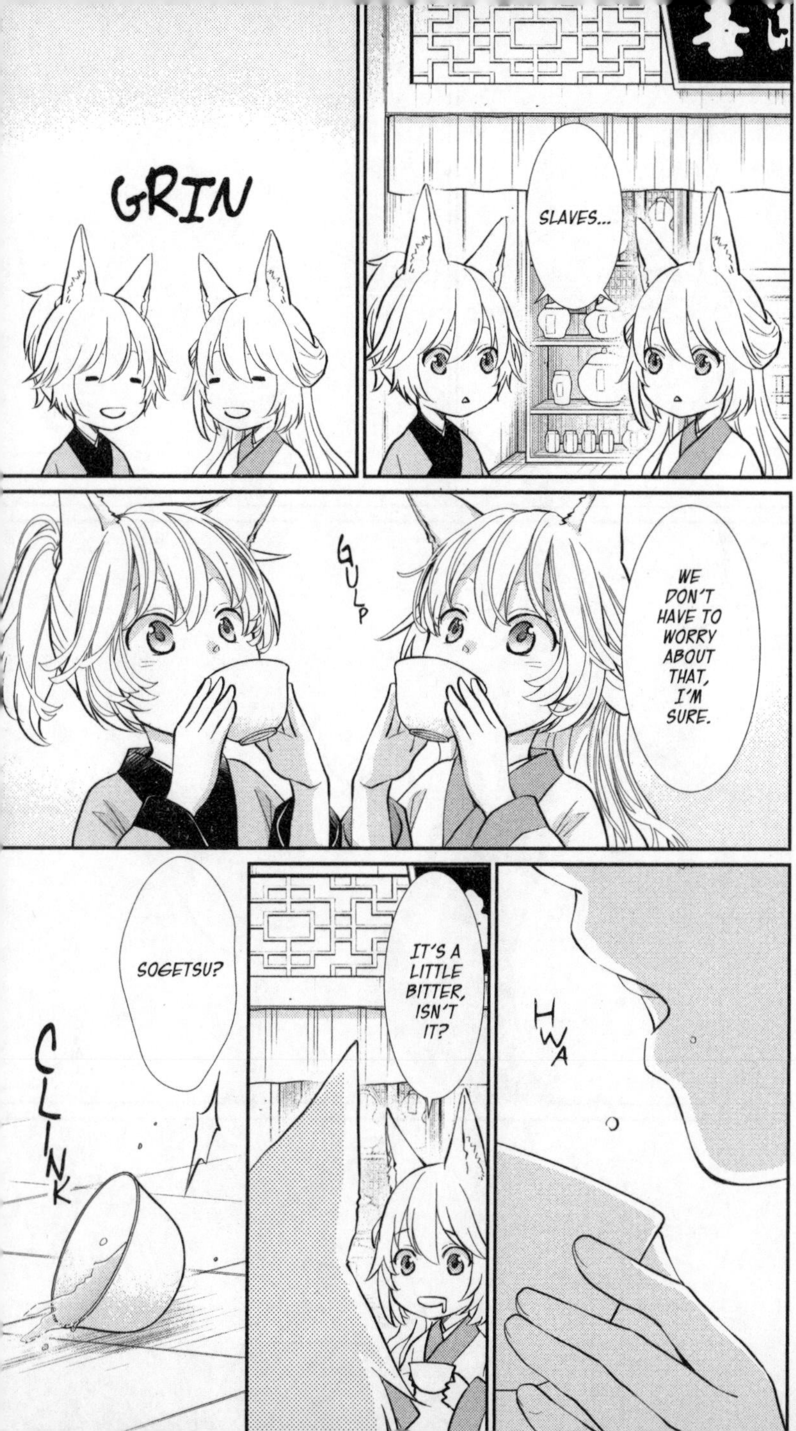
SLAVES...
GRIN
WE DON'T HAVE TO WORRY ABOUT THAT, I'M SURE.
GULP
HWA
IT'S A LITTLE BITTER, ISN'T IT?
SOGETSU?
CLINK

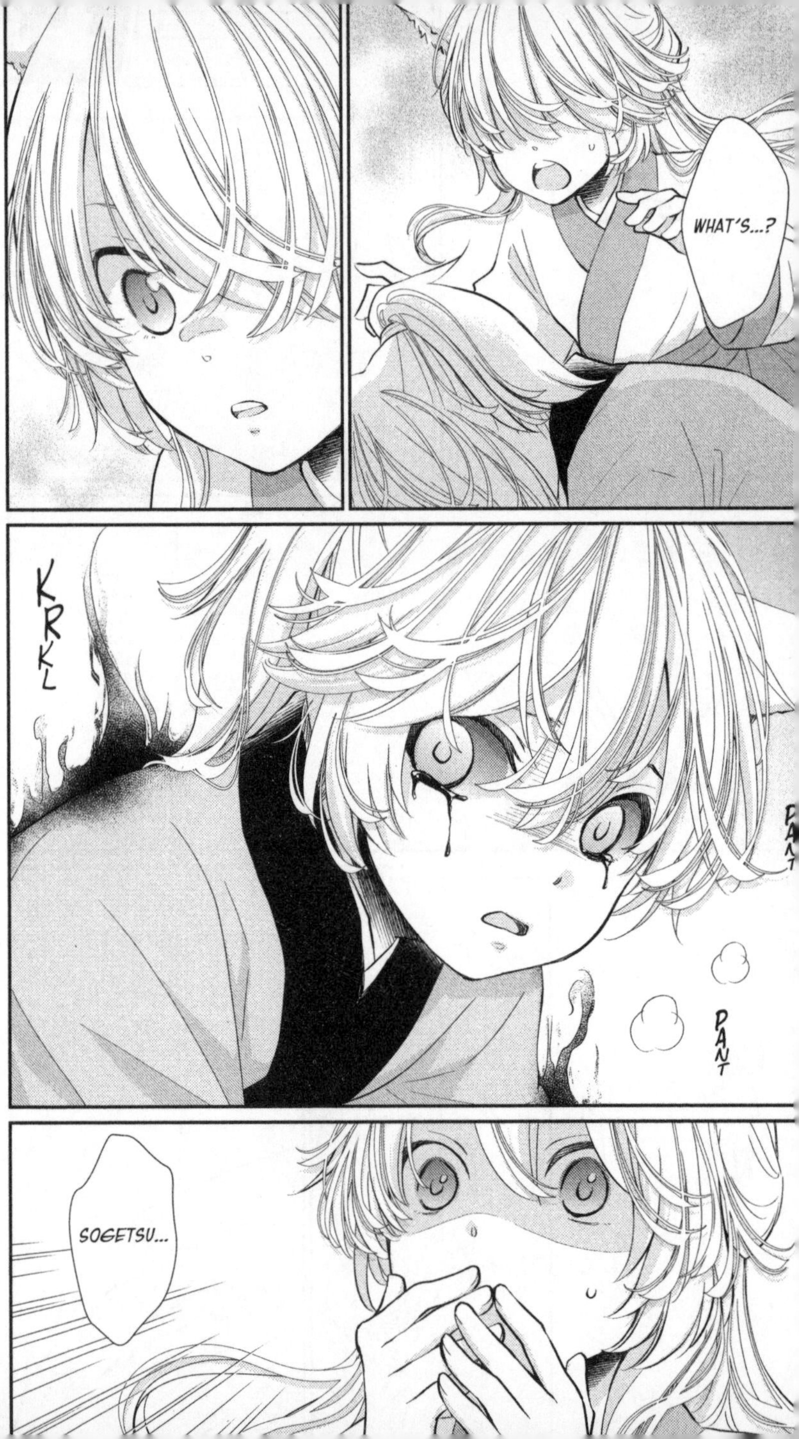
WHAT'S...?
KRKL
PANT
PANT
SOGETSU...

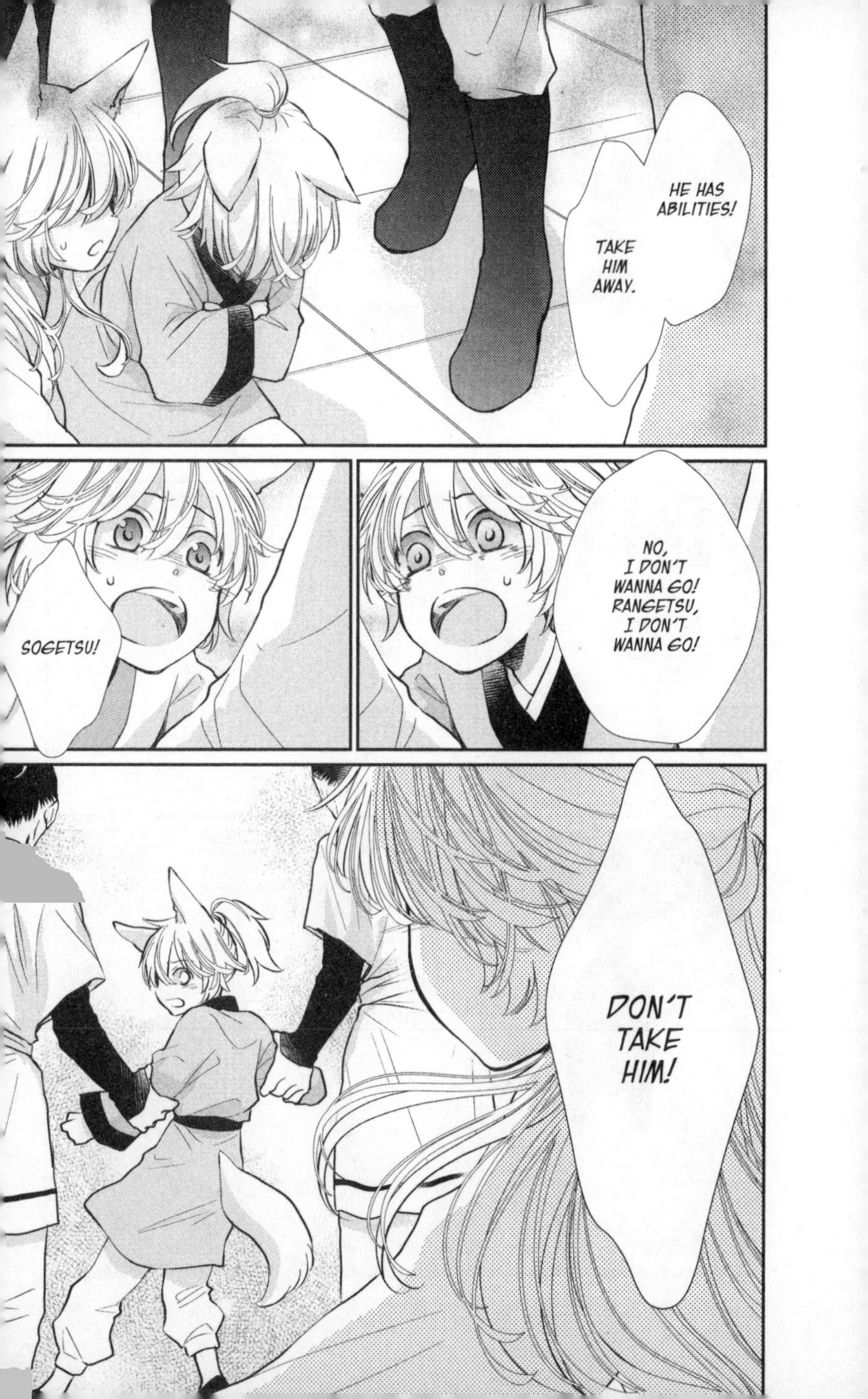
HE HAS ABILITIES!
TAKE HIM AWAY.
NO, I DON'T WANNA GO! RANGETSU, I DON'T WANNA GO!
SOGETSU!
DON'T TAKE HIM!

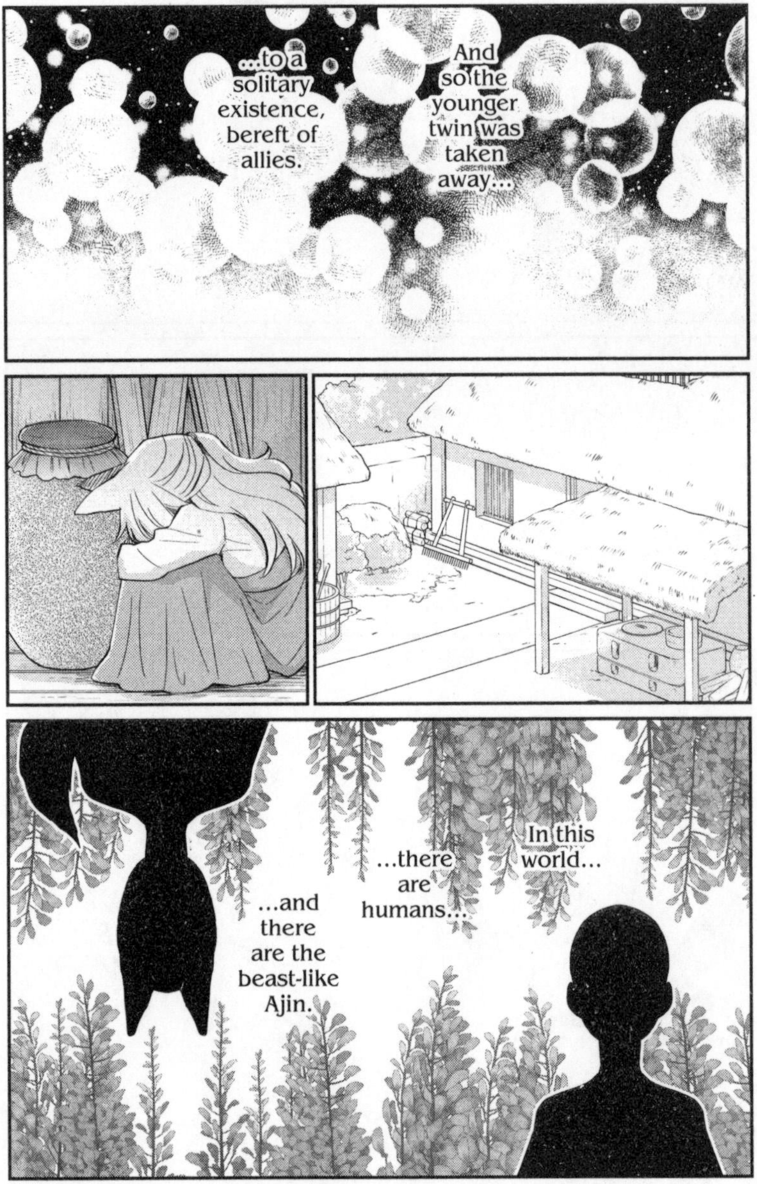
And so the younger twin was taken away...
...to a solitary existence, bereft of allies.
In this world...
...there are humans...
...and there are the beast-like Ajin.

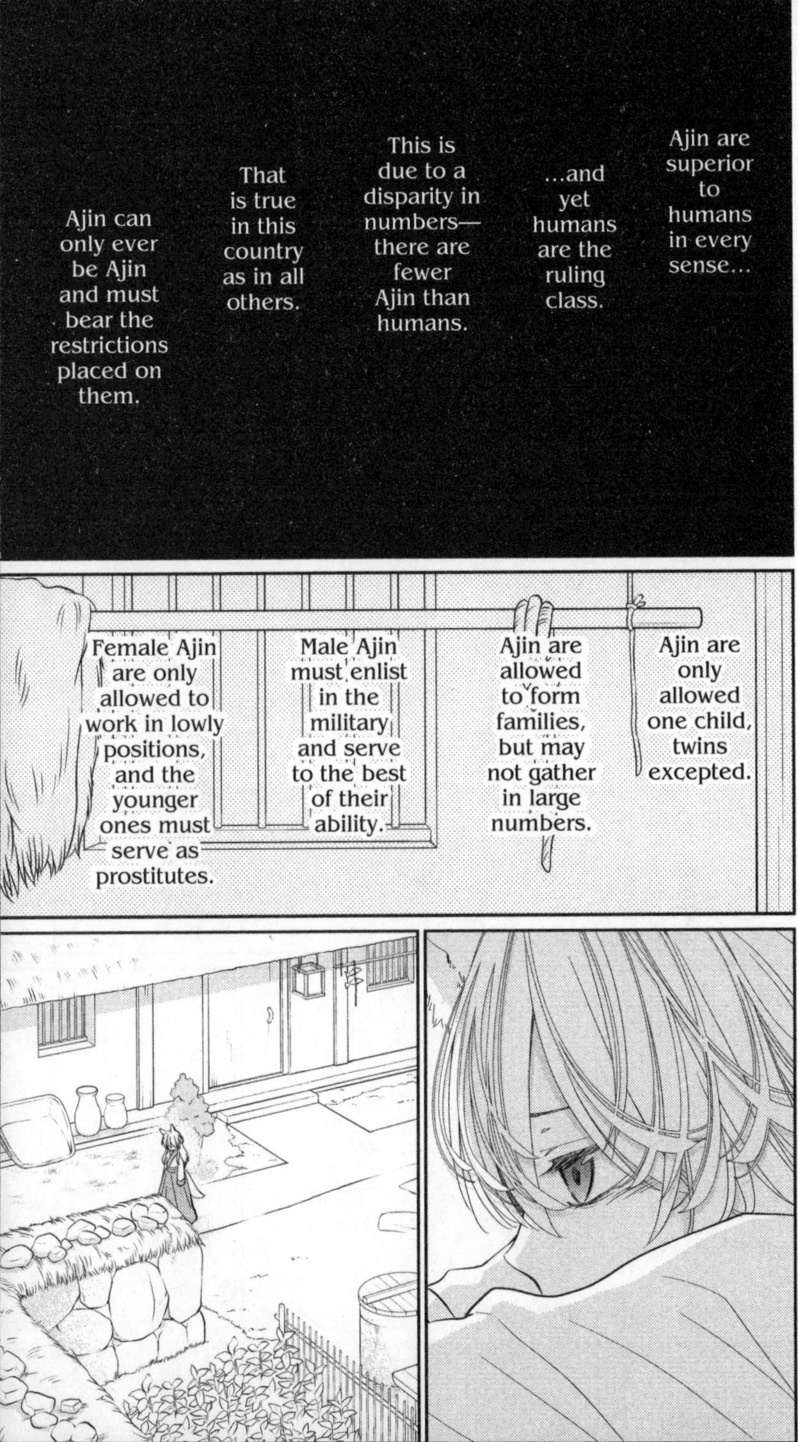
Ajin are superior to humans in every sense...
...and yet humans are the ruling class.
This is due to a disparity in numbers—there are fewer Ajin than humans.
That is true in this country as in all others.
Ajin can only ever be Ajin and must bear the restrictions placed on them.
Ajin are only allowed one child, twins excepted.
Ajin are allowed to form families, but may not gather in large numbers.
Male Ajin must enlist in the military and serve to the best of their ability.
Female Ajin are only allowed to work in lowly positions, and the younger ones must serve as prostitutes.

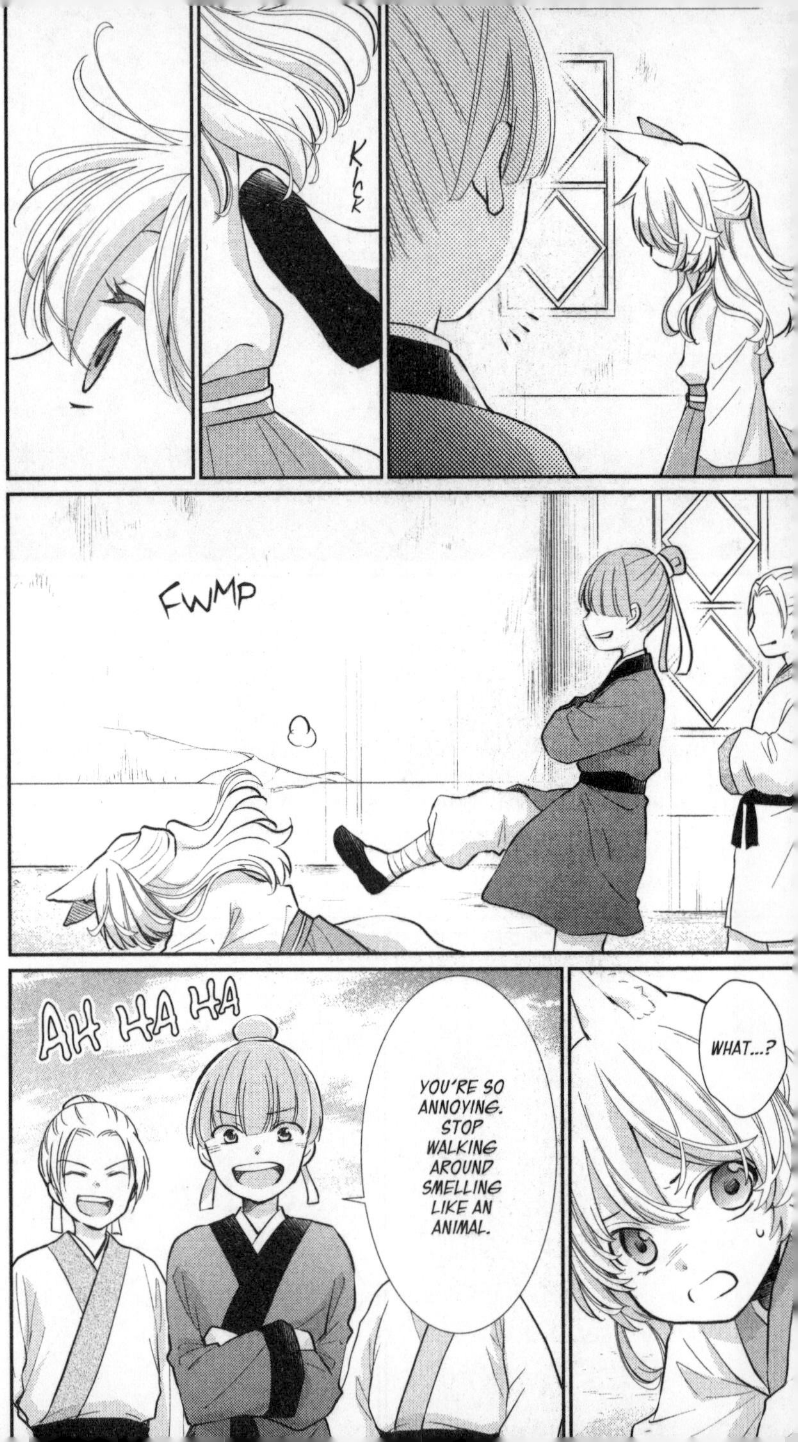
KICK
FWMP
WHAT...?
YOU'RE SO ANNOYING. STOP WALKING AROUND SMELLING LIKE AN ANIMAL.
AH HA HA

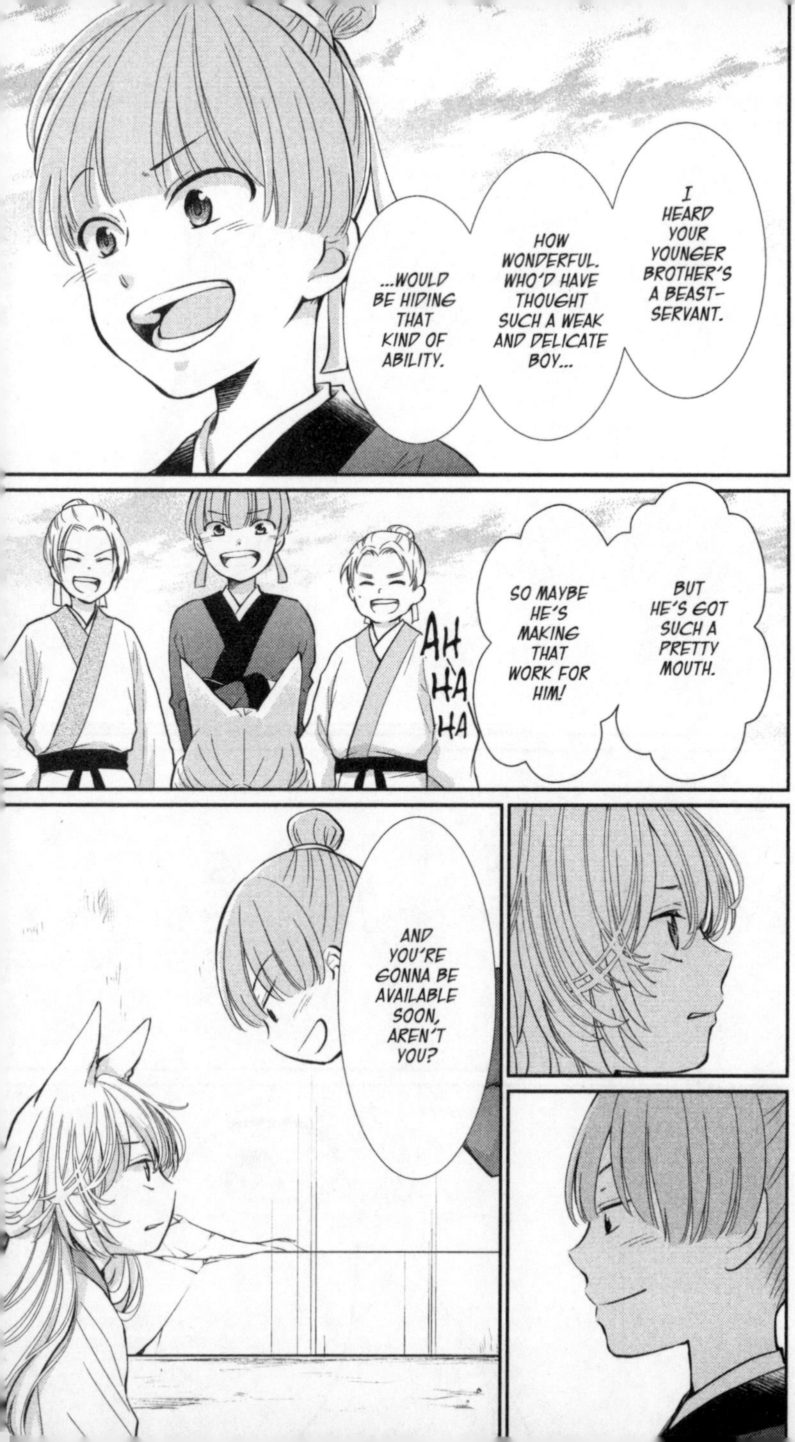
I HEARD YOUR YOUNGER BROTHER'S A BEAST-SERVANT.
HOW WONDERFUL. WHO'D HAVE THOUGHT SUCH A WEAK AND DELICATE BOY...
...WOULD BE HIDING THAT KIND OF ABILITY.
BUT HE'S GOT SUCH A PRETTY MOUTH.
SO MAYBE HE'S MAKING THAT WORK FOR HIM!
AH HA HA
AND YOU'RE GONNA BE AVAILABLE SOON, AREN'T YOU?

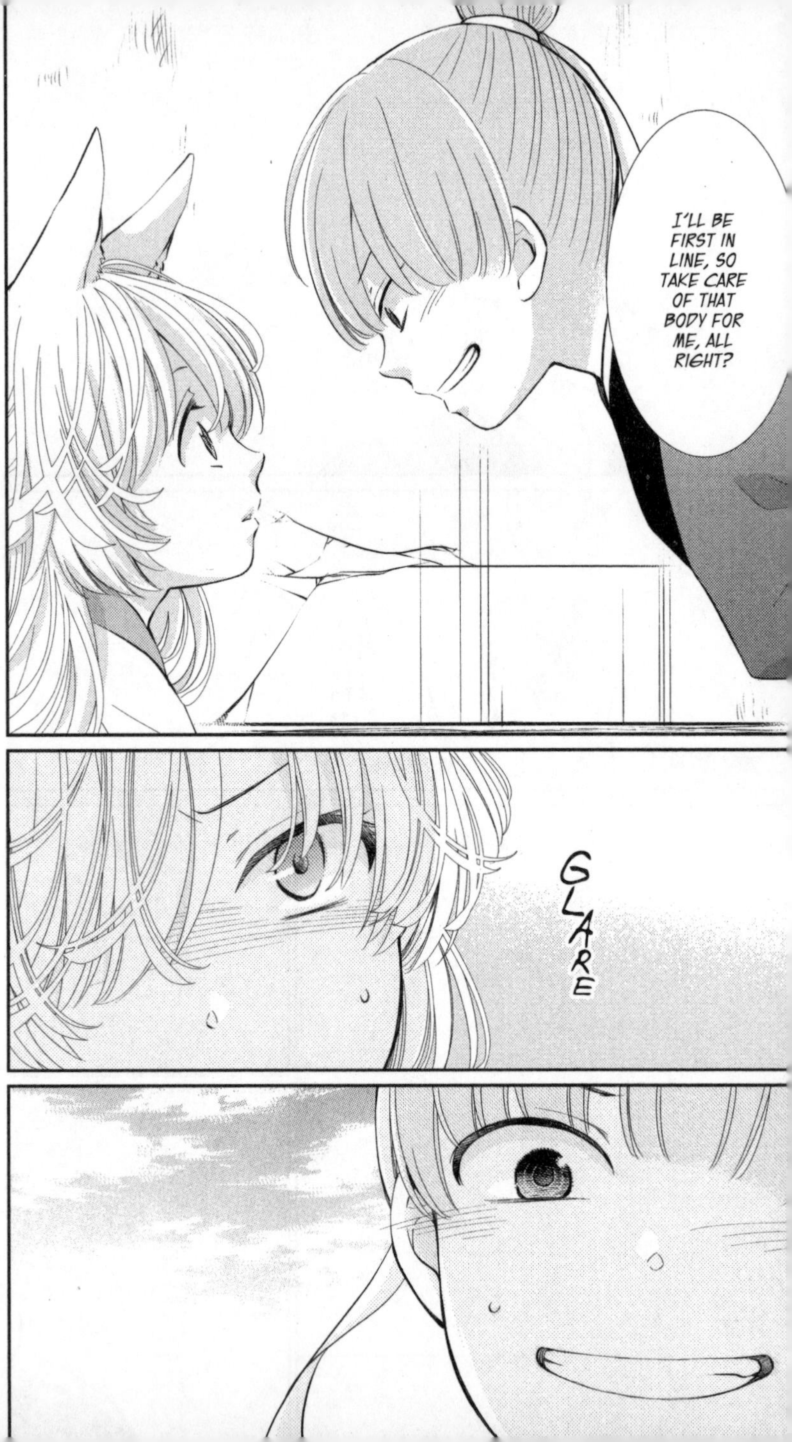
I'LL BE FIRST IN LINE, SO TAKE CARE OF THAT BODY FOR ME, ALL RIGHT?
GLARE

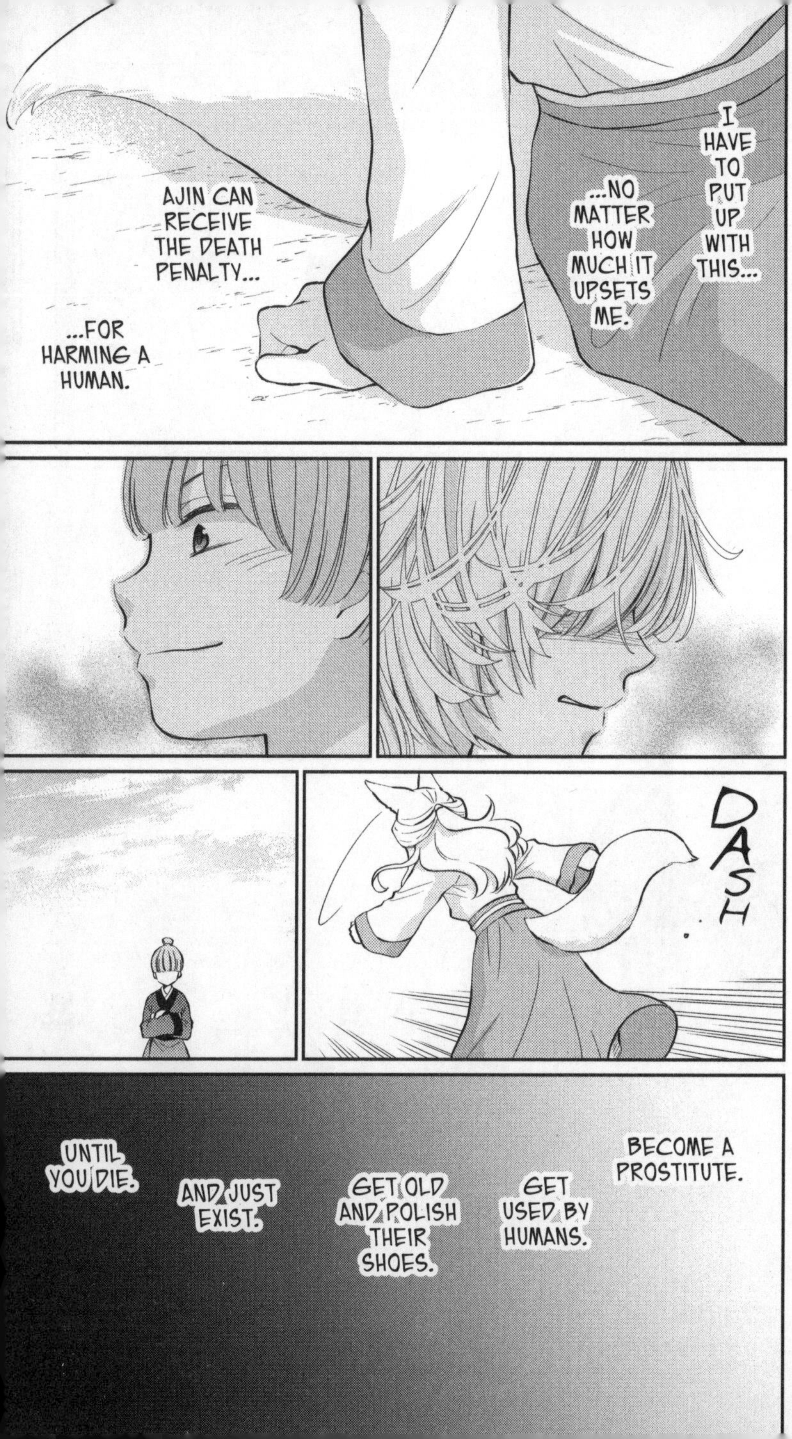
I HAVE TO PUT UP WITH THIS...
...NO MATTER HOW MUCH IT UPSETS ME.
AJIN CAN RECEIVE THE DEATH PENALTY...
...FOR HARMING A HUMAN.
DASH
BECOME A PROSTITUTE.
GET USED BY HUMANS.
GET OLD AND POLISH THEIR SHOES.
AND JUST EXIST.
UNTIL YOU DIE.

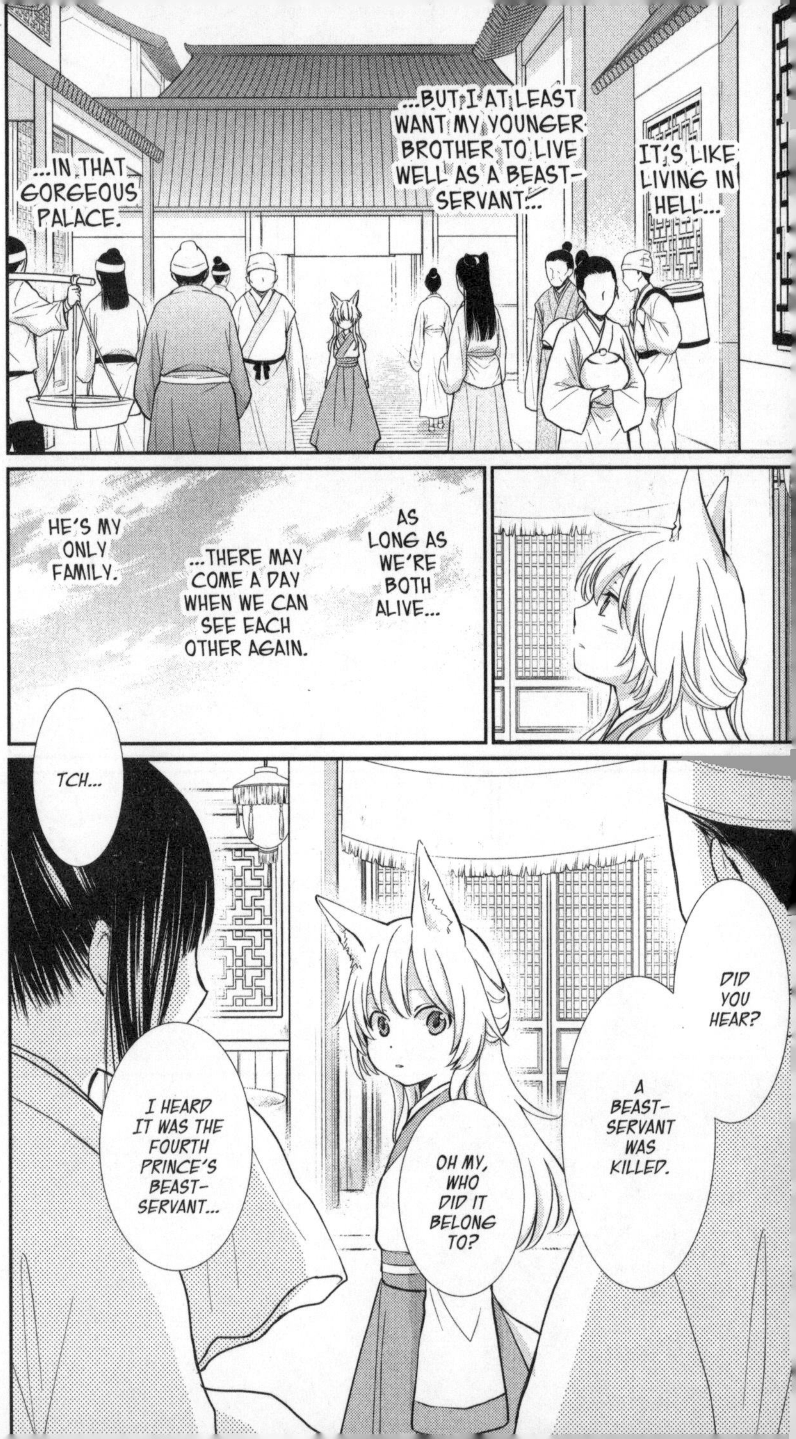
IT'S LIKE LIVING IN HELL...
...BUT I AT LEAST WANT MY YOUNGER BROTHER TO LIVE WELL AS A BEAST-SERVANT...
...IN THAT GORGEOUS PALACE.
AS LONG AS WE'RE BOTH ALIVE...
...THERE MAY COME A DAY WHEN WE CAN SEE EACH OTHER AGAIN.
HE'S MY ONLY FAMILY.
DID YOU HEAR?
A BEAST-SERVANT WAS KILLED.
OH MY, WHO DID IT BELONG TO?
I HEARD IT WAS THE FOURTH PRINCE'S BEAST-SERVANT...
TCH...

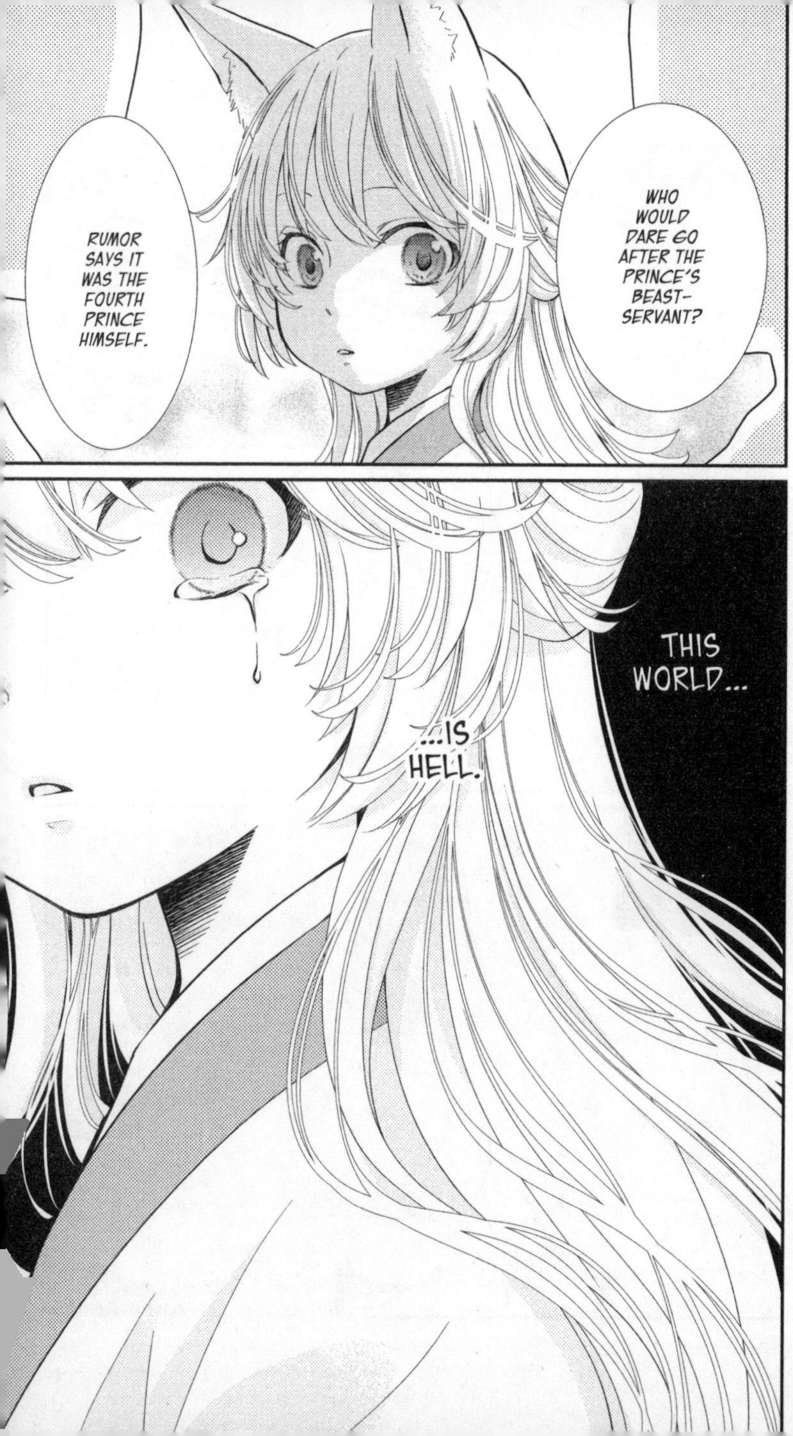
WHO WOULD DARE GO AFTER THE PRINCE'S BEAST-SERVANT?
RUMOR SAYS IT WAS THE FOURTH PRINCE HIMSELF.
THIS WORLD...
...IS HELL.

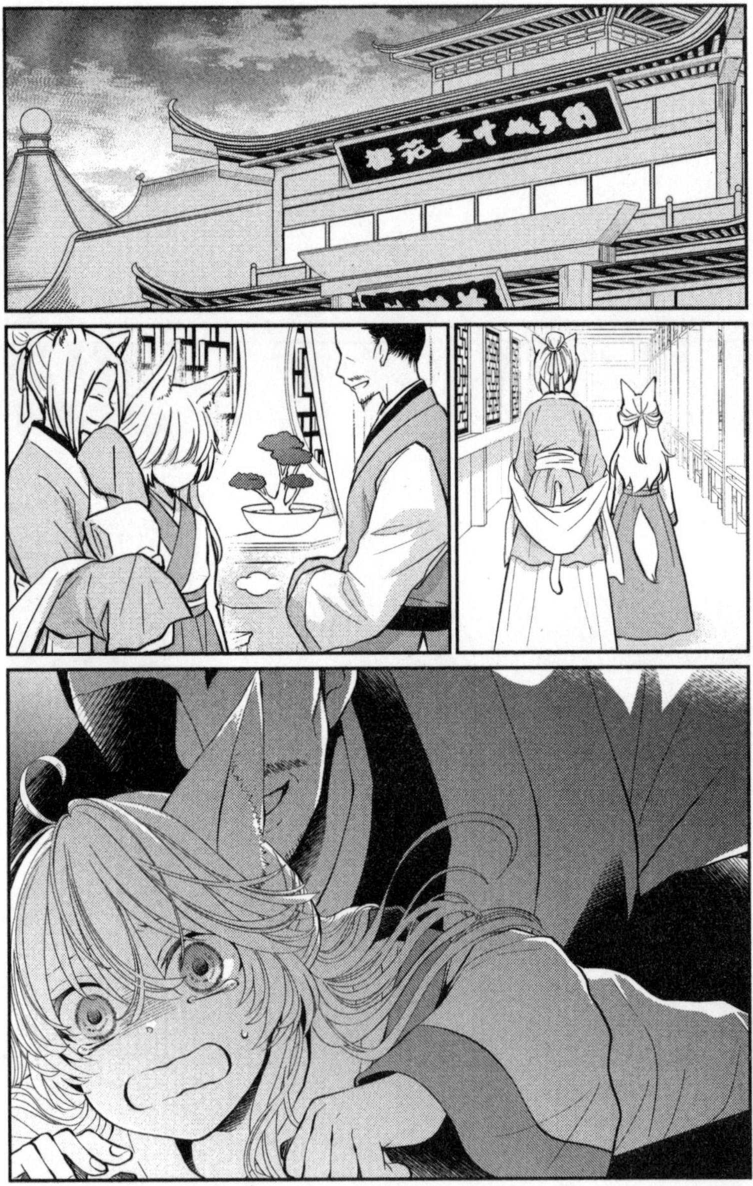

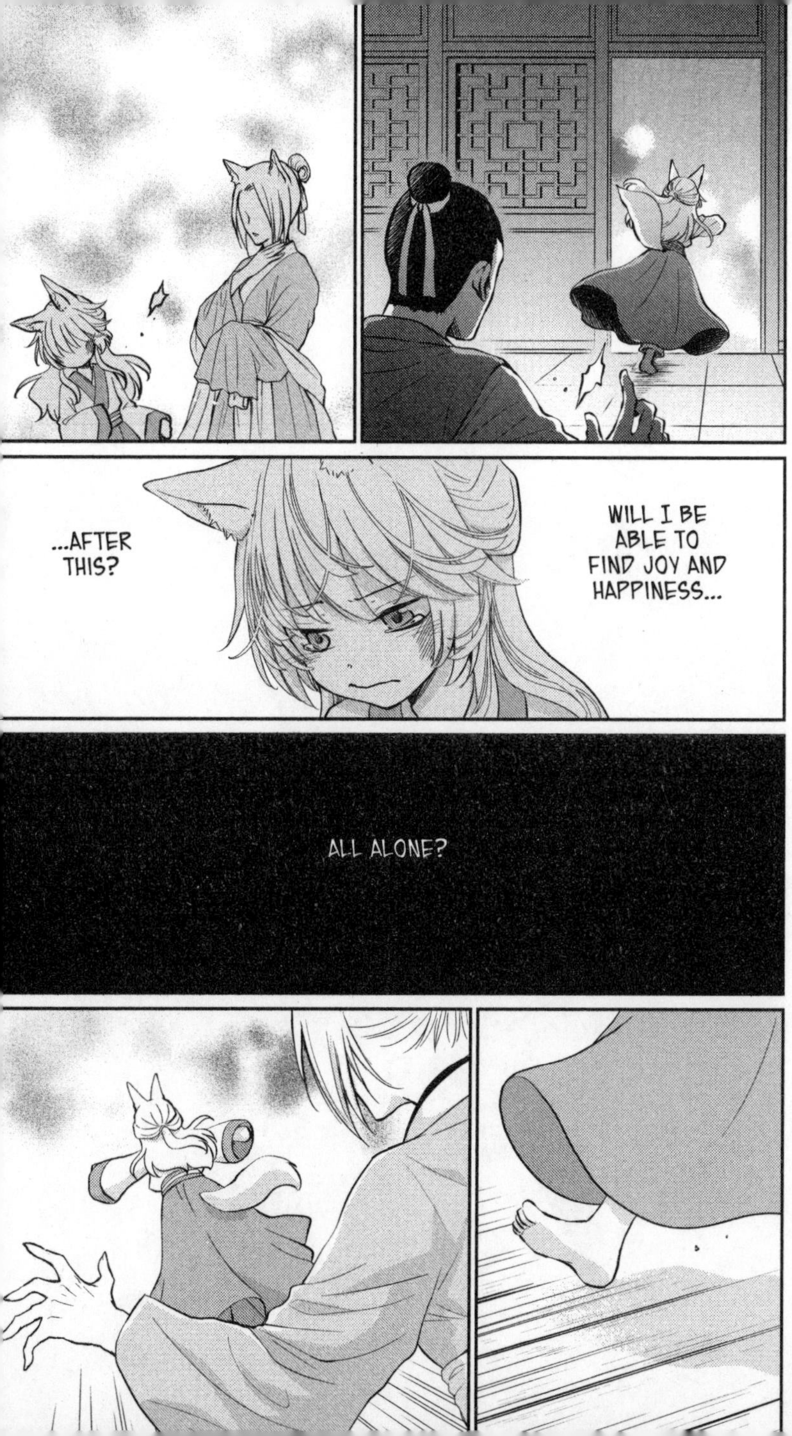
WILL I BE ABLE TO FIND JOY AND HAPPINESS...
...AFTER THIS?
ALL ALONE?

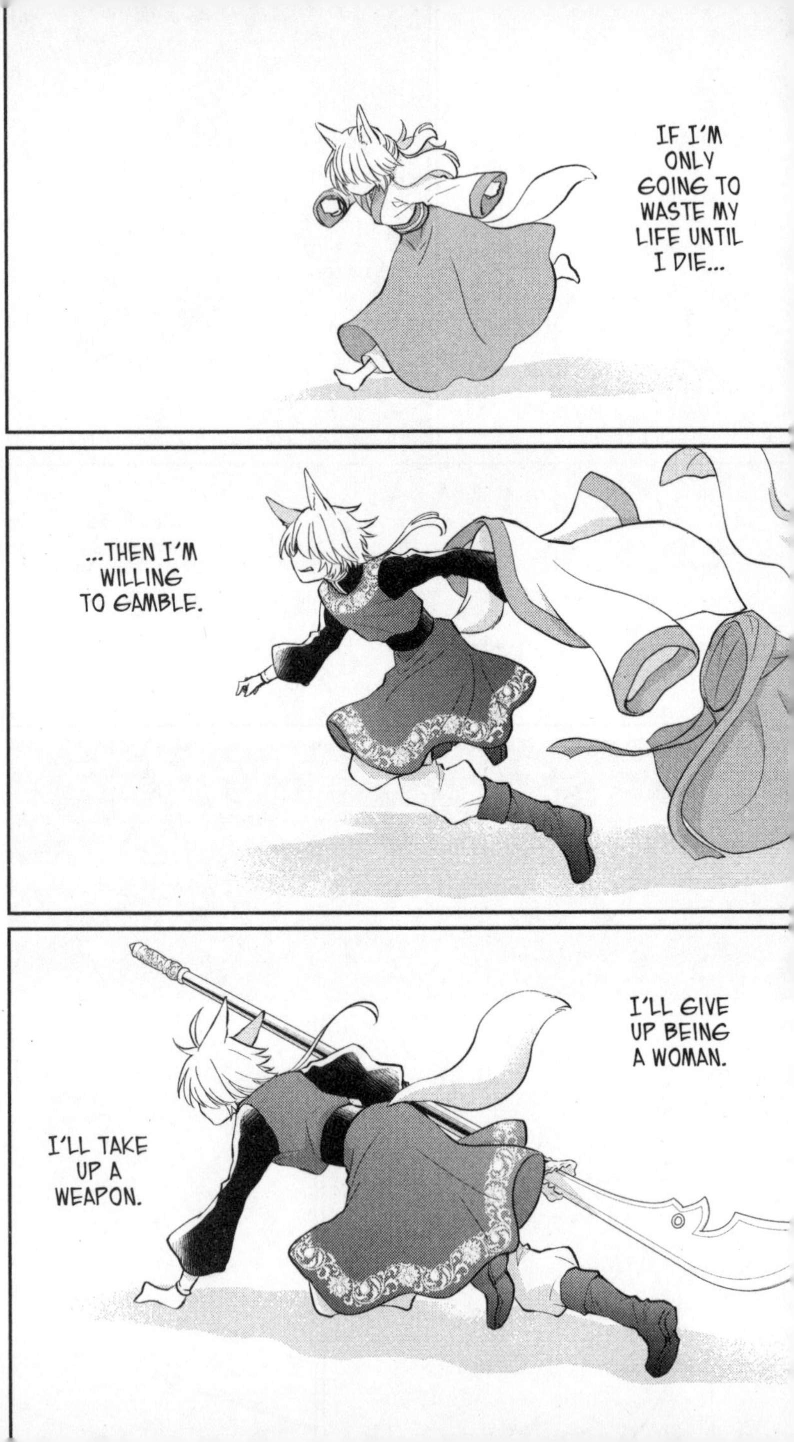
IF I'M ONLY GOING TO WASTE MY LIFE UNTIL I DIE...
...THEN I'M WILLING TO GAMBLE.
I'LL GIVE UP BEING A WOMAN.
I'LL TAKE UP A WEAPON.

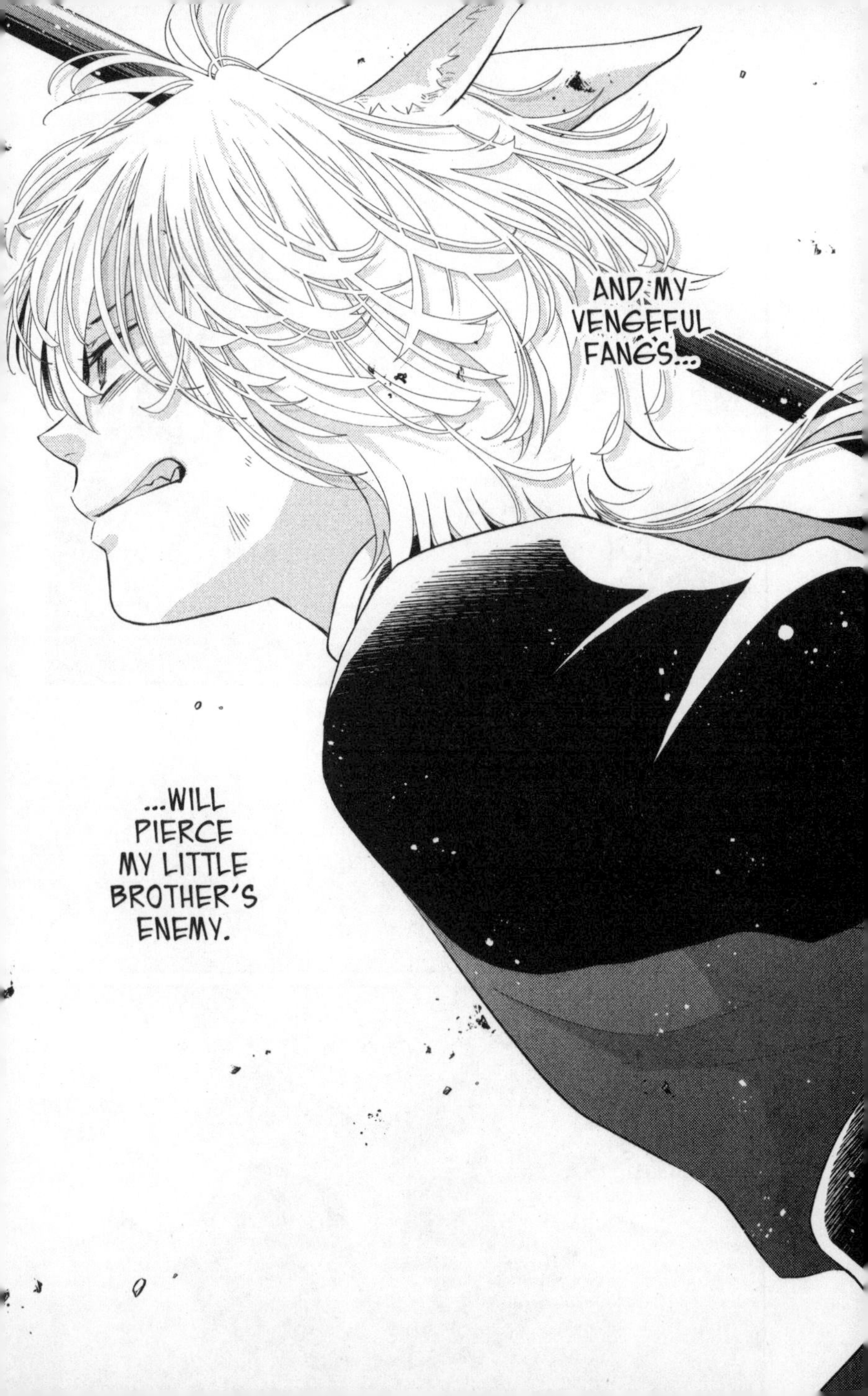
AND MY VENGEFUL FANGS...
...WILL PIERCE MY LITTLE BROTHER'S ENEMY.

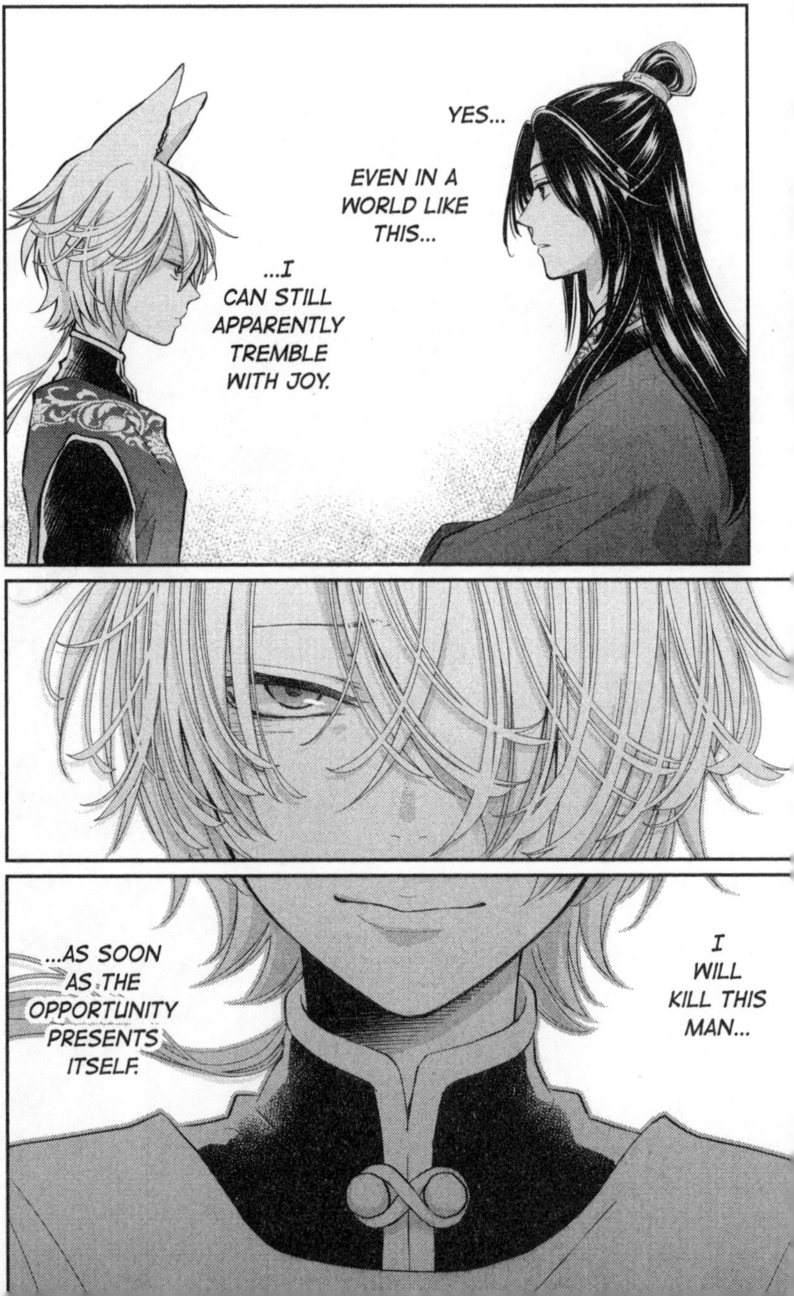
YES...
EVEN IN A WORLD LIKE THIS...
...I CAN STILL APPARENTLY TREMBLE WITH JOY.
I WILL KILL THIS MAN...
...AS SOON AS THE OPPORTUNITY PRESENTS ITSELF.

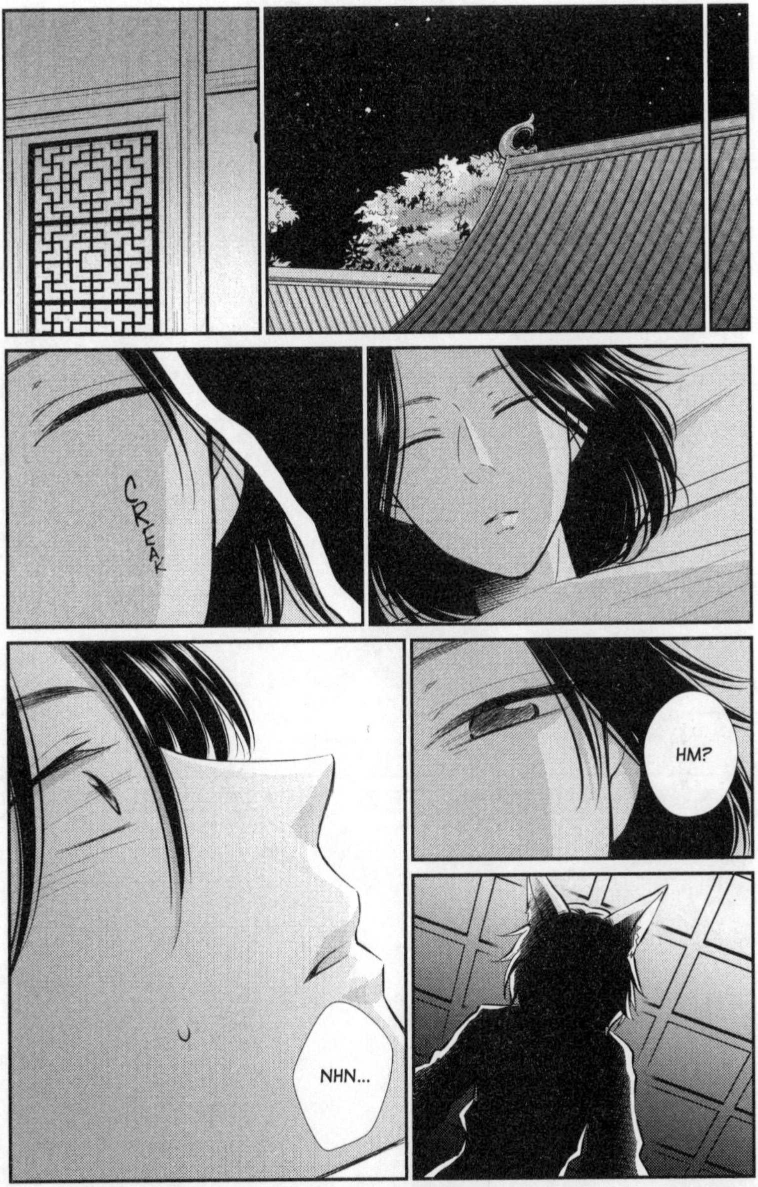
CREAK
HM?
NHN...

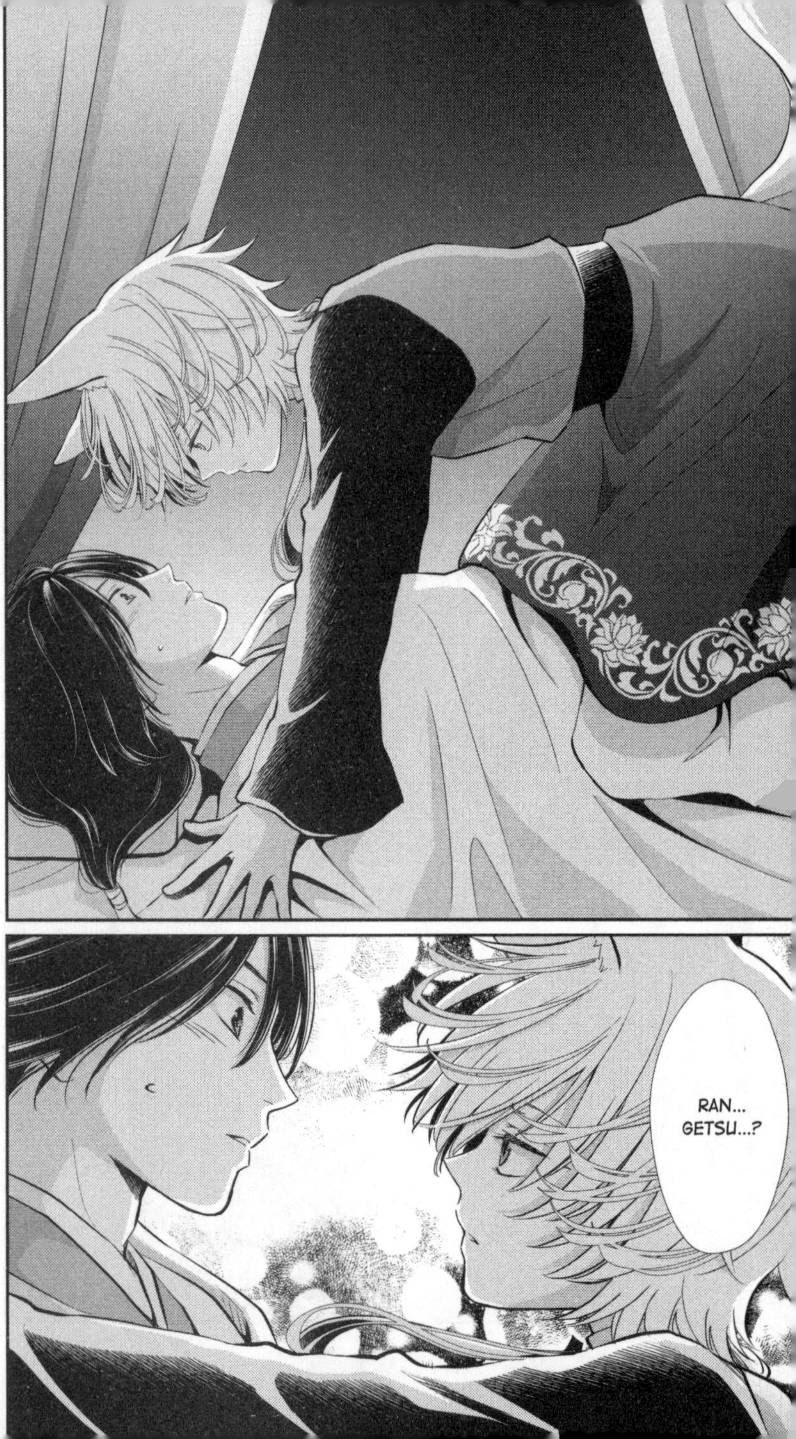
RAN... GETSU...?

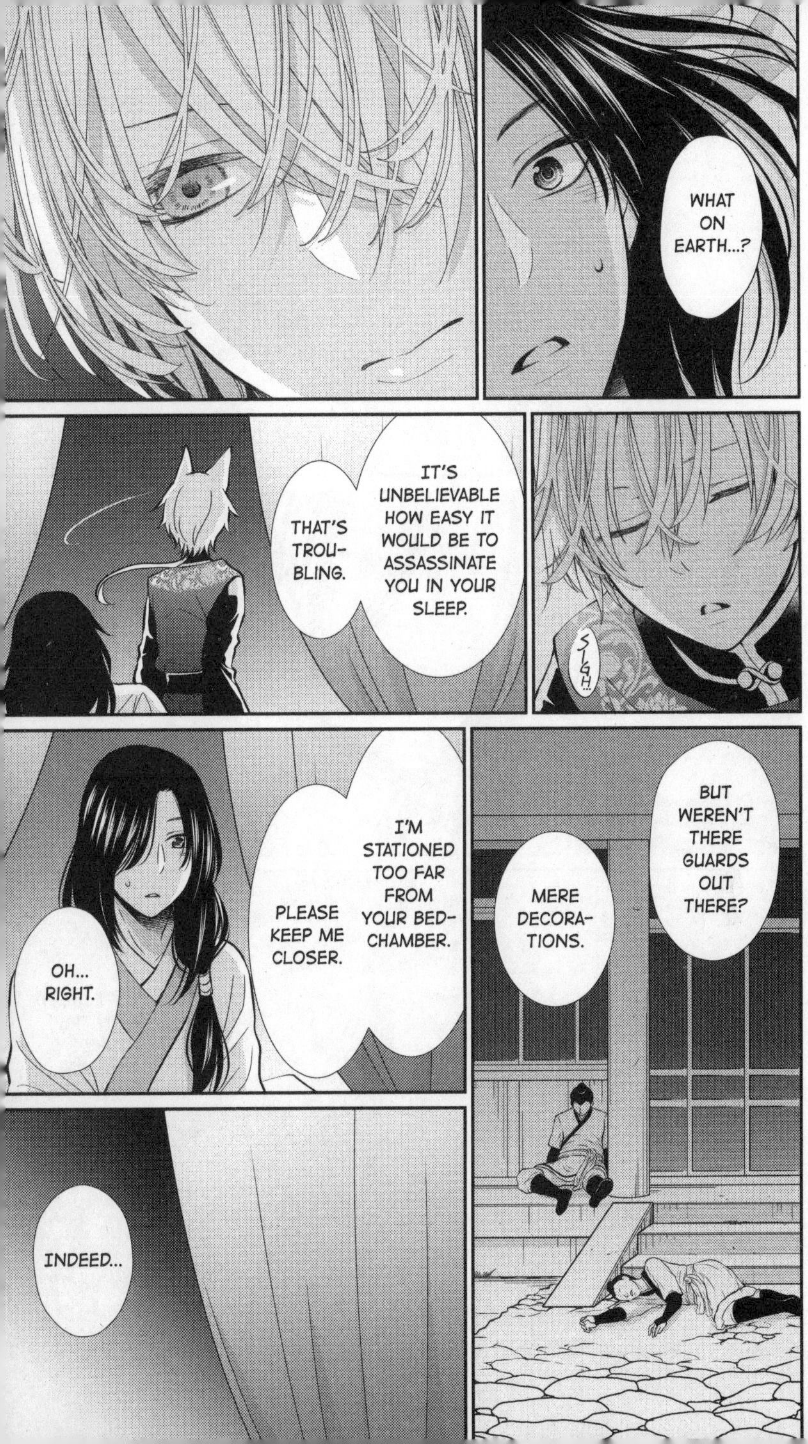
WHAT ON EARTH...?
SIGH...
IT'S UNBELIEVABLE HOW EASY IT WOULD BE TO ASSASSINATE YOU IN YOUR SLEEP.
THAT'S TROU-BLING.
BUT WEREN'T THERE GUARDS OUT THERE?
MERE DECORA-TIONS.
I'M STATIONED TOO FAR FROM YOUR BED-CHAMBER.
PLEASE KEEP ME CLOSER.
OH... RIGHT.
INDEED...

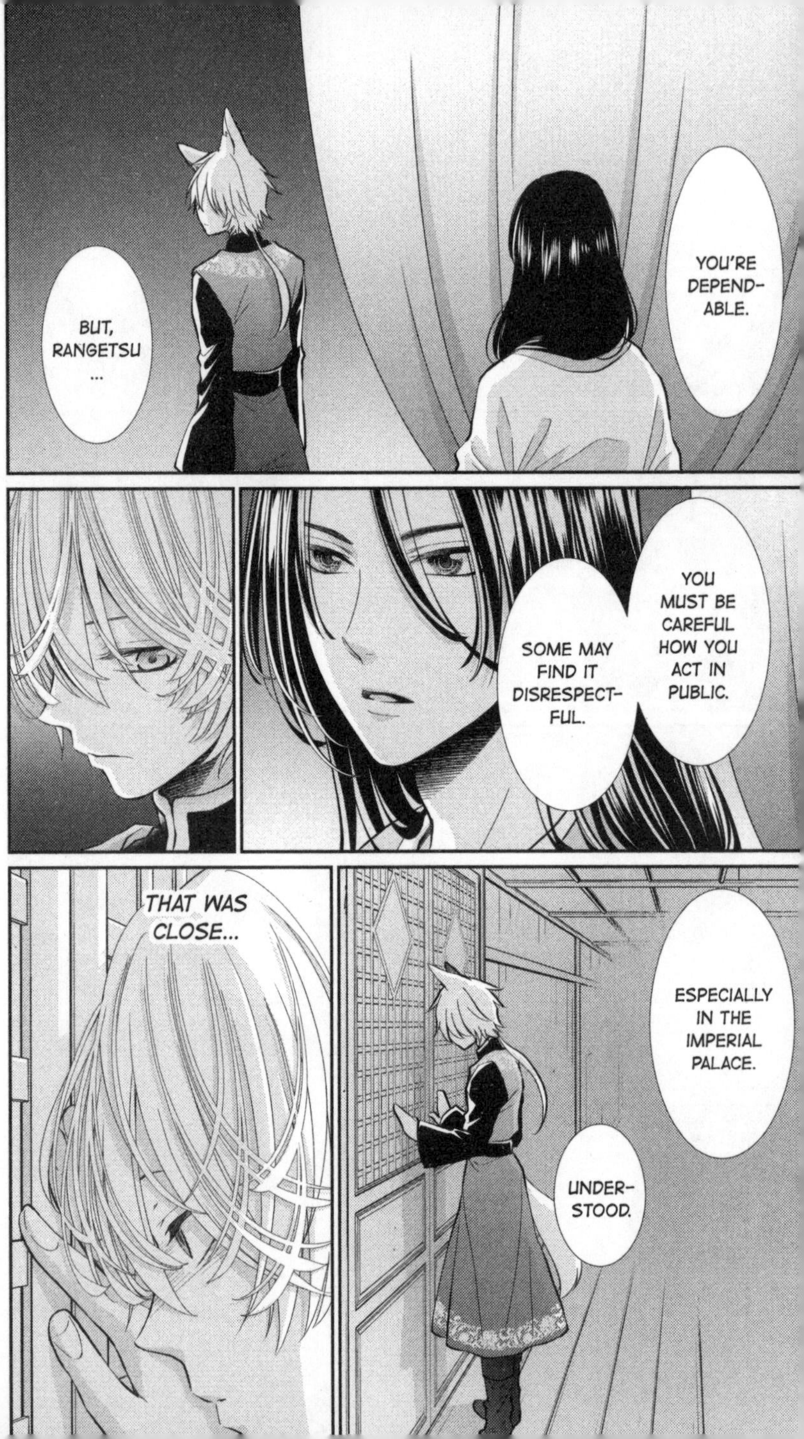
YOU'RE DEPEND-ABLE.
BUT, RANGETSU ...
YOU MUST BE CAREFUL HOW YOU ACT IN PUBLIC.
SOME MAY FIND IT DISRESPECT-FUL.
ESPECIALLY IN THE IMPERIAL PALACE.
UNDER-STOOD.
THAT WAS CLOSE...

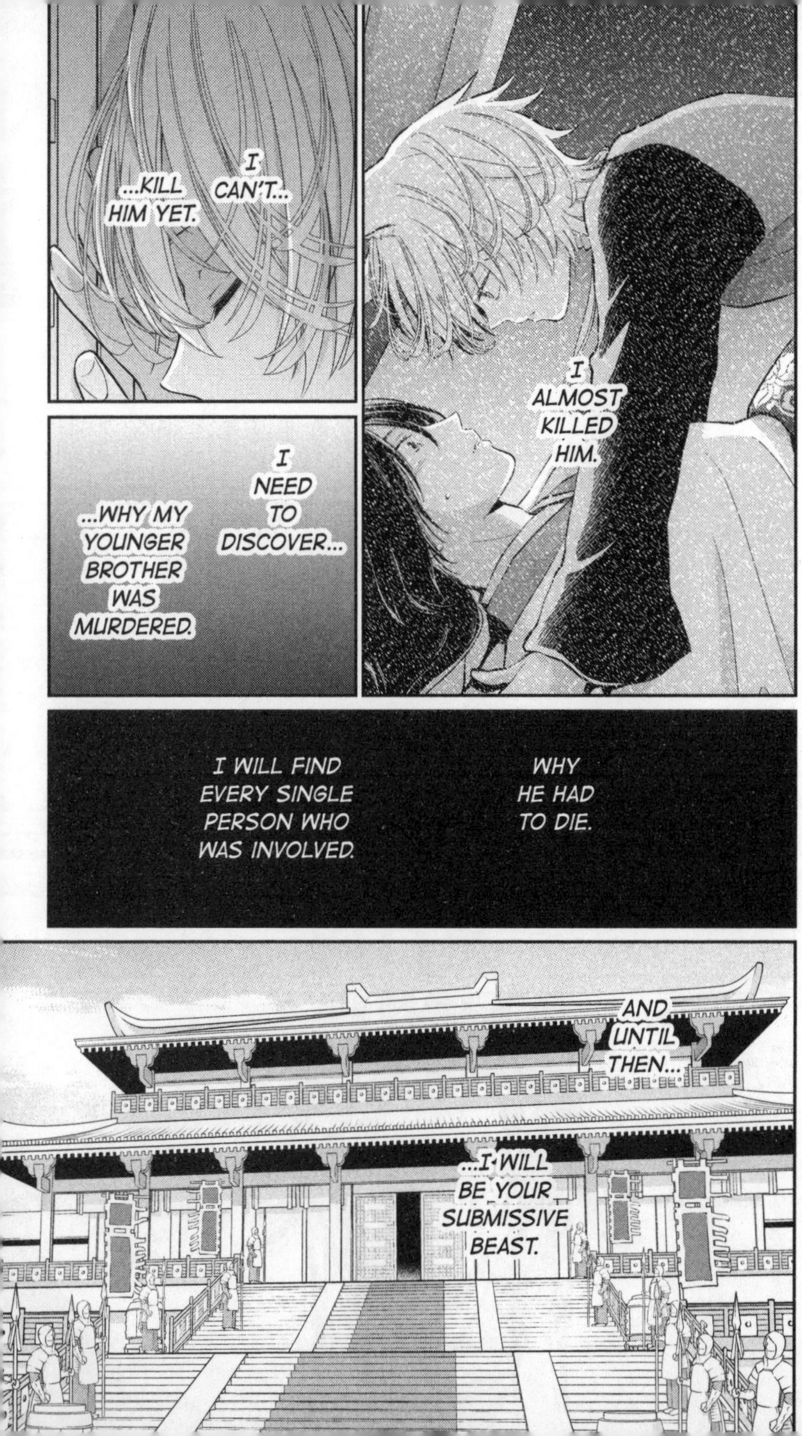
I ALMOST KILLED HIM.
I CAN'T...
...KILL HIM YET.
I NEED TO DISCOVER...
...WHY MY YOUNGER BROTHER WAS MURDERED.
WHY HE HAD TO DIE.
I WILL FIND EVERY SINGLE PERSON WHO WAS INVOLVED.
AND UNTIL THEN...
...I WILL BE YOUR SUBMISSIVE BEAST.

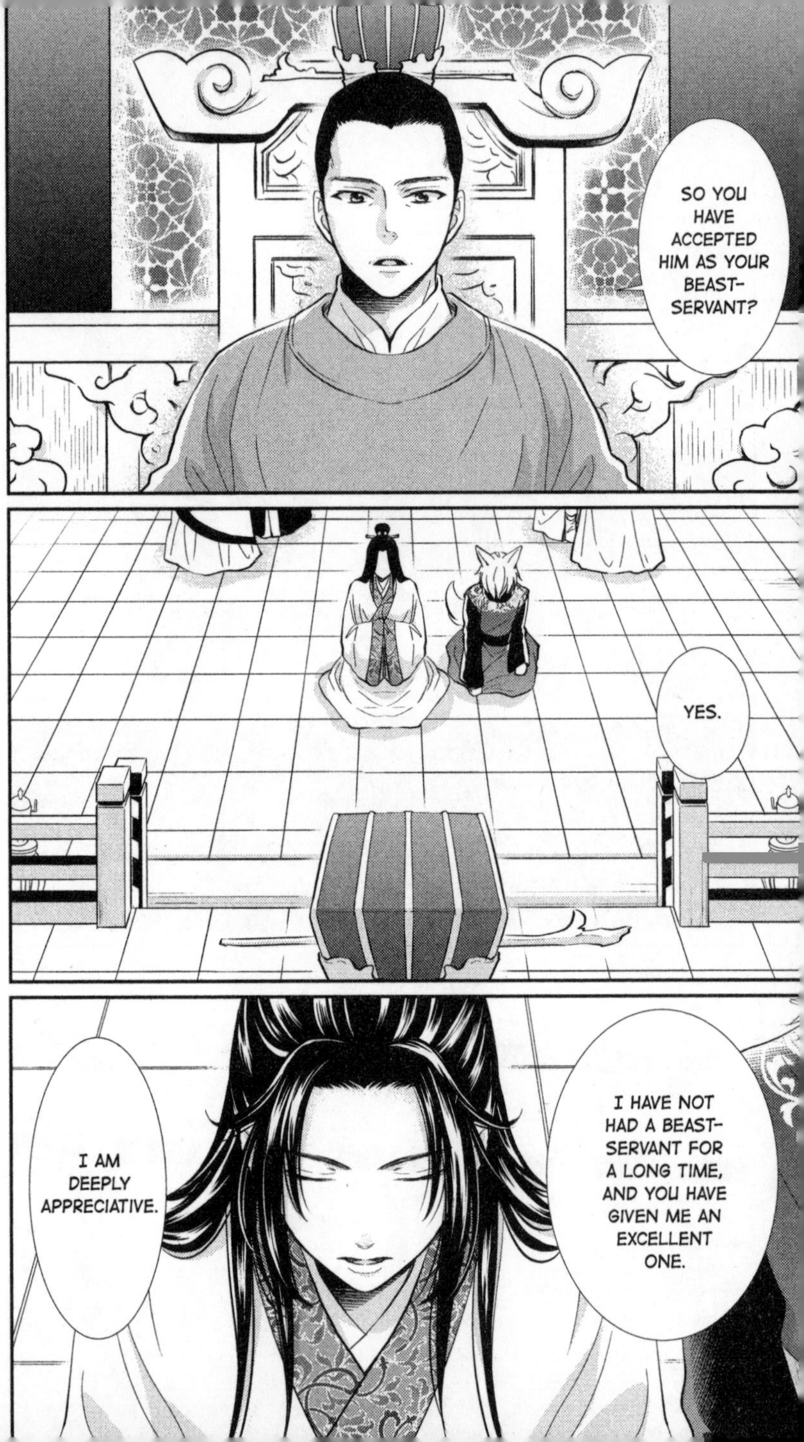
SO YOU HAVE ACCEPTED HIM AS YOUR BEAST-SERVANT?
YES.
I HAVE NOT HAD A BEAST-SERVANT FOR A LONG TIME, AND YOU HAVE GIVEN ME AN EXCELLENT ONE.
I AM DEEPLY APPRECIATIVE.

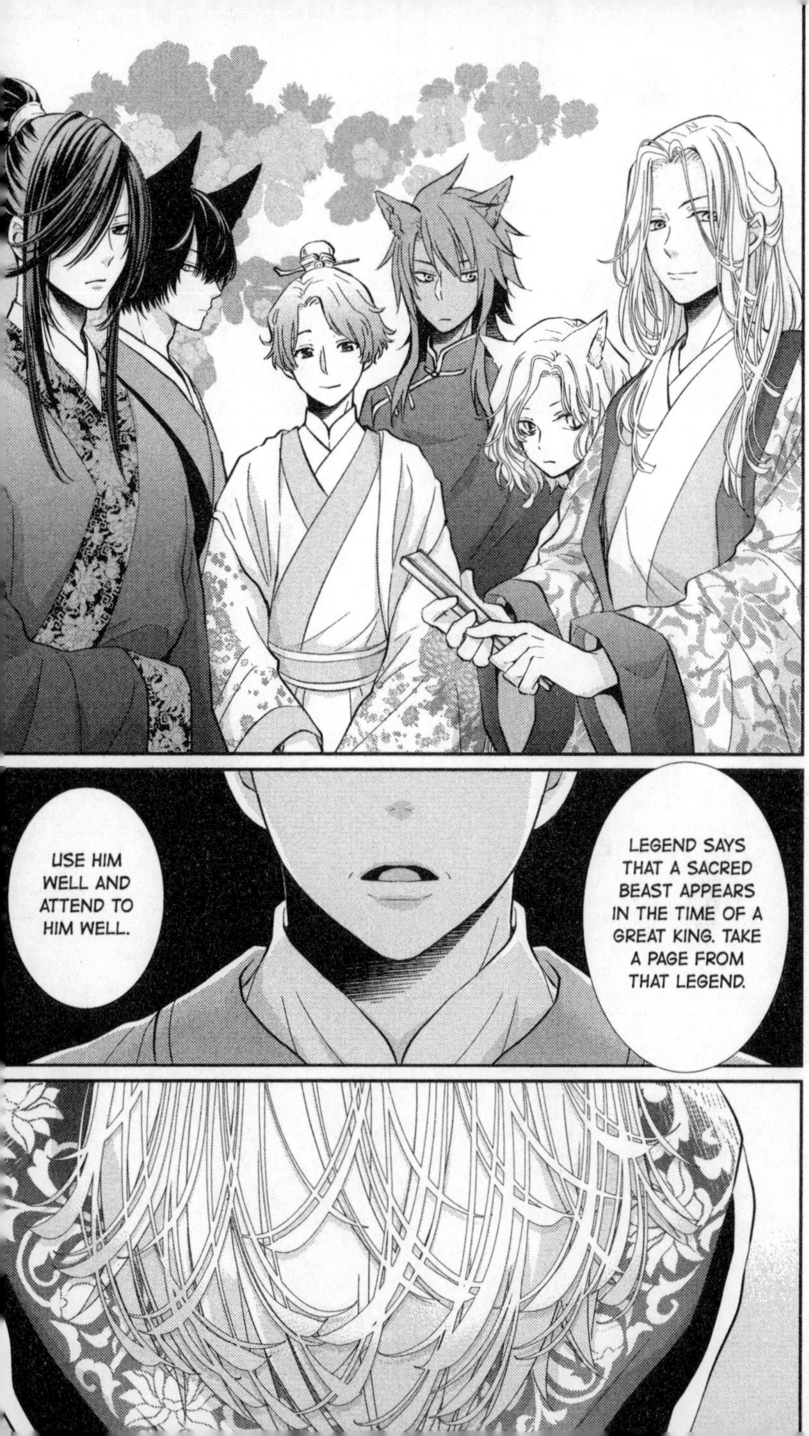
LEGEND SAYS THAT A SACRED BEAST APPEARS IN THE TIME OF A GREAT KING. TAKE A PAGE FROM THAT LEGEND.
USE HIM WELL AND ATTEND TO HIM WELL.

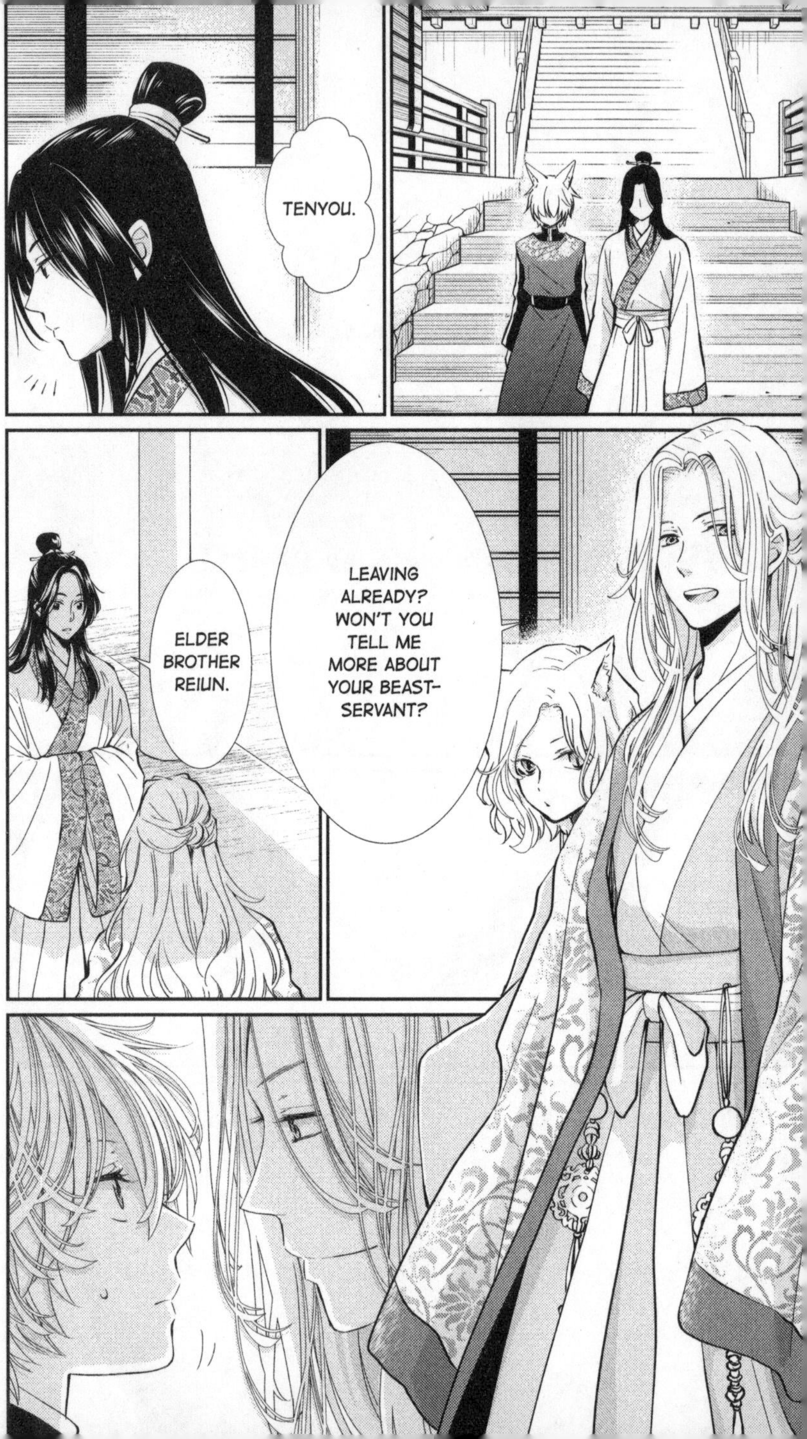
TENYOU.
LEAVING ALREADY? WON'T YOU TELL ME MORE ABOUT YOUR BEAST-SERVANT?
ELDER BROTHER REIUN.

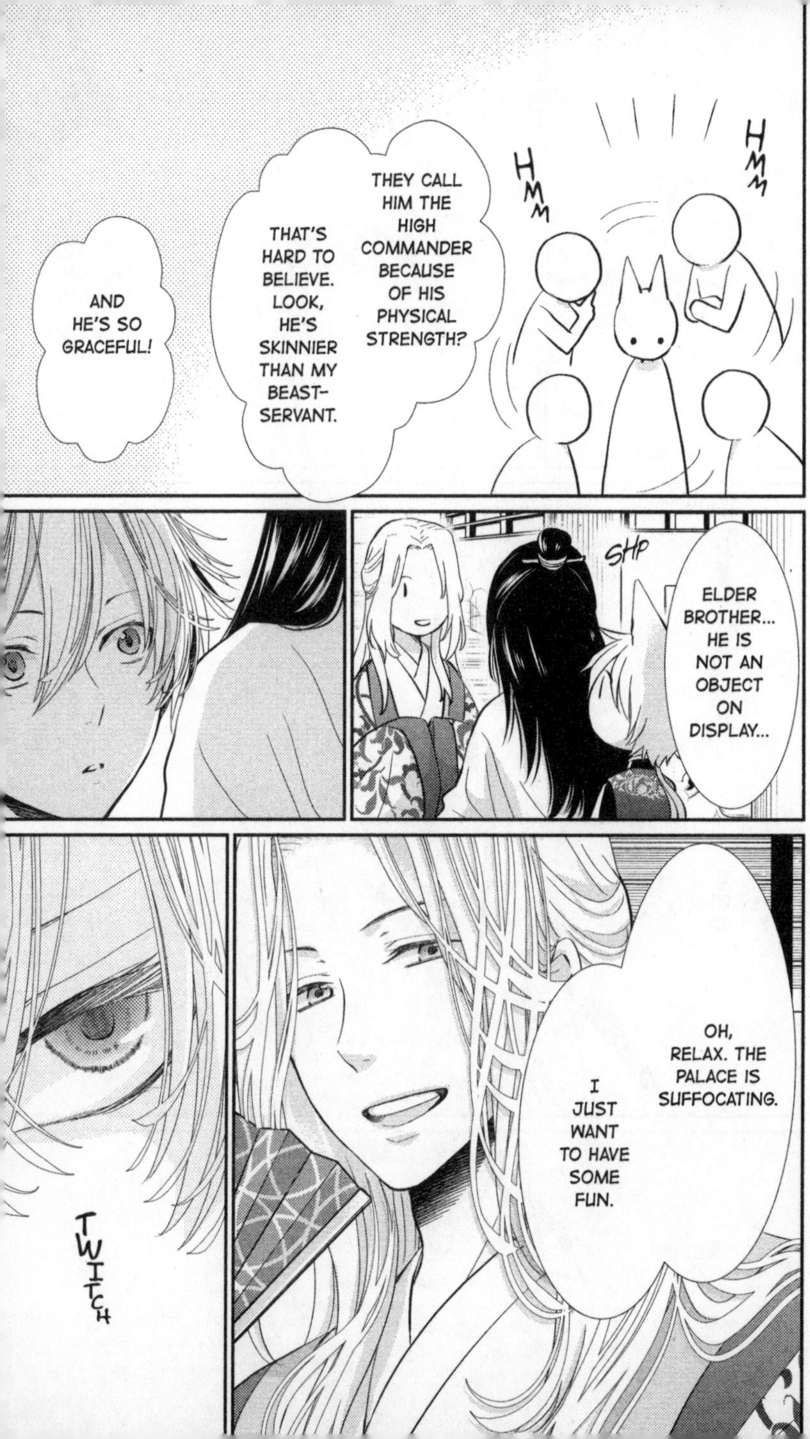
HMM
HMM
THEY CALL HIM THE HIGH COMMANDER BECAUSE OF HIS PHYSICAL STRENGTH?
THAT'S HARD TO BELIEVE. LOOK, HE'S SKINNIER THAN MY BEAST-SERVANT.
AND HE'S SO GRACEFUL!
SHP
ELDER BROTHER... HE IS NOT AN OBJECT ON DISPLAY...
OH, RELAX. THE PALACE IS SUFFOCATING.
I JUST WANT TO HAVE SOME FUN.
TWITCH

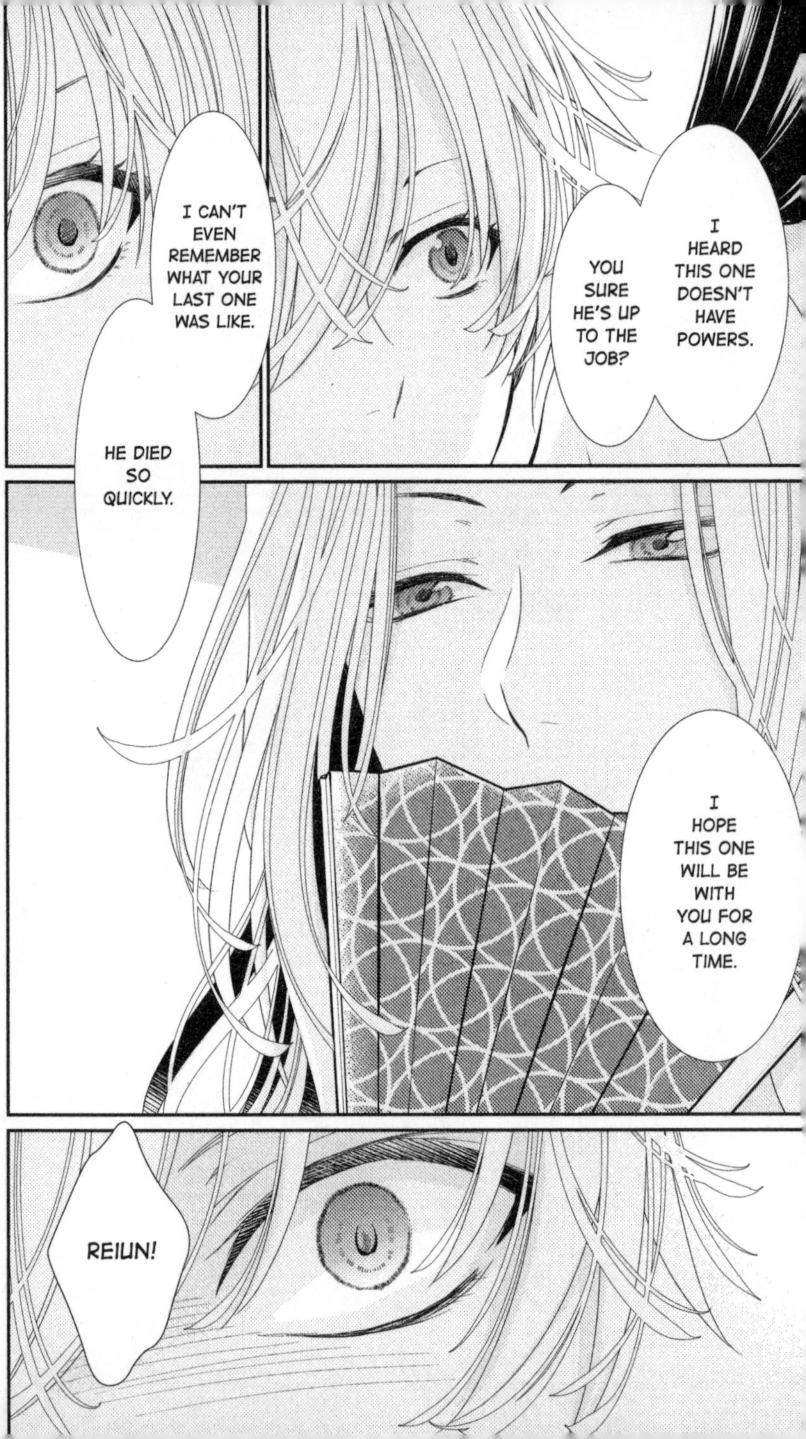
I HEARD THIS ONE DOESN'T HAVE POWERS.
YOU SURE HE'S UP TO THE JOB?
I CAN'T EVEN REMEMBER WHAT YOUR LAST ONE WAS LIKE.
HE DIED SO QUICKLY.
I HOPE THIS ONE WILL BE WITH YOU FOR A LONG TIME.
REIUN!

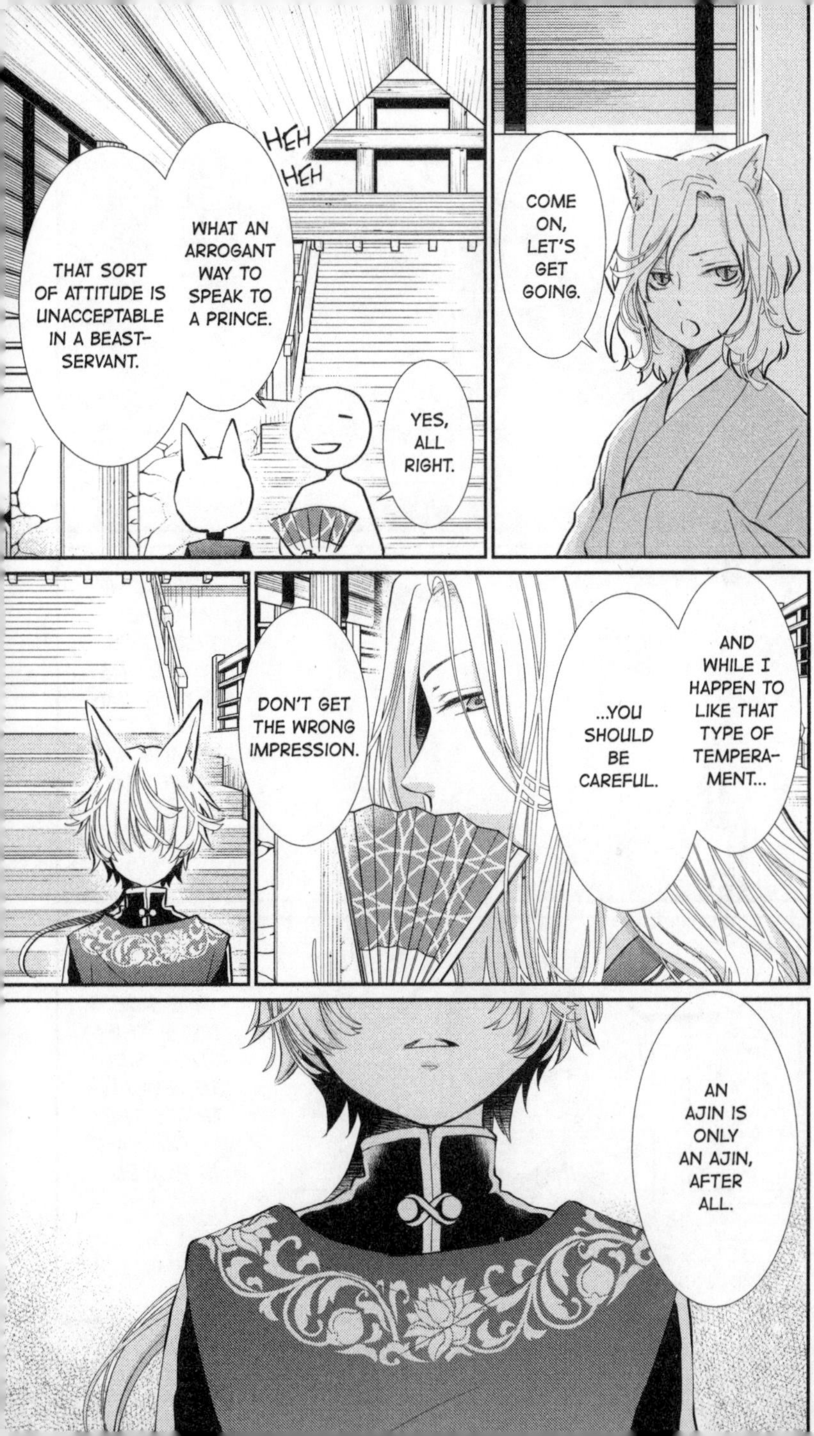
COME ON, LET'S GET GOING.
YES, ALL RIGHT.
HEH HEH
WHAT AN ARROGANT WAY TO SPEAK TO A PRINCE.
THAT SORT OF ATTITUDE IS UNACCEPTABLE IN A BEAST-SERVANT.
AND WHILE I HAPPEN TO LIKE THAT TYPE OF TEMPERA-MENT...
...YOU SHOULD BE CAREFUL.
DON'T GET THE WRONG IMPRESSION.
AN AJIN IS ONLY AN AJIN, AFTER ALL.

I KNEW...

...THE WORLD WAS LIKE THIS.

WE BECOME ANOTHER PERSON'S TOY ALL JUST SO THEY CAN HAVE A LITTLE FUN AND KILL SOME TIME.

ONE SIDE USES, THE OTHER SIDE GETS USED. THAT'S THE WAY THE GAME IS PLAYED.

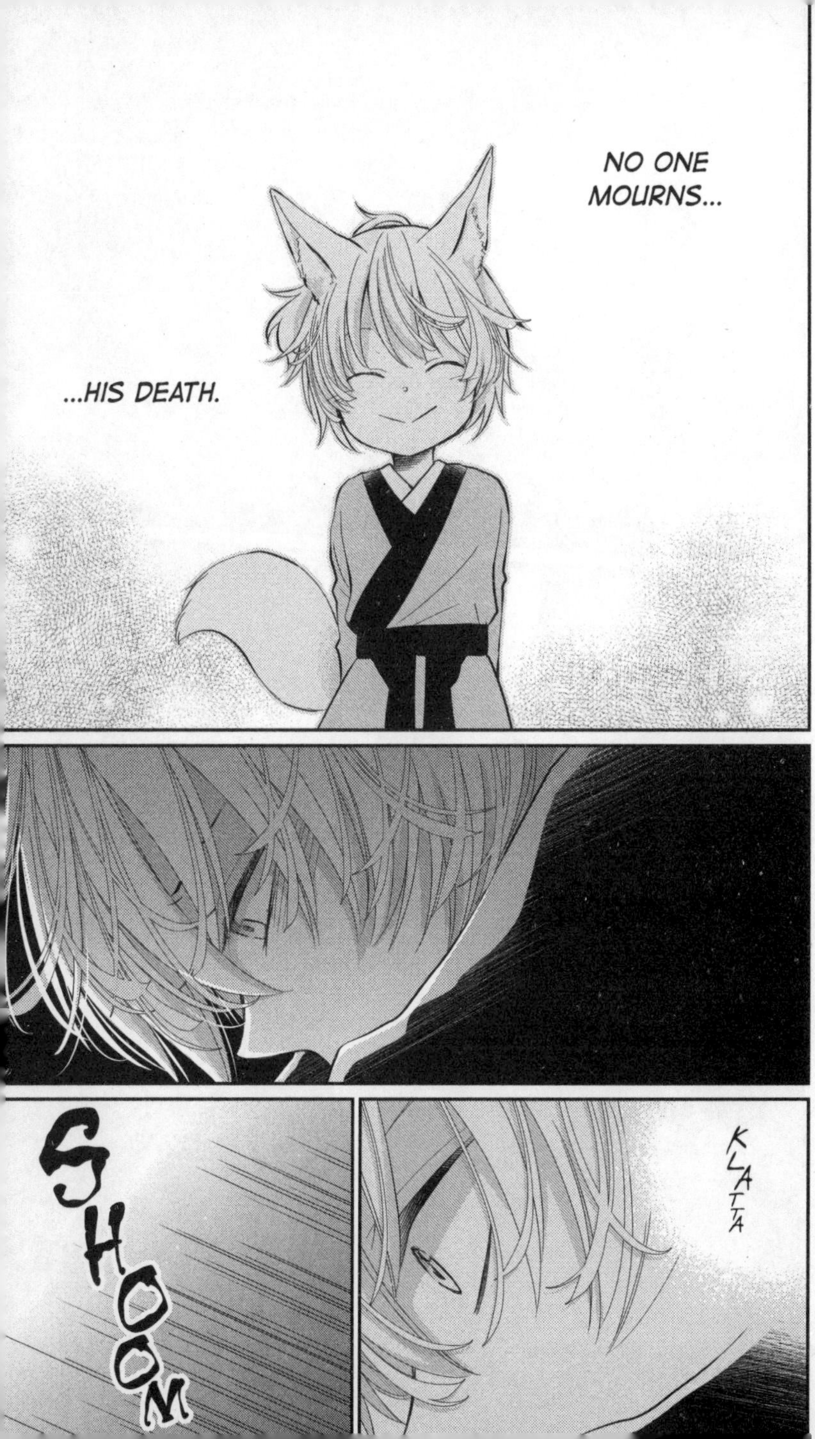
NO ONE MOURNS...
...HIS DEATH.
KLATTA
SHOOM

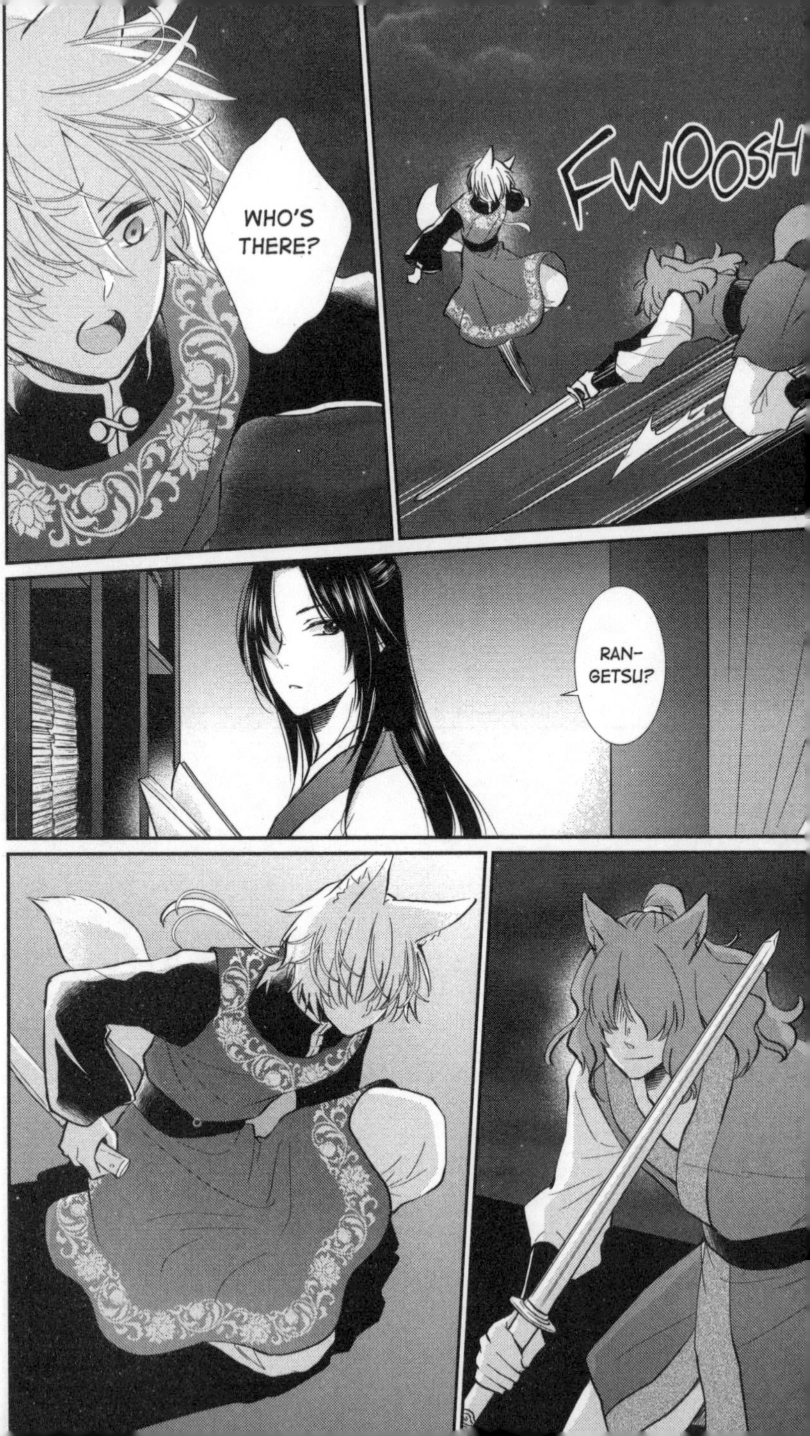
FWOOSH
WHO'S THERE?
RAN-GETSU?

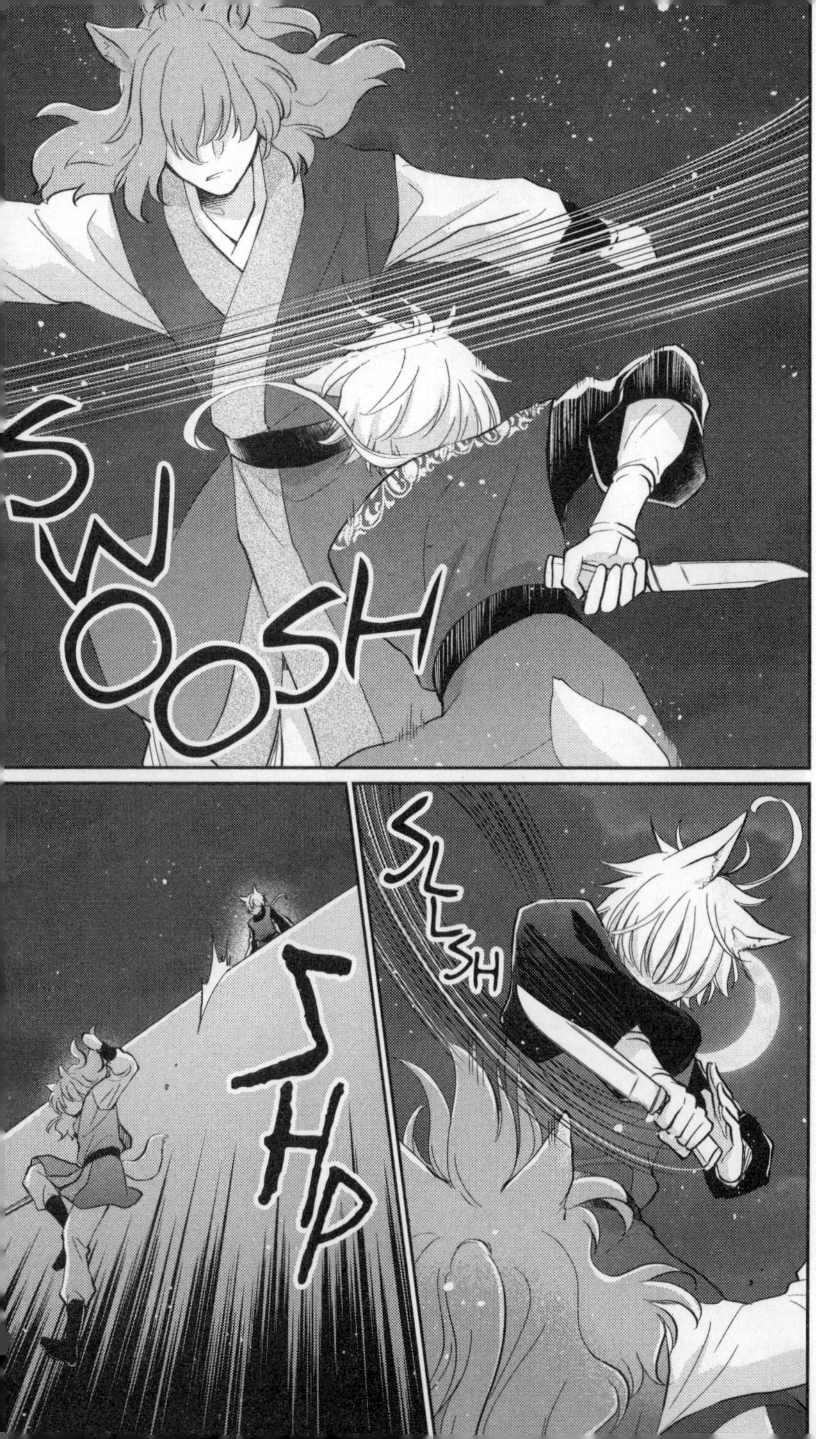
SWOOSH
SLLSH
SHP

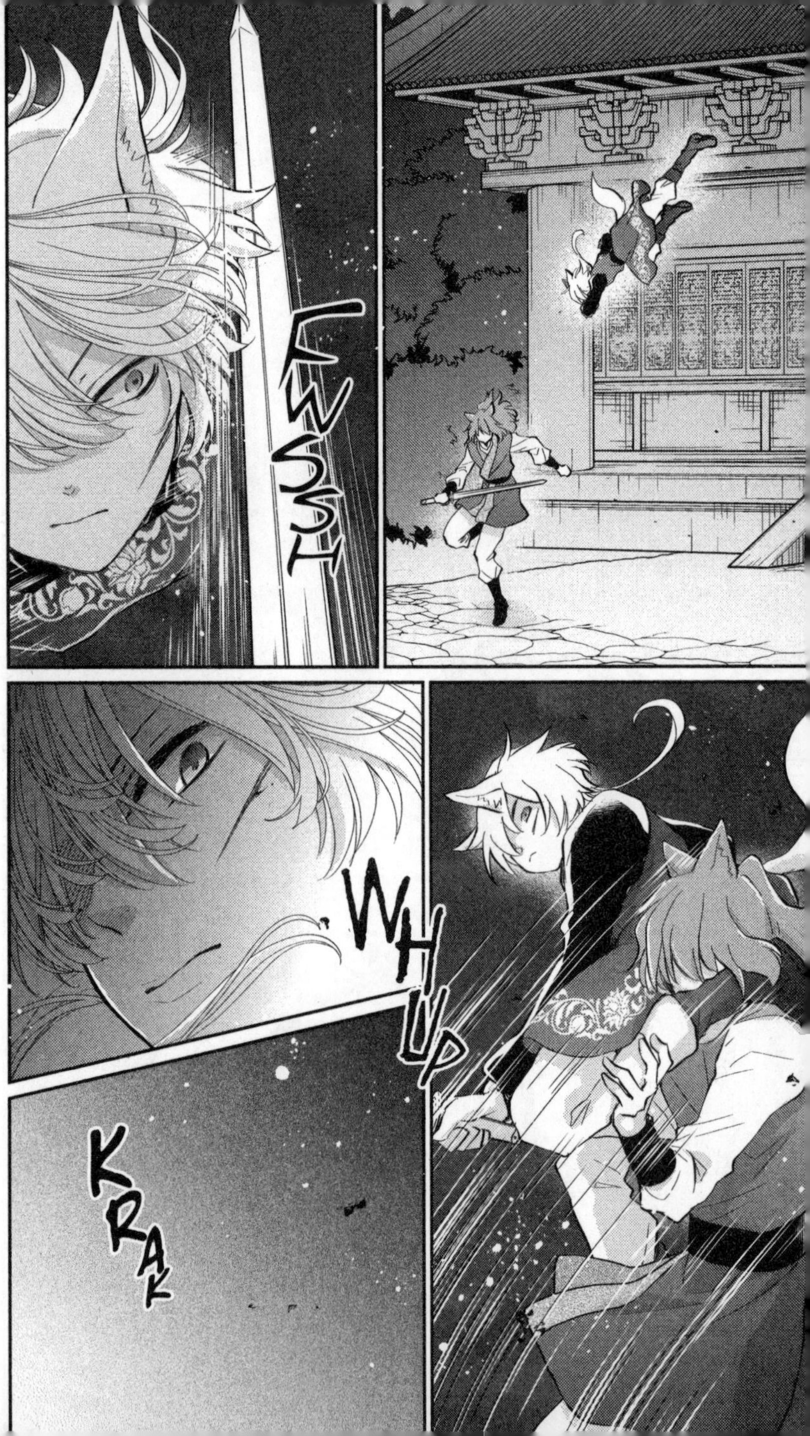
FWSSH
WHUP
KRAK

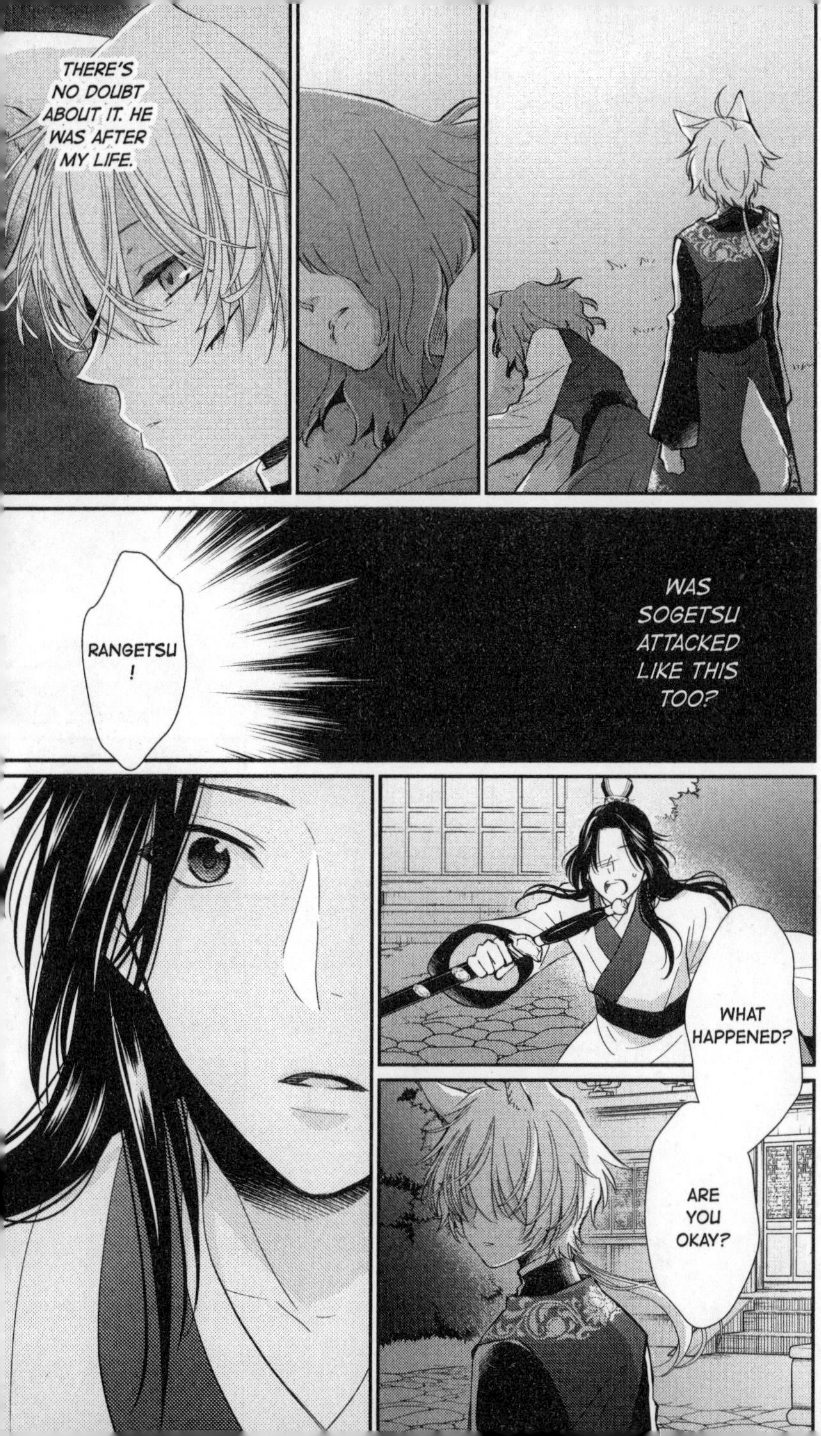
THERE'S NO DOUBT ABOUT IT. HE WAS AFTER MY LIFE.
WAS SOGETSU ATTACKED LIKE THIS TOO?
RANGETSU!
WHAT HAPPENED?
ARE YOU OKAY?

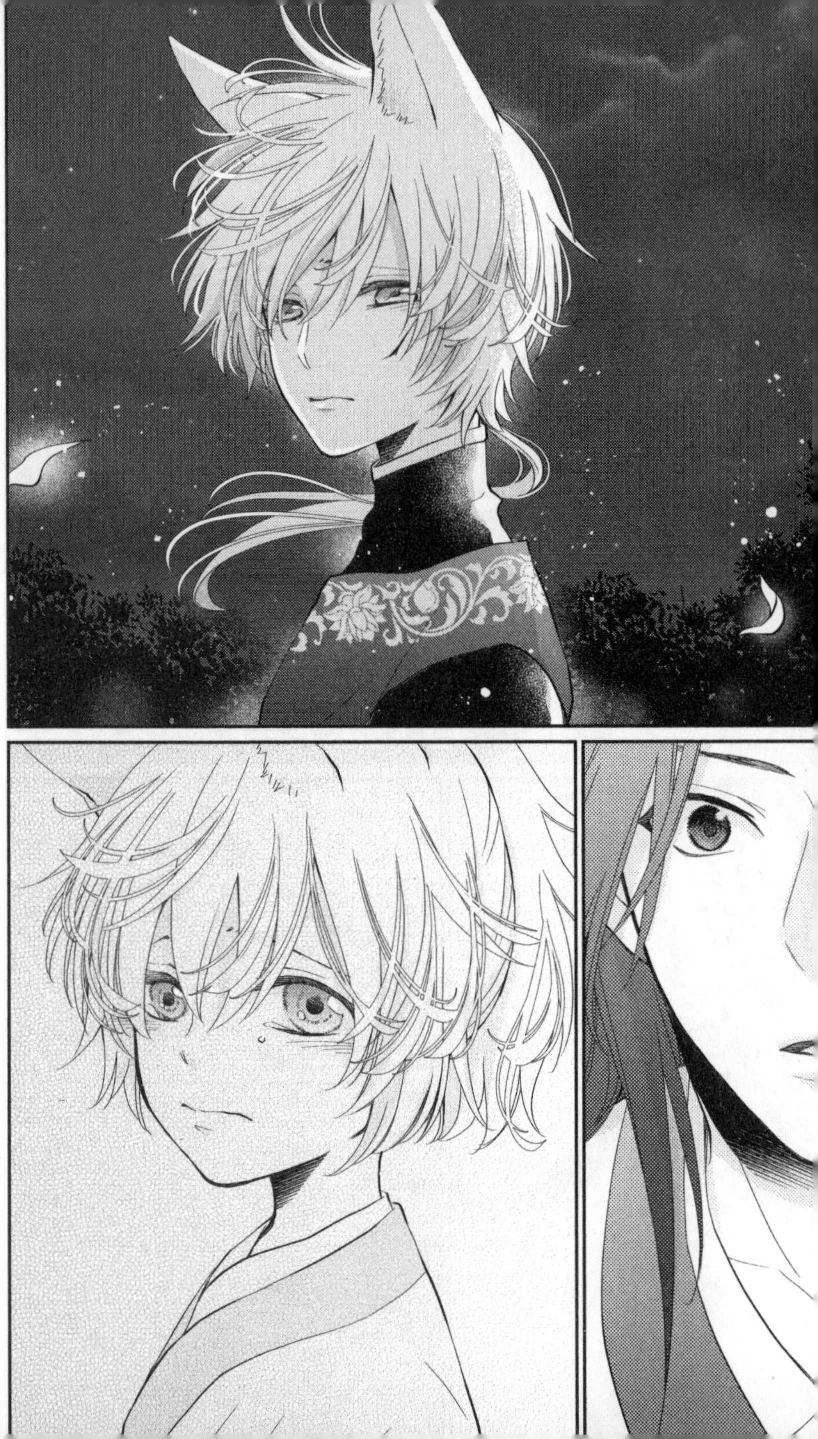

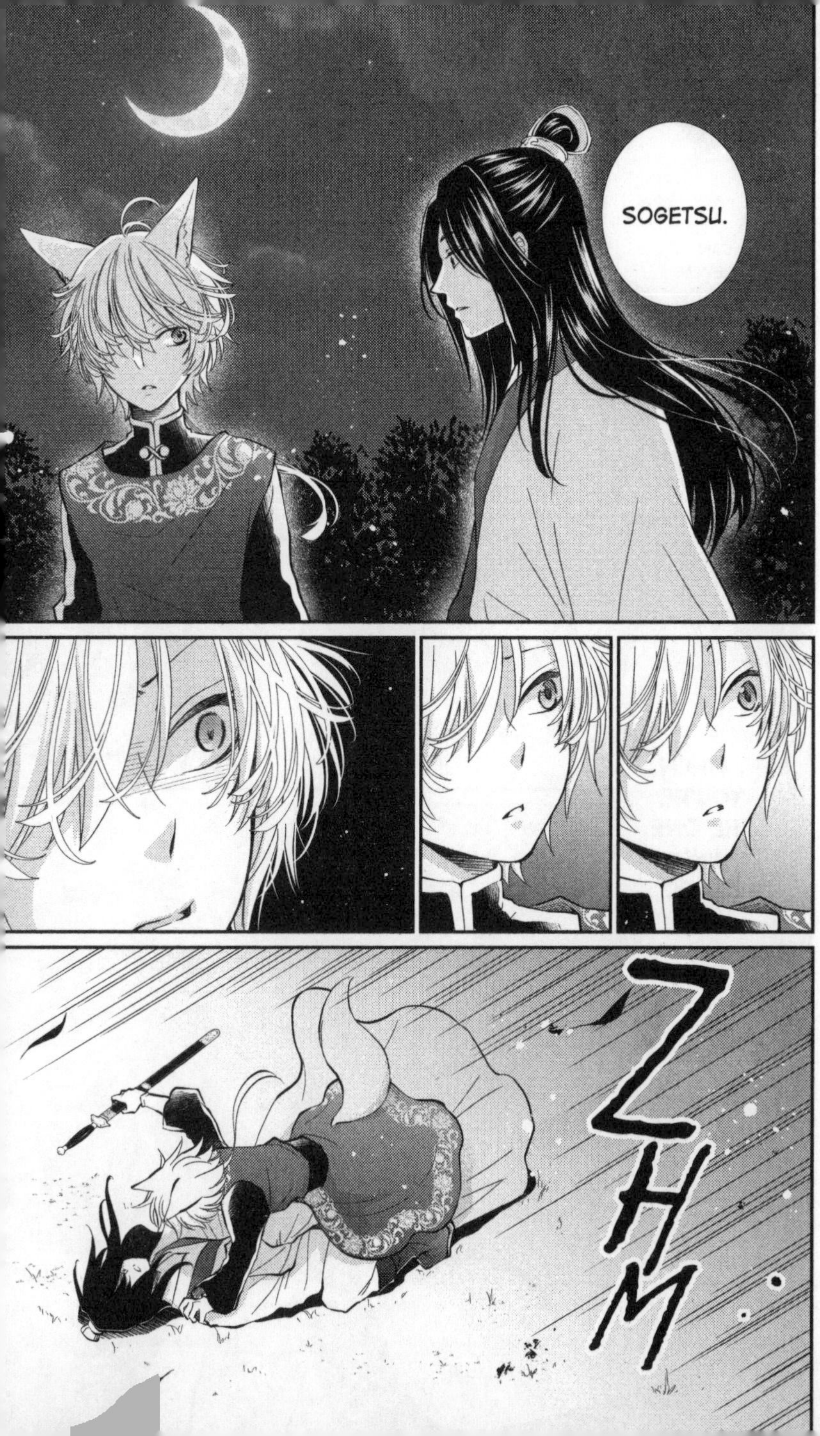
SOGETSU.
ZHM

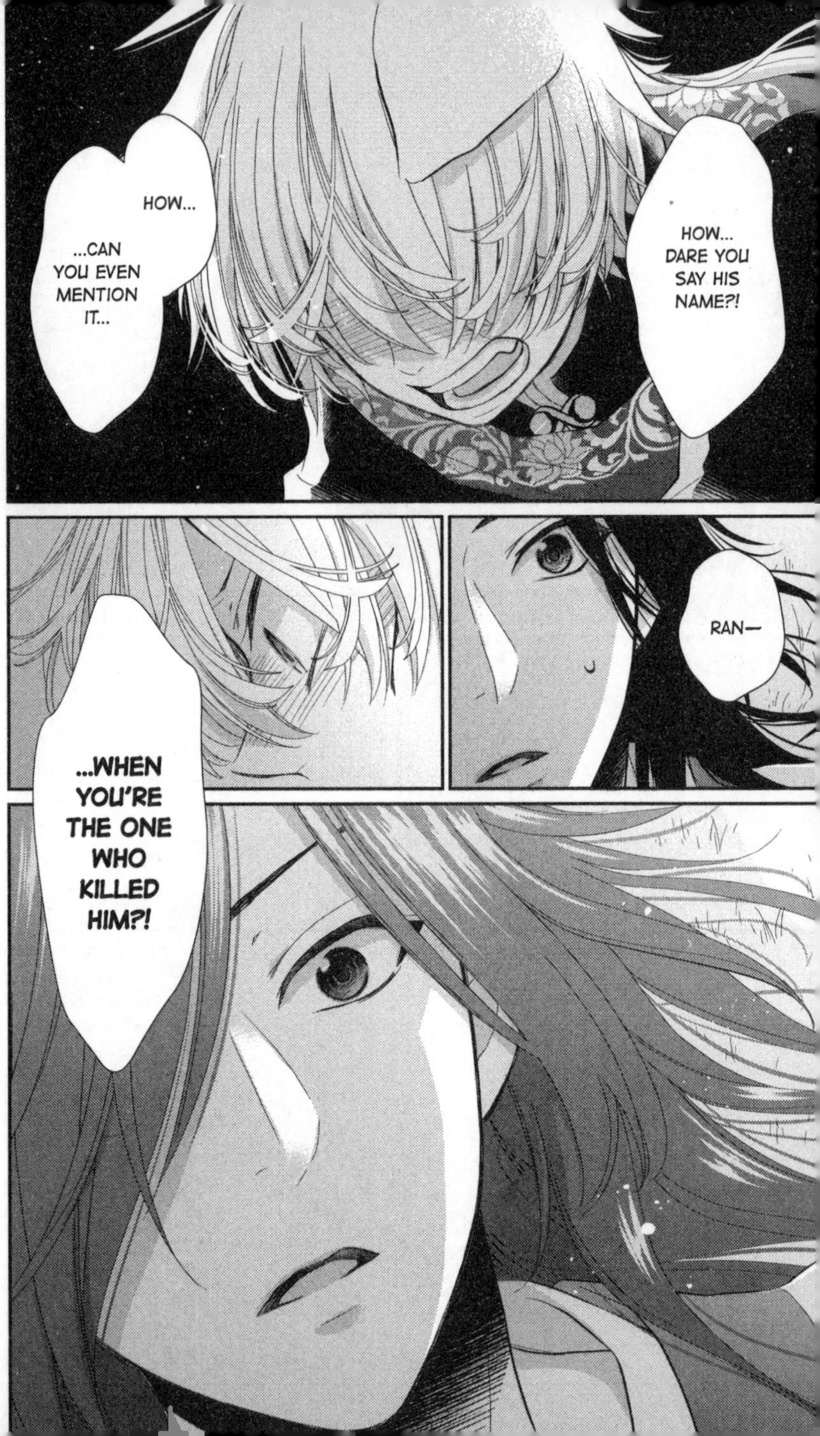
HOW... DARE YOU SAY HIS NAME?!
HOW...
...CAN YOU EVEN MENTION IT...
RAN—
...WHEN YOU'RE THE ONE WHO KILLED HIM?!

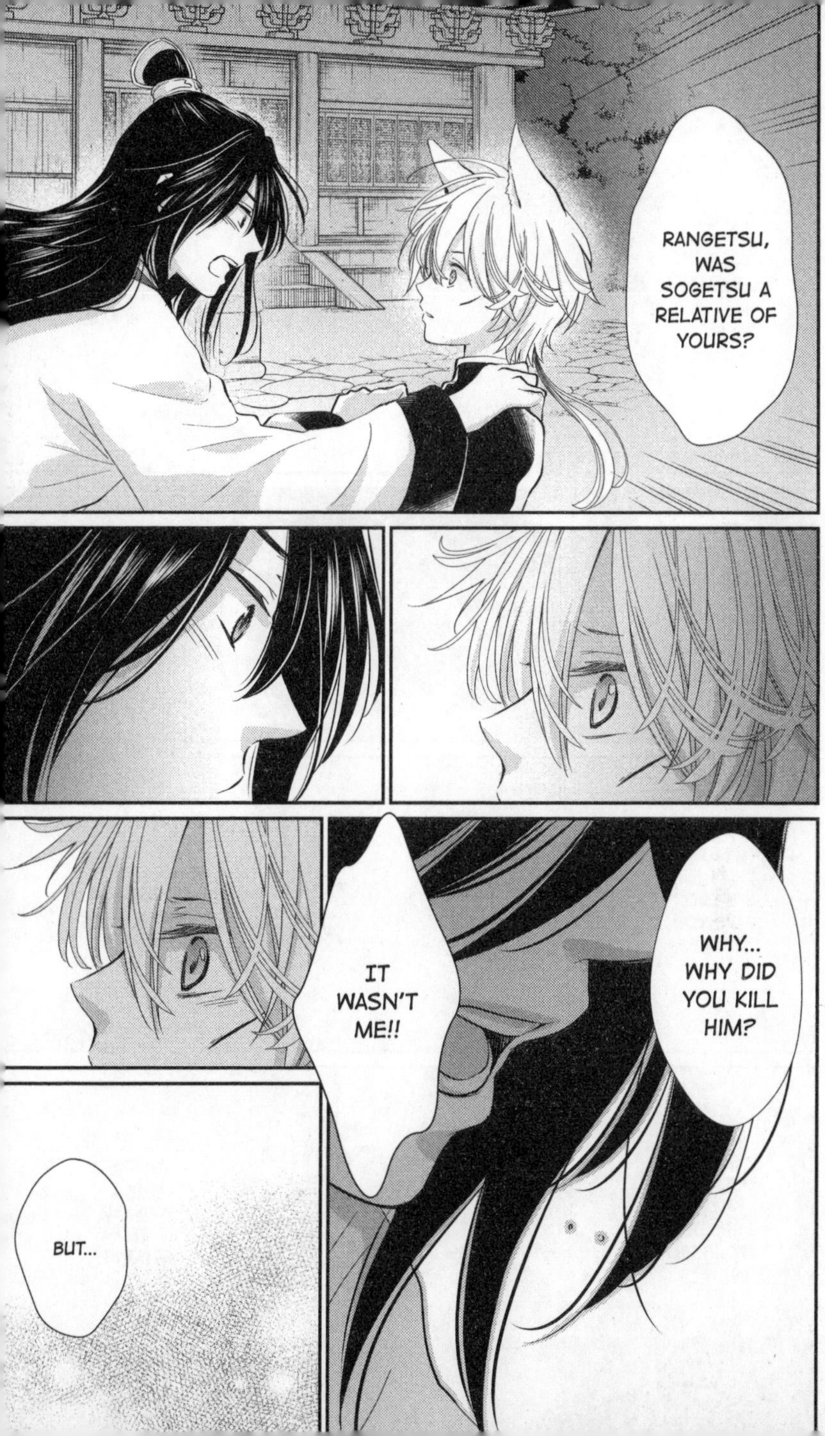
RANGETSU, WAS SOGETSU A RELATIVE OF YOURS?
WHY... WHY DID YOU KILL HIM?
IT WASN'T ME!!
BUT...

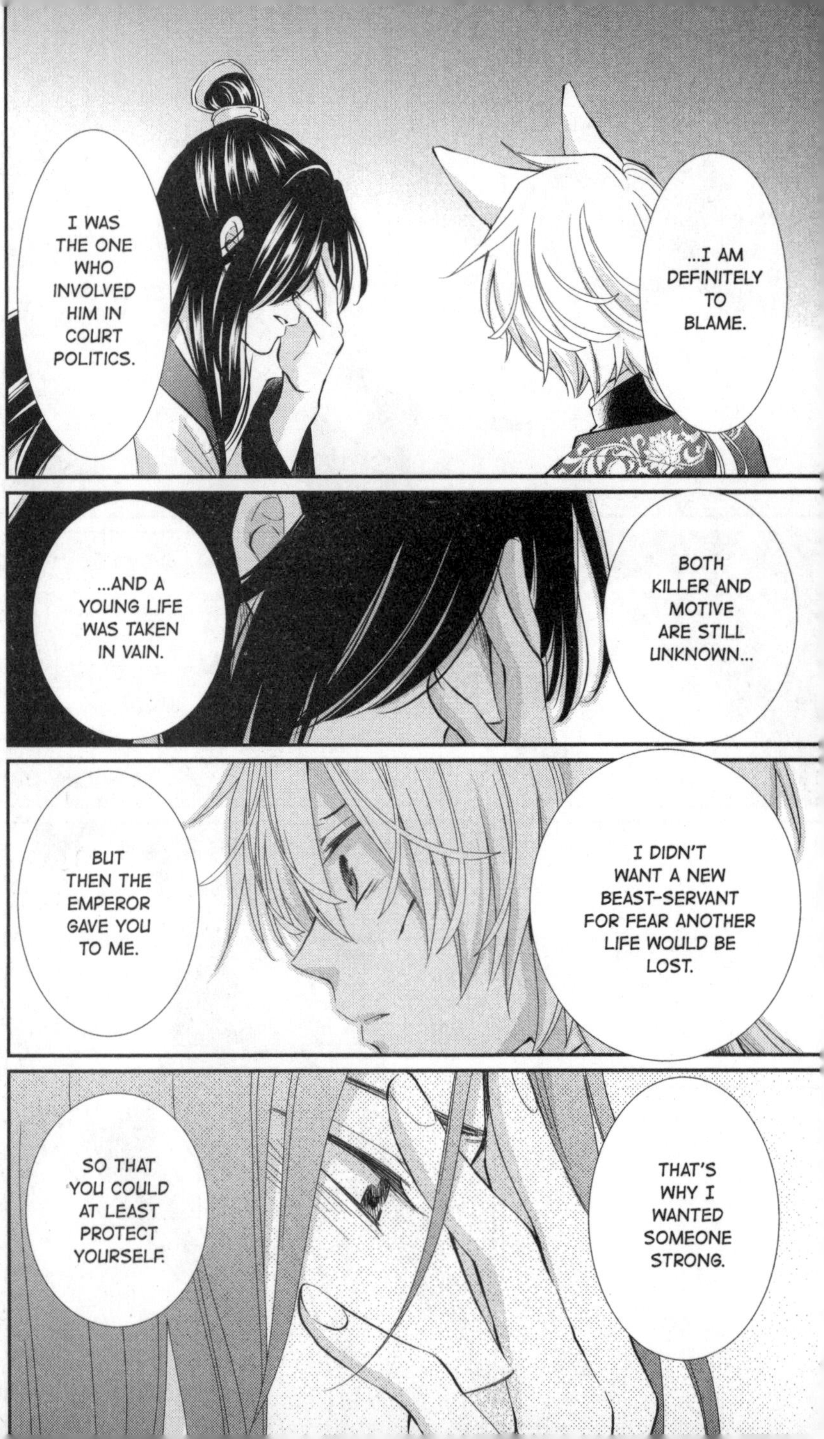
...I AM DEFINITELY TO BLAME.
I WAS THE ONE WHO INVOLVED HIM IN COURT POLITICS.
BOTH KILLER AND MOTIVE ARE STILL UNKNOWN...
...AND A YOUNG LIFE WAS TAKEN IN VAIN.
I DIDN'T WANT A NEW BEAST-SERVANT FOR FEAR ANOTHER LIFE WOULD BE LOST.
BUT THEN THE EMPEROR GAVE YOU TO ME.
THAT'S WHY I WANTED SOMEONE STRONG.
SO THAT YOU COULD AT LEAST PROTECT YOURSELF.

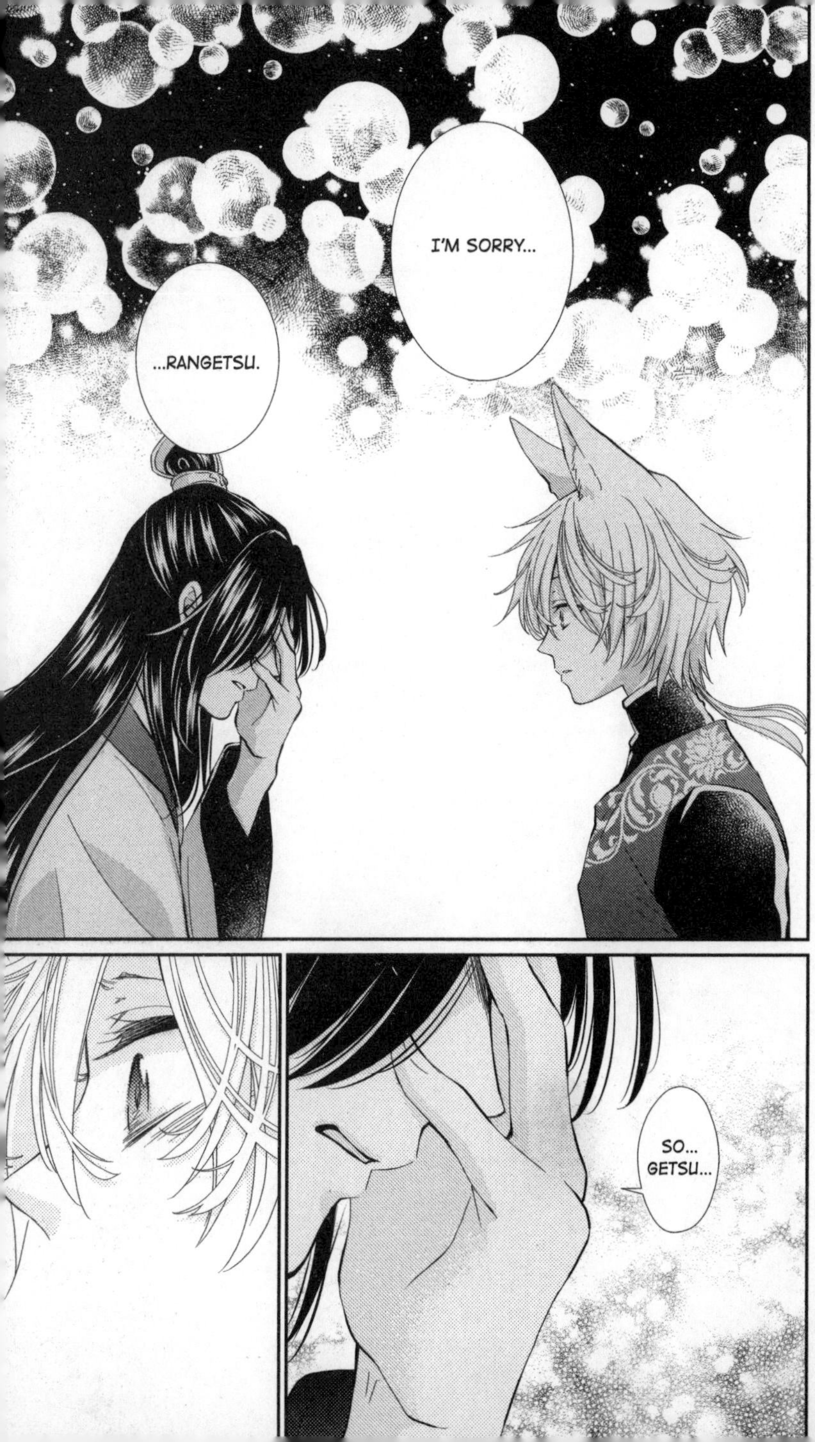
I'M SORRY...
...RANGETSU.
SO... GETSU...

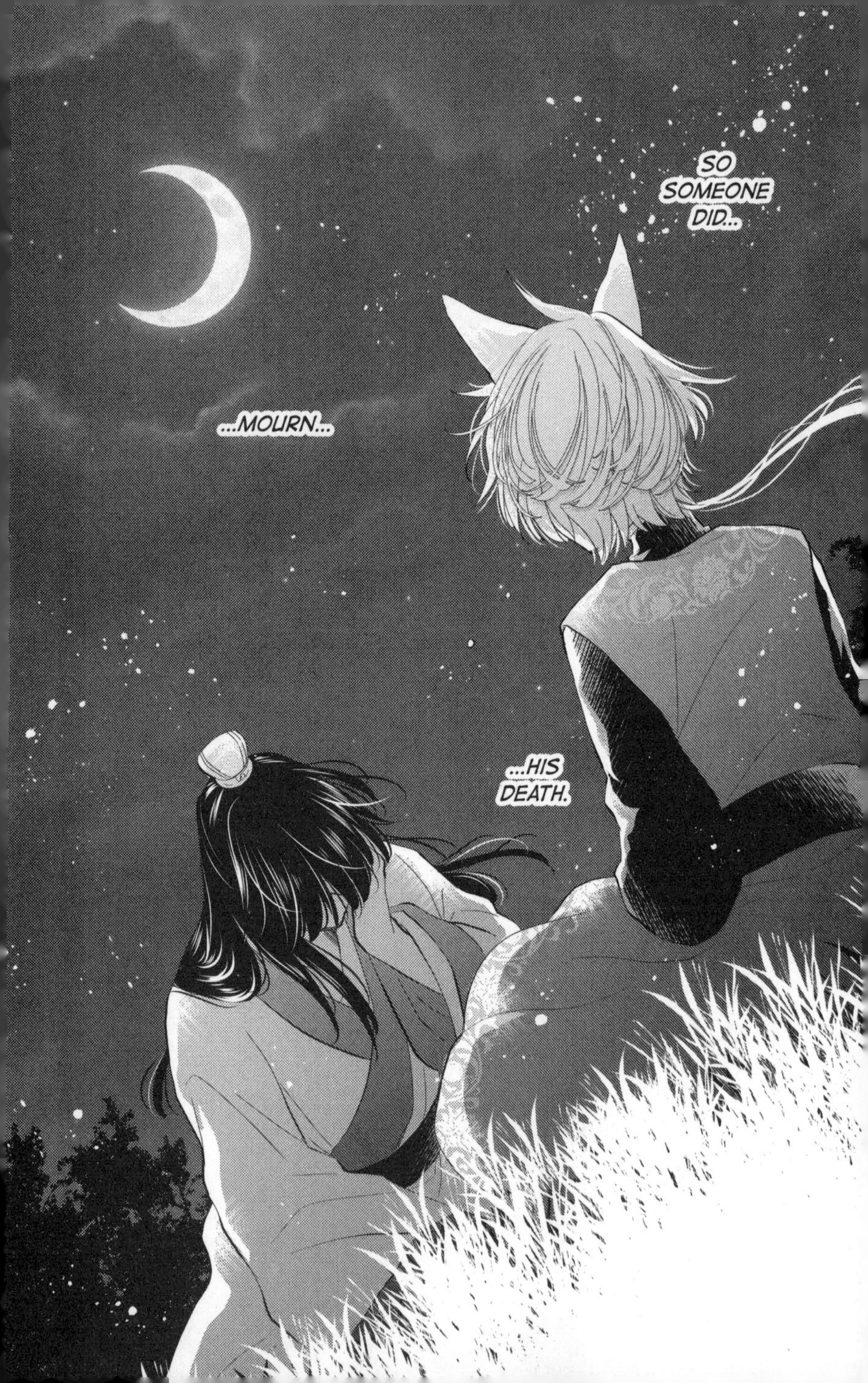
SO SOMEONE DID...
...MOURN...
...HIS DEATH.

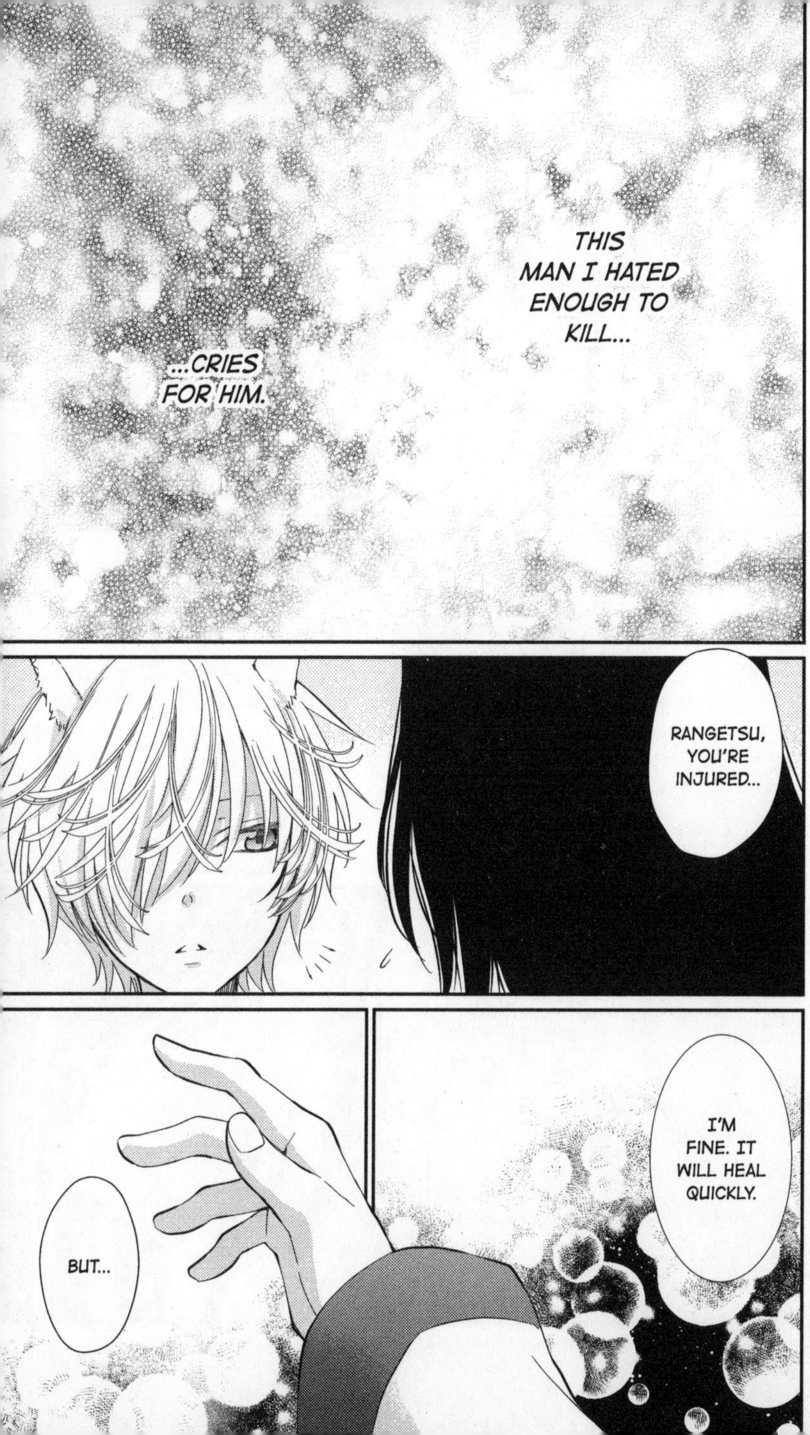
THIS MAN I HATED ENOUGH TO KILL...
...CRIES FOR HIM.
RANGETSU, YOU'RE INJURED...
I'M FINE. IT WILL HEAL QUICKLY.
BUT...

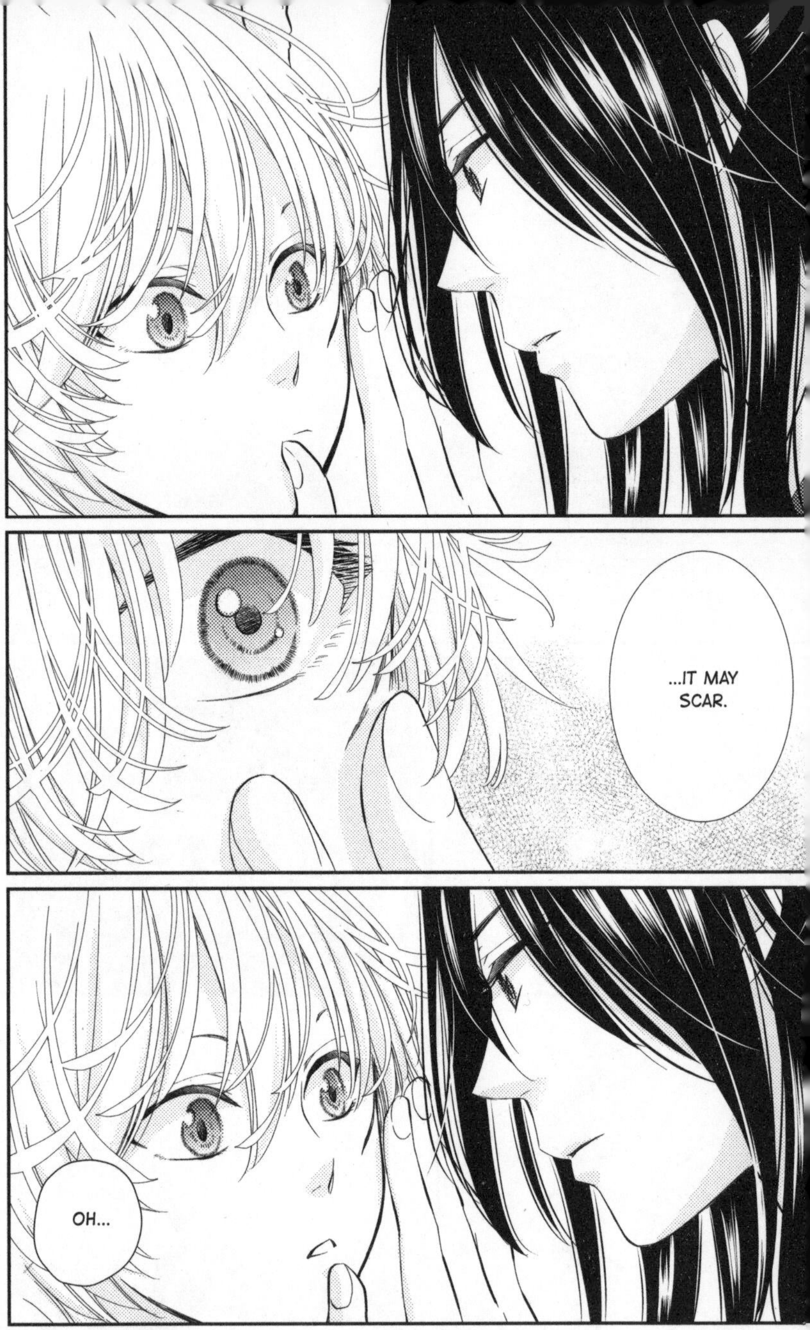
...IT MAY SCAR.
OH...

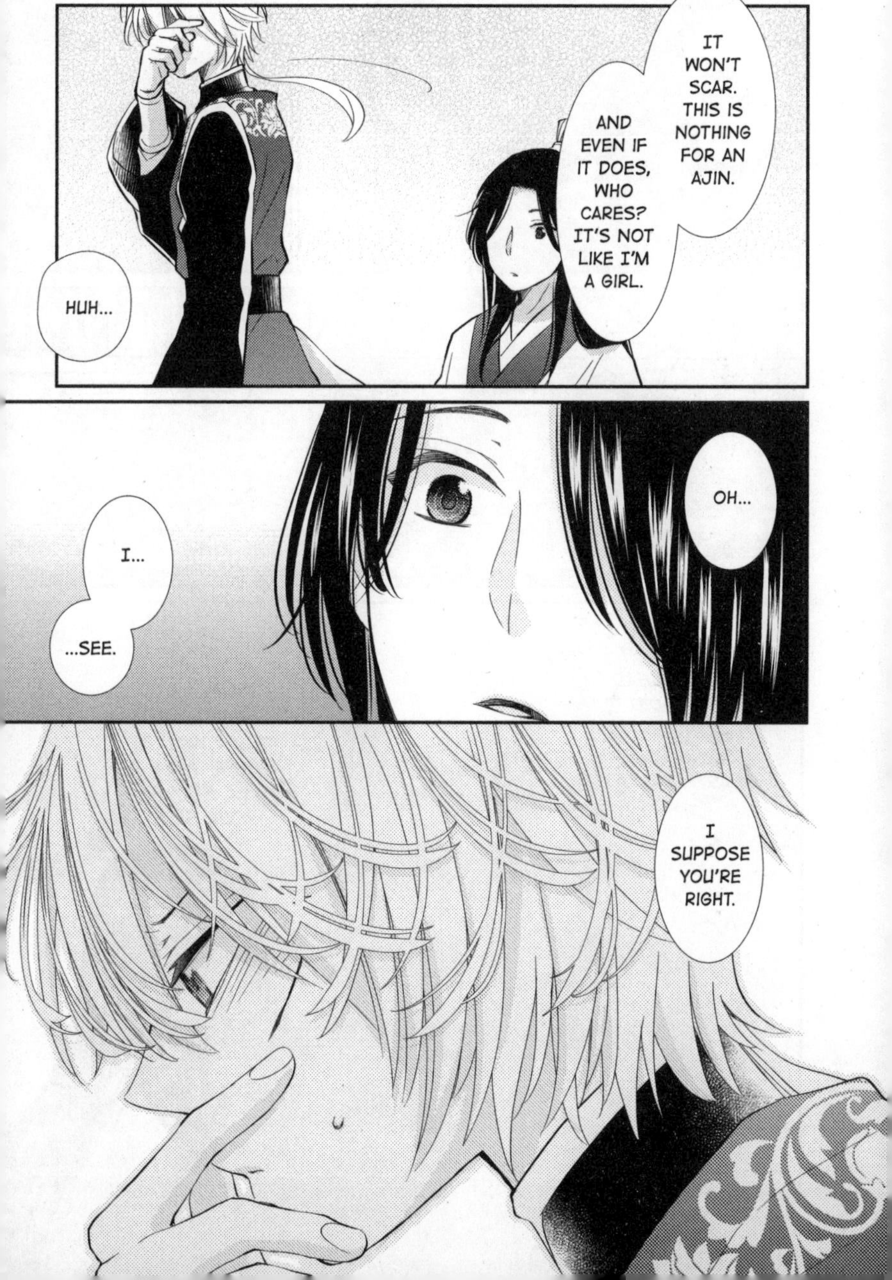
IT WON'T SCAR. THIS IS NOTHING FOR AN AJIN.
AND EVEN IF IT DOES, WHO CARES? IT'S NOT LIKE I'M A GIRL.
HUH...
OH...
I...
...SEE.
I SUPPOSE YOU'RE RIGHT.

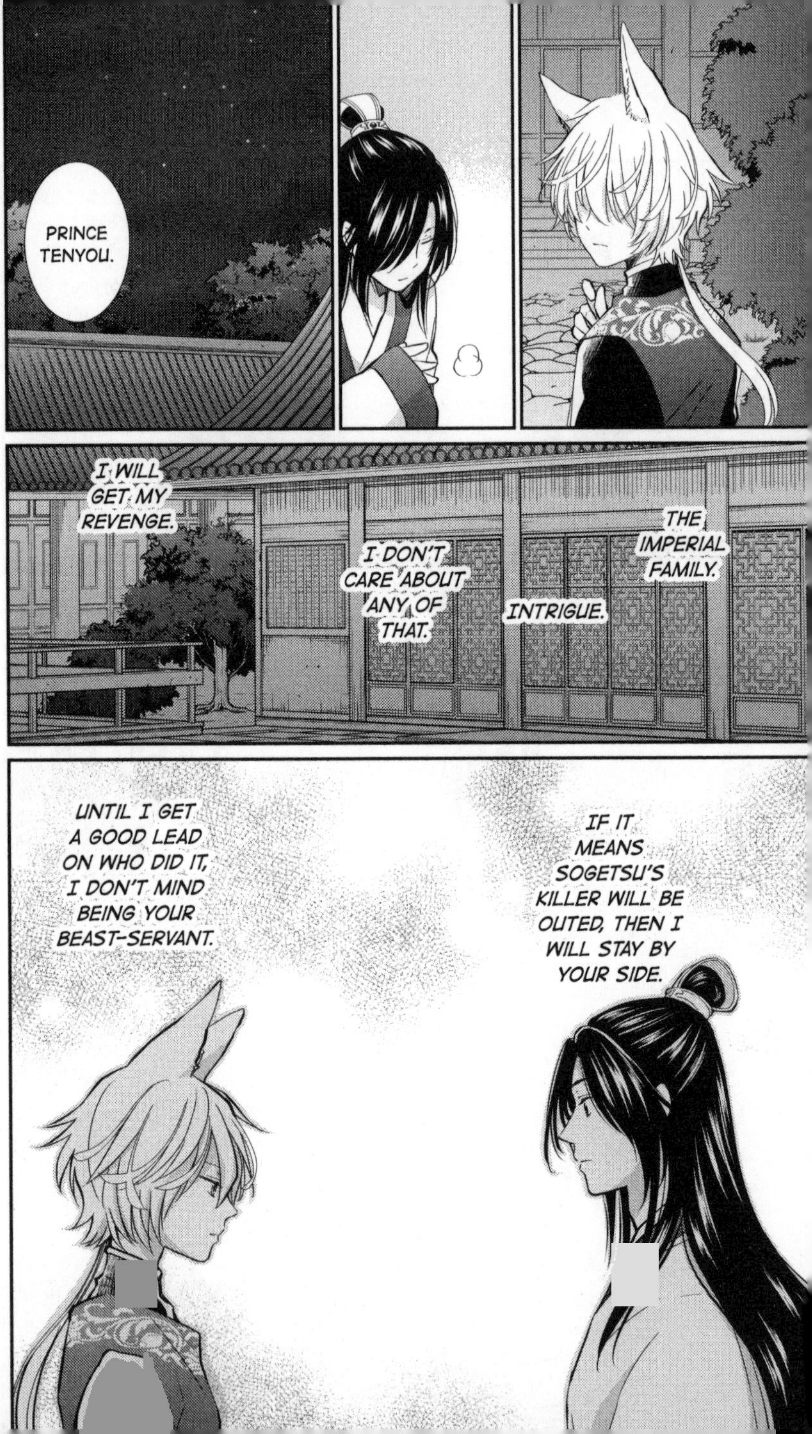
PRINCE TENYOU.
THE IMPERIAL FAMILY.
INTRIGUE.
I DON'T CARE ABOUT ANY OF THAT.
I WILL GET MY REVENGE.
IF IT MEANS SOGETSU'S KILLER WILL BE OUTED, THEN I WILL STAY BY YOUR SIDE.
UNTIL I GET A GOOD LEAD ON WHO DID IT, I DON'T MIND BEING YOUR BEAST-SERVANT.

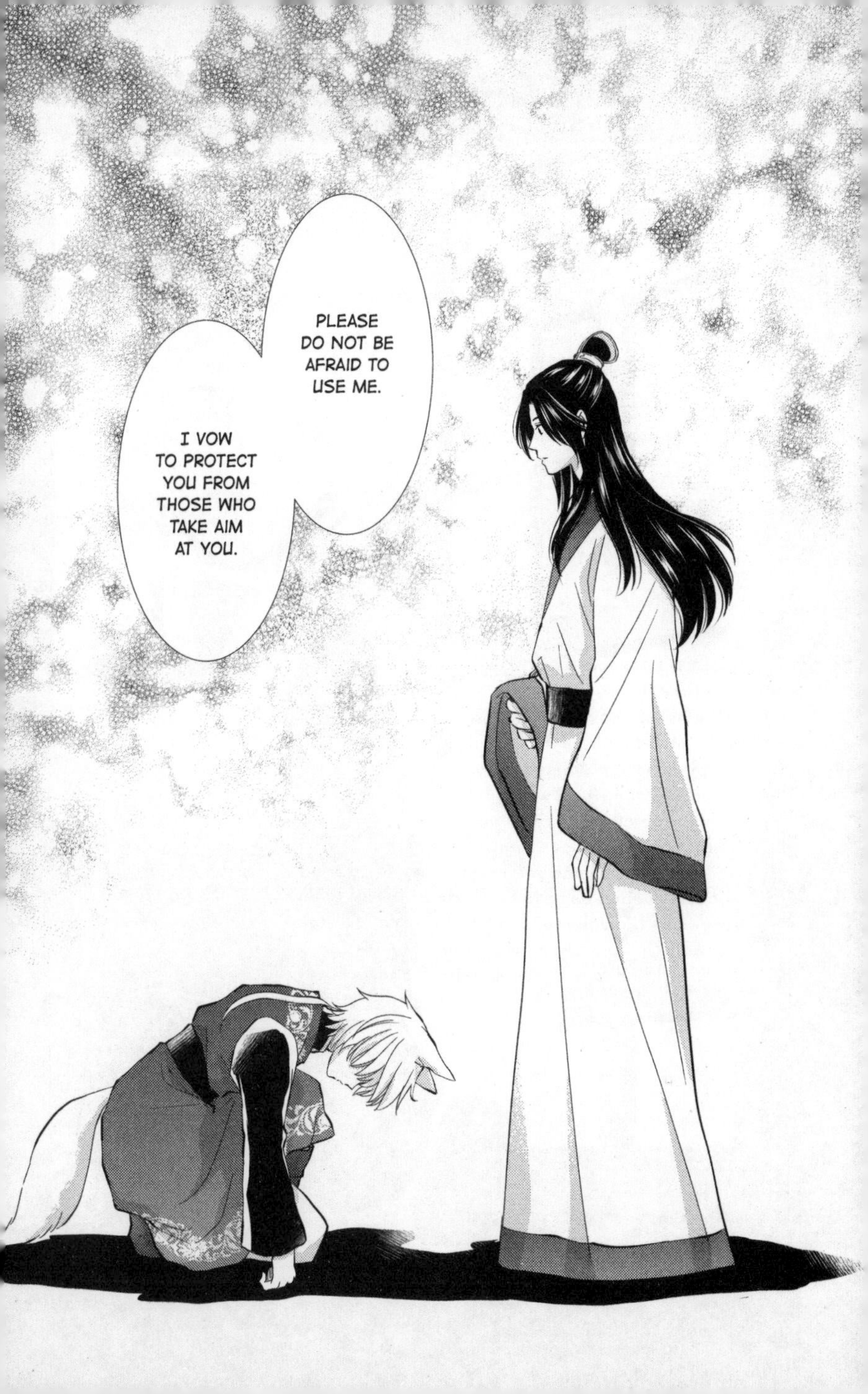
PLEASE DO NOT BE AFRAID TO USE ME.
I VOW TO PROTECT YOU FROM THOSE WHO TAKE AIM AT YOU.

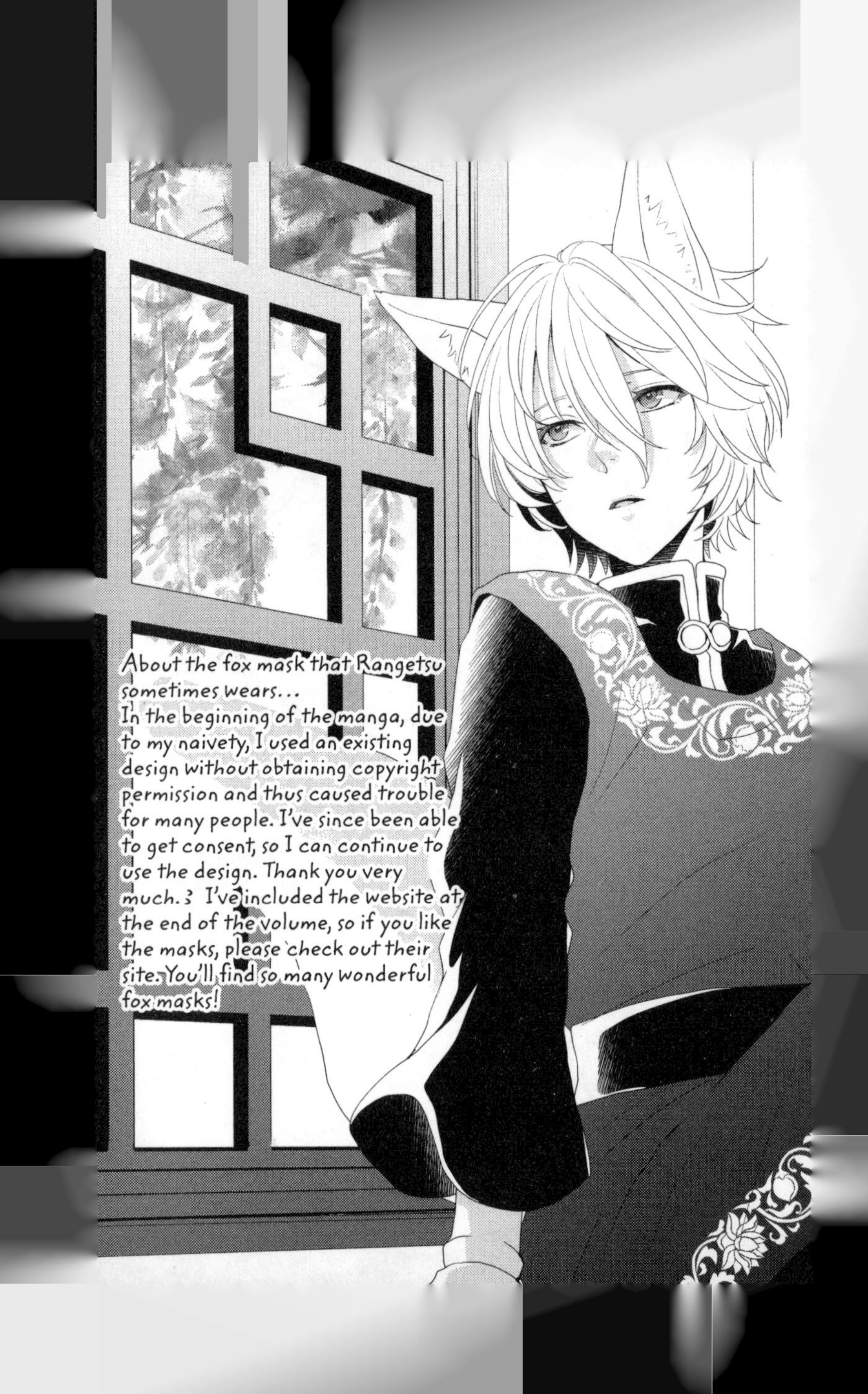
About the fox mask that Rangetsu sometimes wears...
In the beginning of the manga, due to my naivety, I used an existing design without obtaining copyright permission and thus caused trouble for many people. I've since been able to get consent, so I can continue to use the design. Thank you very much. I've included the website at the end of the volume, so if you like the masks, please check out their site. You'll find so many wonderful fox masks!

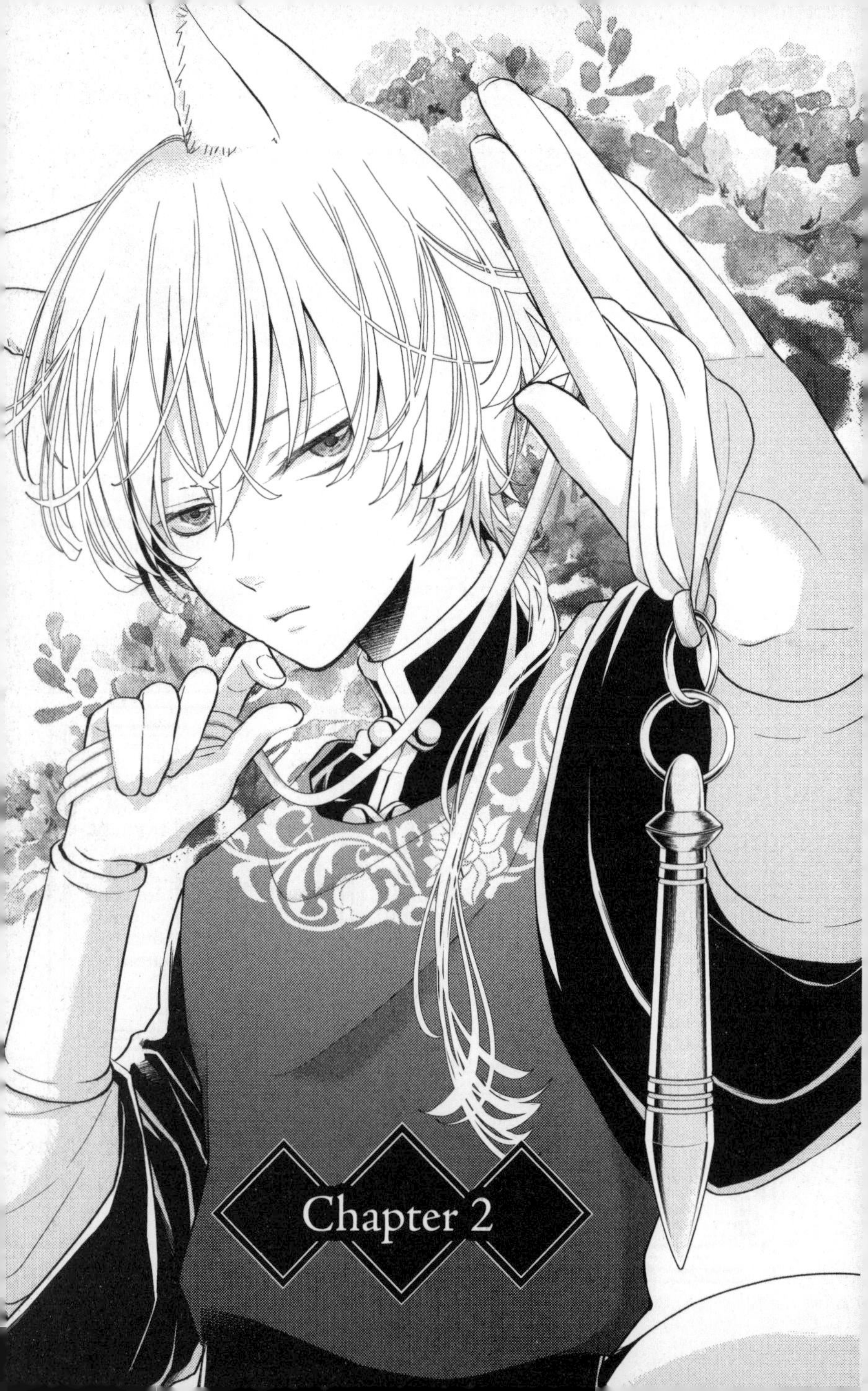
Chapter 2

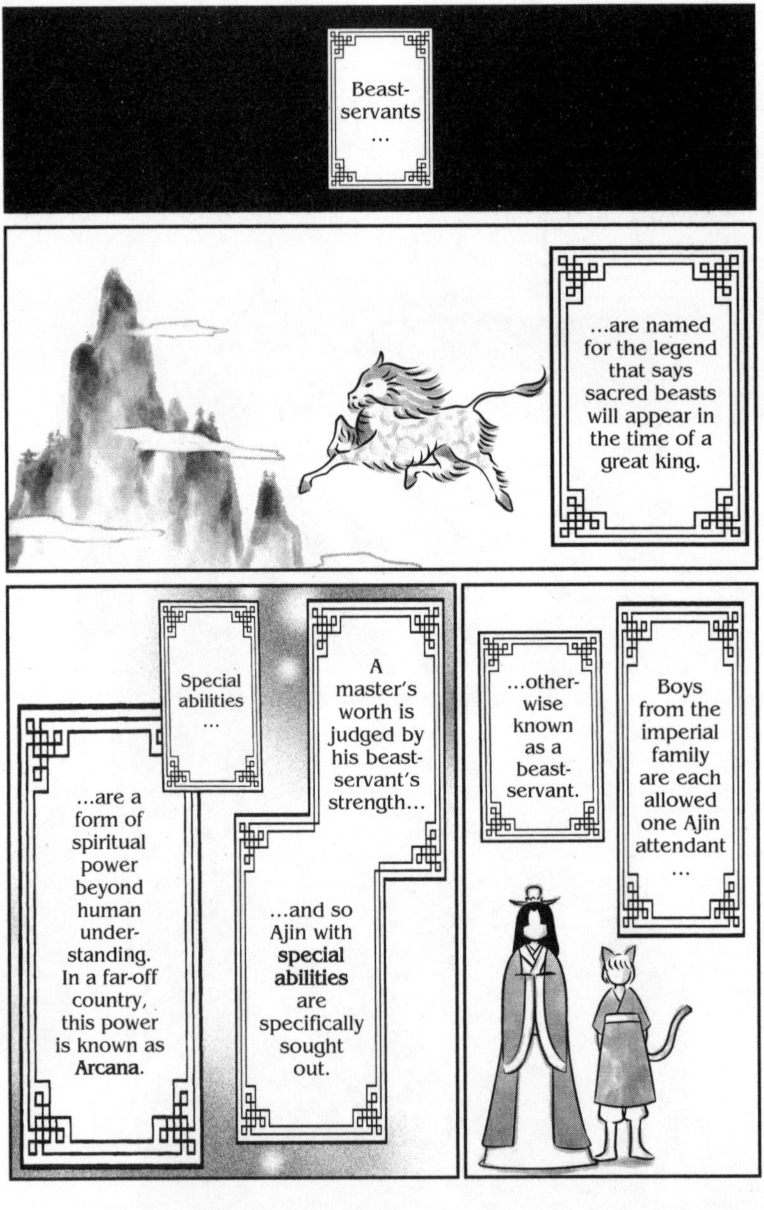
Beast-servants…
…are named for the legend that says sacred beasts will appear in the time of a great king.
Boys from the imperial family are each allowed one Ajin attendant…
…otherwise known as a beast-servant.
A master's worth is judged by his beast-servant's strength…
…and so Ajin with **special abilities** are specifically sought out.
Special abilities…
…are a form of spiritual power beyond human understanding. In a far-off country, this power is known as **Arcana**.

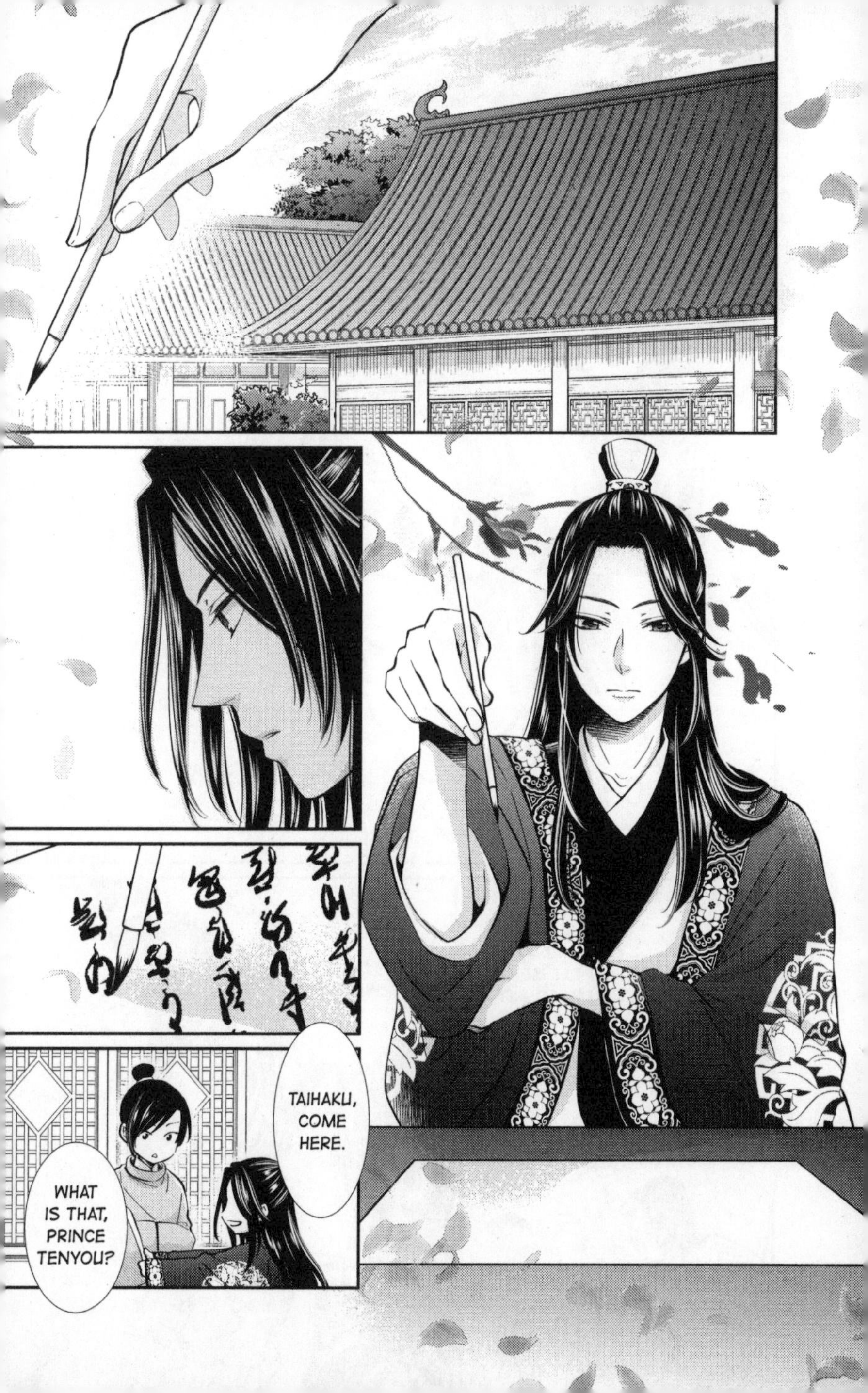
TAIHAKU, COME HERE.
WHAT IS THAT, PRINCE TENYOU?

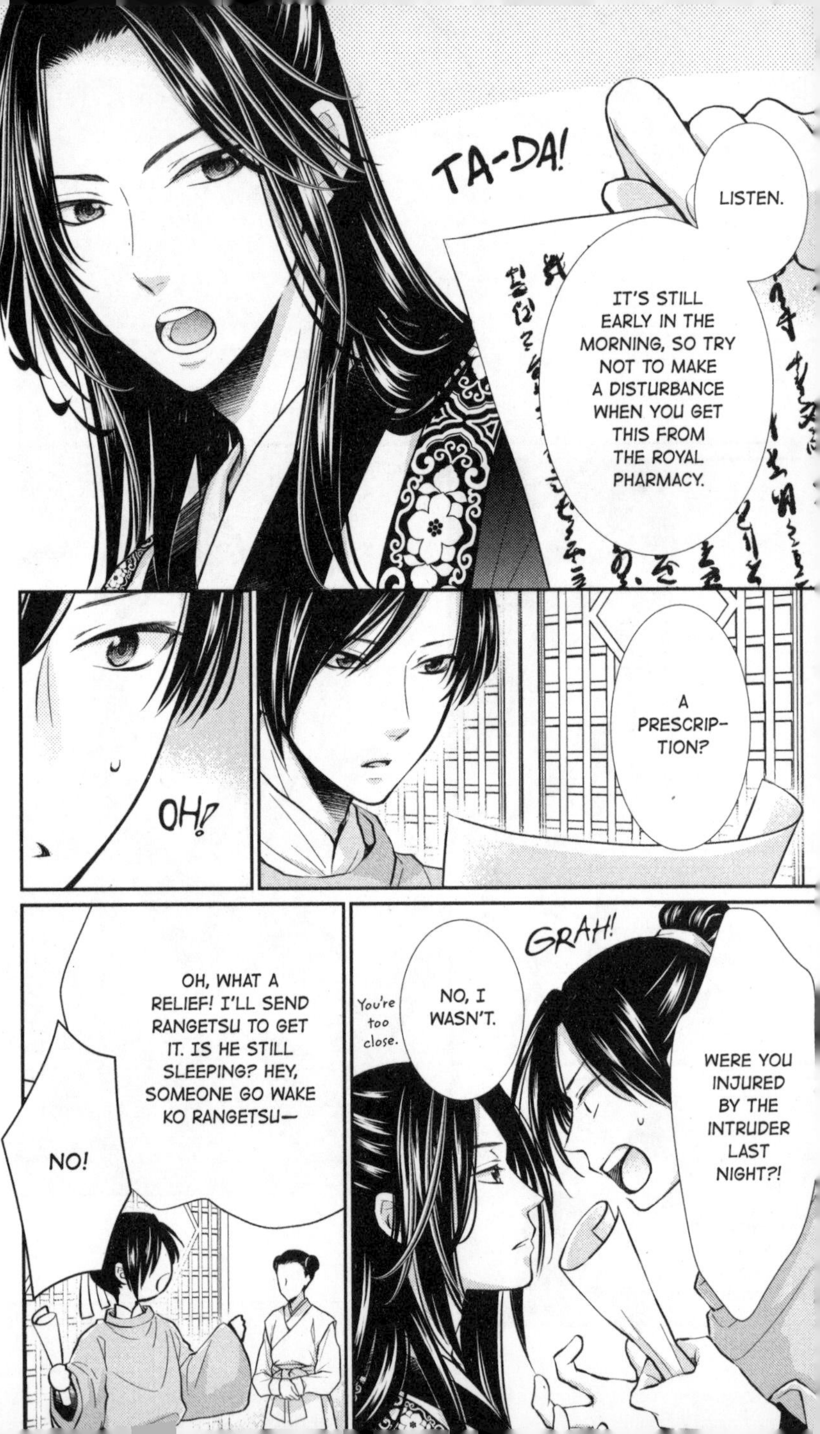
LISTEN.
TA-DA!
IT'S STILL EARLY IN THE MORNING, SO TRY NOT TO MAKE A DISTURBANCE WHEN YOU GET THIS FROM THE ROYAL PHARMACY.
A PRESCRIP-TION?
OH!
GRAH!
WERE YOU INJURED BY THE INTRUDER LAST NIGHT?!
NO, I WASN'T.
You're too close.
OH, WHAT A RELIEF! I'LL SEND RANGETSU TO GET IT. IS HE STILL SLEEPING? HEY, SOMEONE GO WAKE KO RANGETSU—
NO!

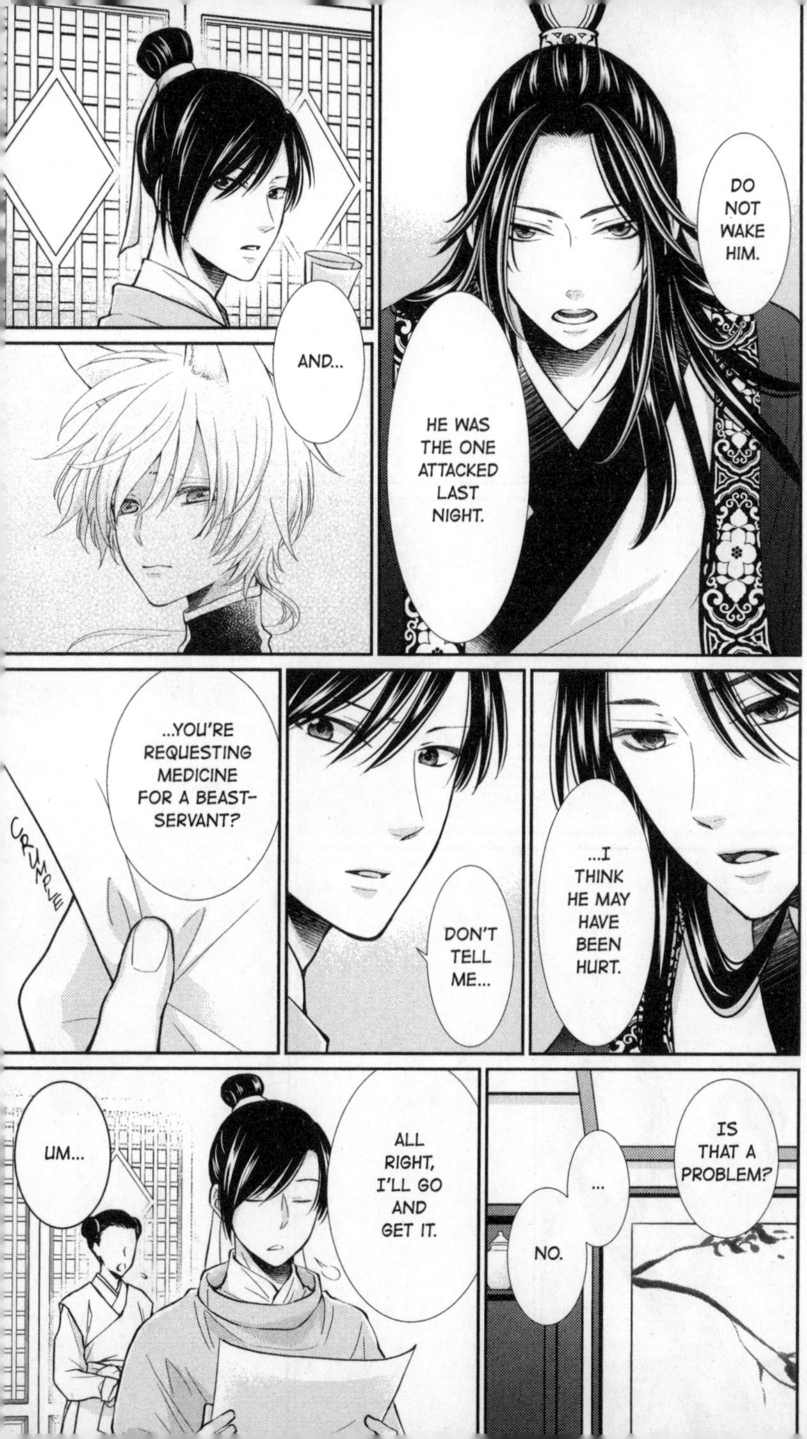
DO NOT WAKE HIM.
AND...
HE WAS THE ONE ATTACKED LAST NIGHT.
...I THINK HE MAY HAVE BEEN HURT.
DON'T TELL ME...
...YOU'RE REQUESTING MEDICINE FOR A BEAST-SERVANT?
CRUMPLE
IS THAT A PROBLEM?
...
NO.
ALL RIGHT, I'LL GO AND GET IT.
UM...

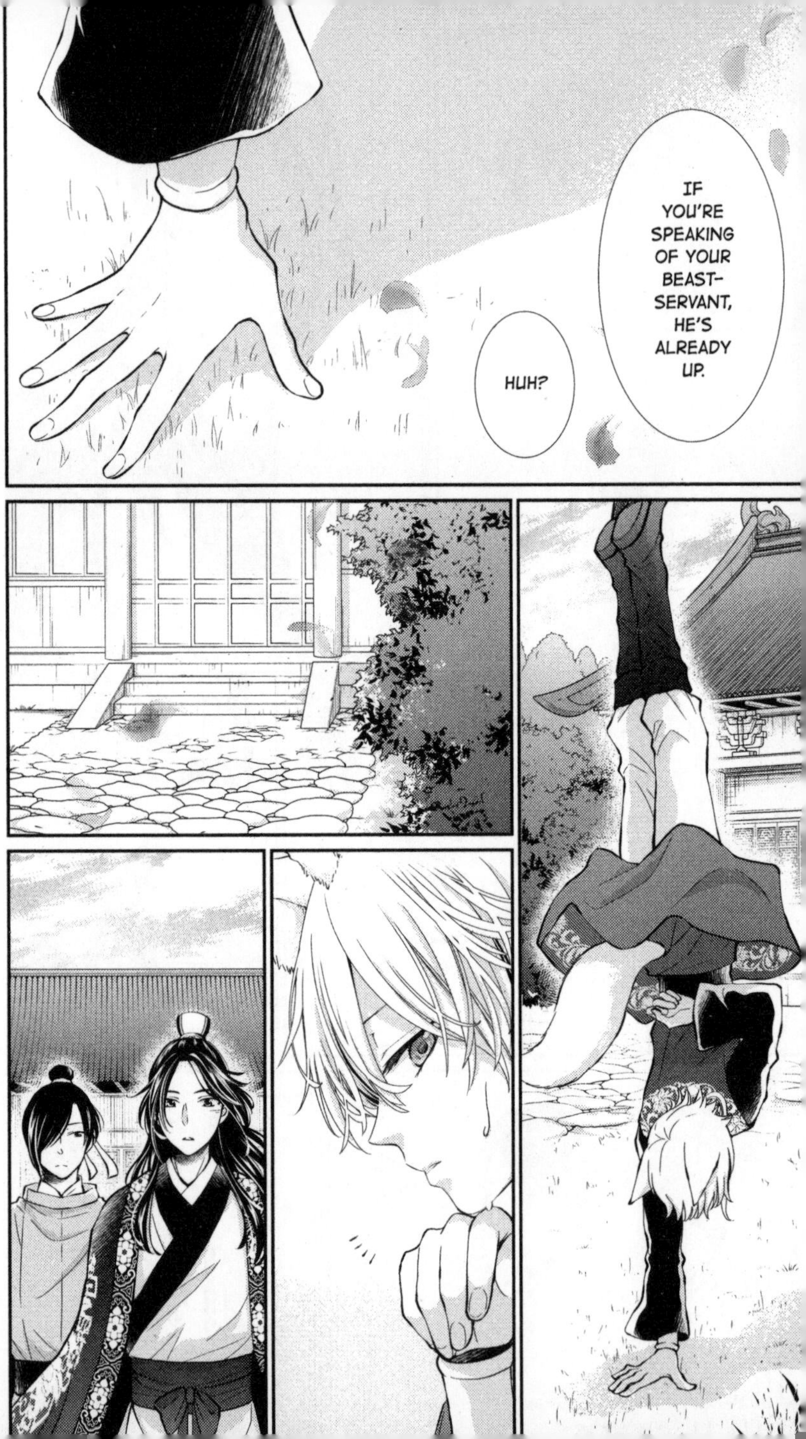
IF YOU'RE SPEAKING OF YOUR BEAST-SERVANT, HE'S ALREADY UP.
HUH?

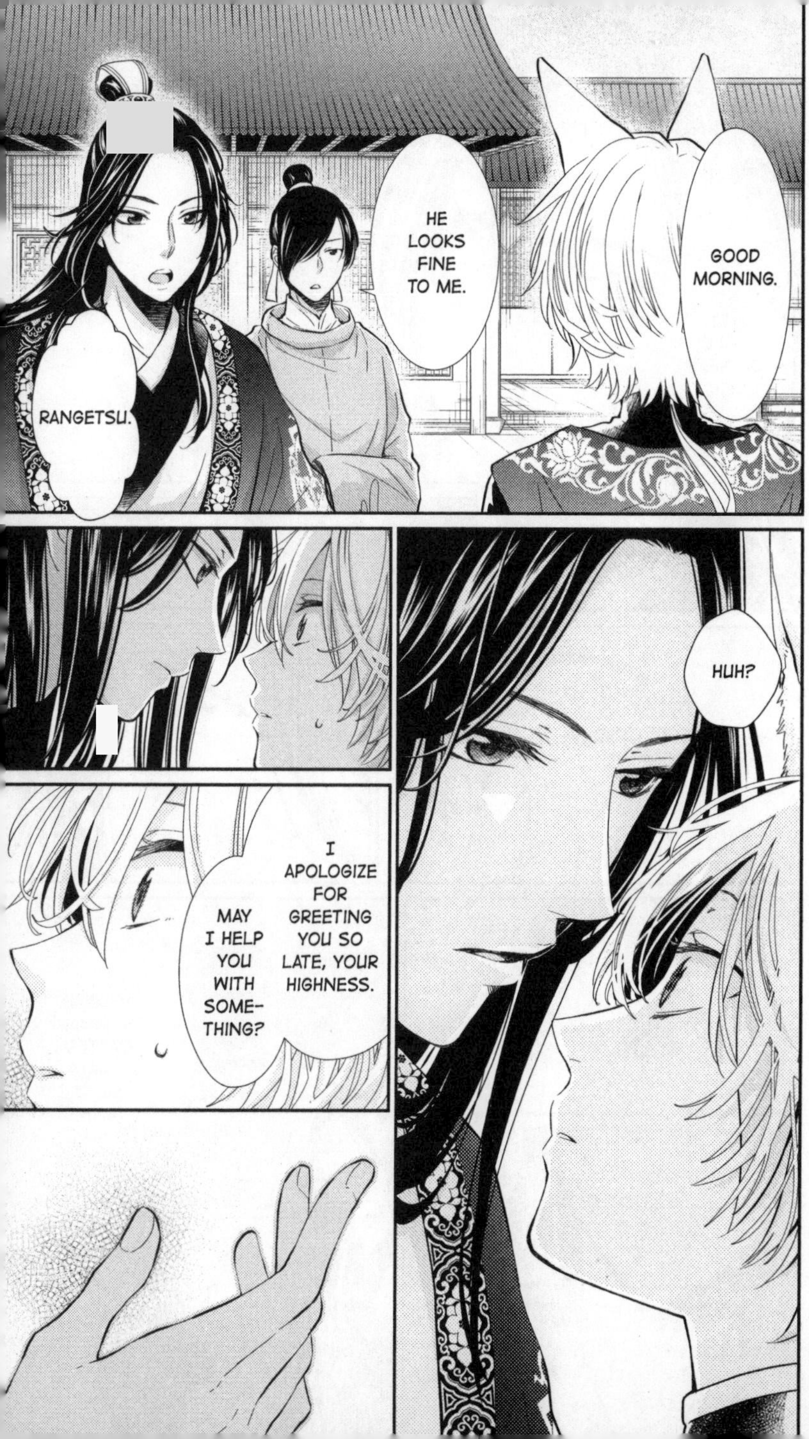
GOOD MORNING.
HE LOOKS FINE TO ME.
RANGETSU.
HUH?
I APOLOGIZE FOR GREETING YOU SO LATE, YOUR HIGHNESS.
MAY I HELP YOU WITH SOME-THING?

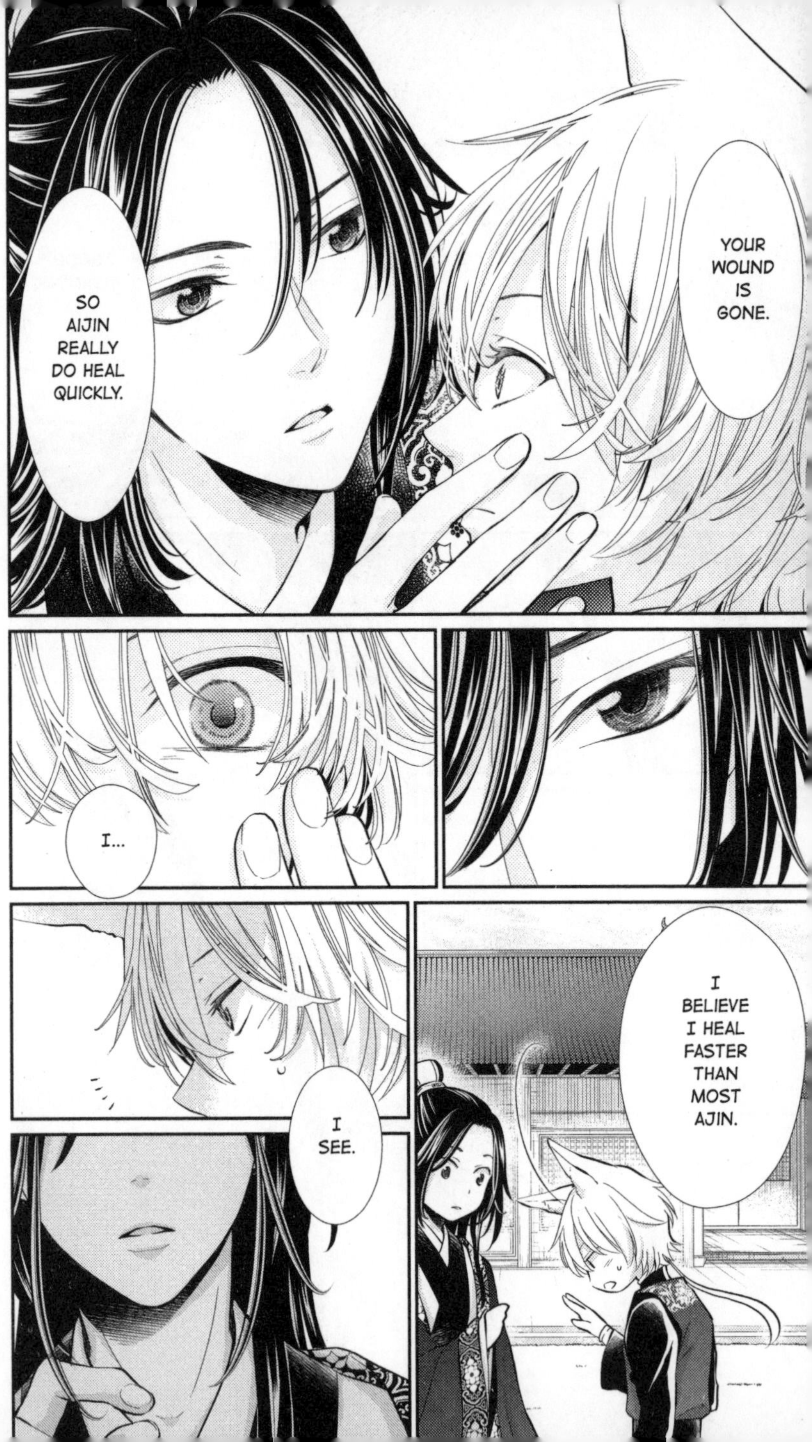
YOUR WOUND IS GONE.
SO AIJIN REALLY DO HEAL QUICKLY.
I...
I BELIEVE I HEAL FASTER THAN MOST AJIN.
I SEE.

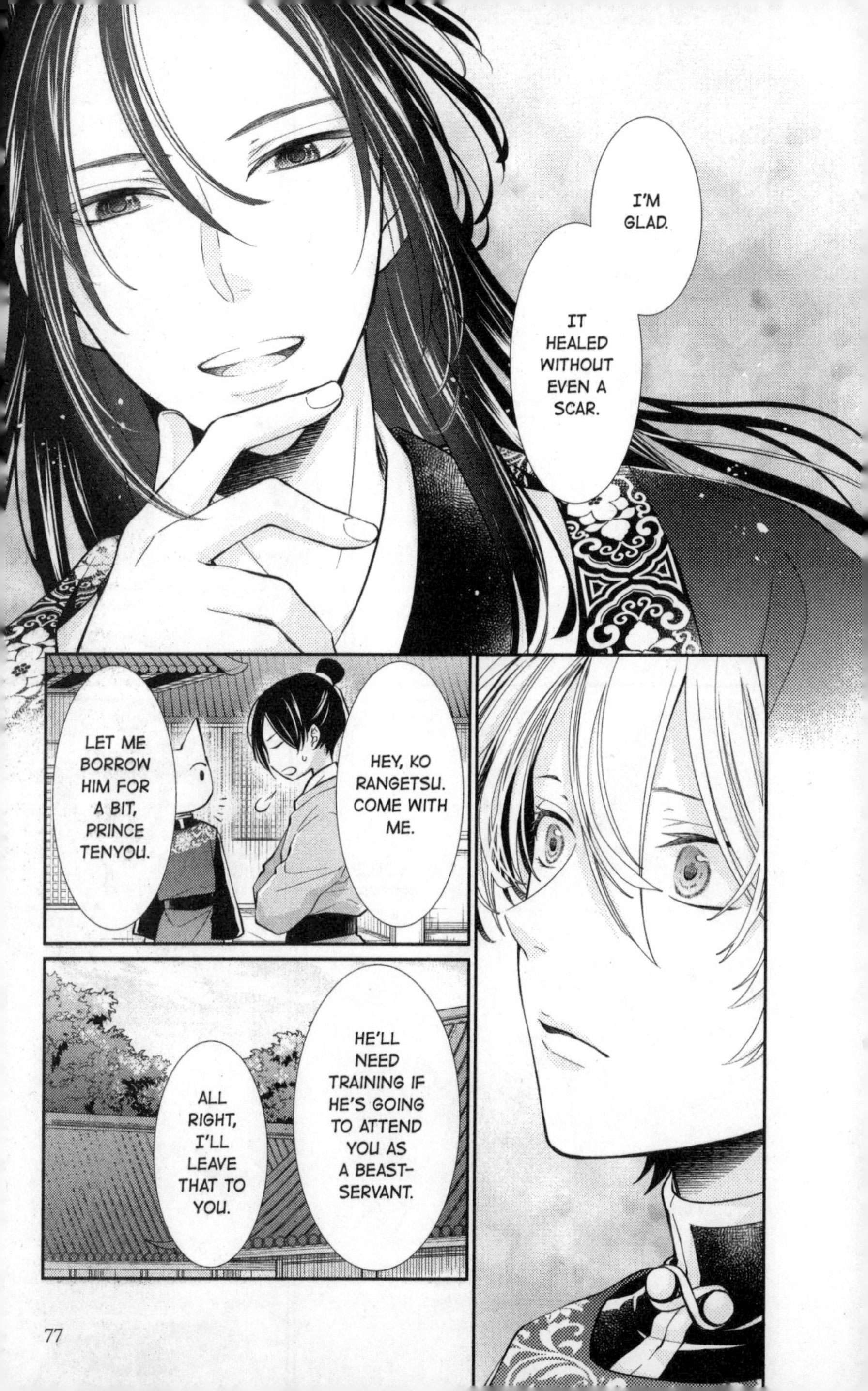
I'M GLAD.
IT HEALED WITHOUT EVEN A SCAR.
HEY, KO RANGETSU. COME WITH ME.
LET ME BORROW HIM FOR A BIT, PRINCE TENYOU.
HE'LL NEED TRAINING IF HE'S GOING TO ATTEND YOU AS A BEAST-SERVANT.
ALL RIGHT, I'LL LEAVE THAT TO YOU.

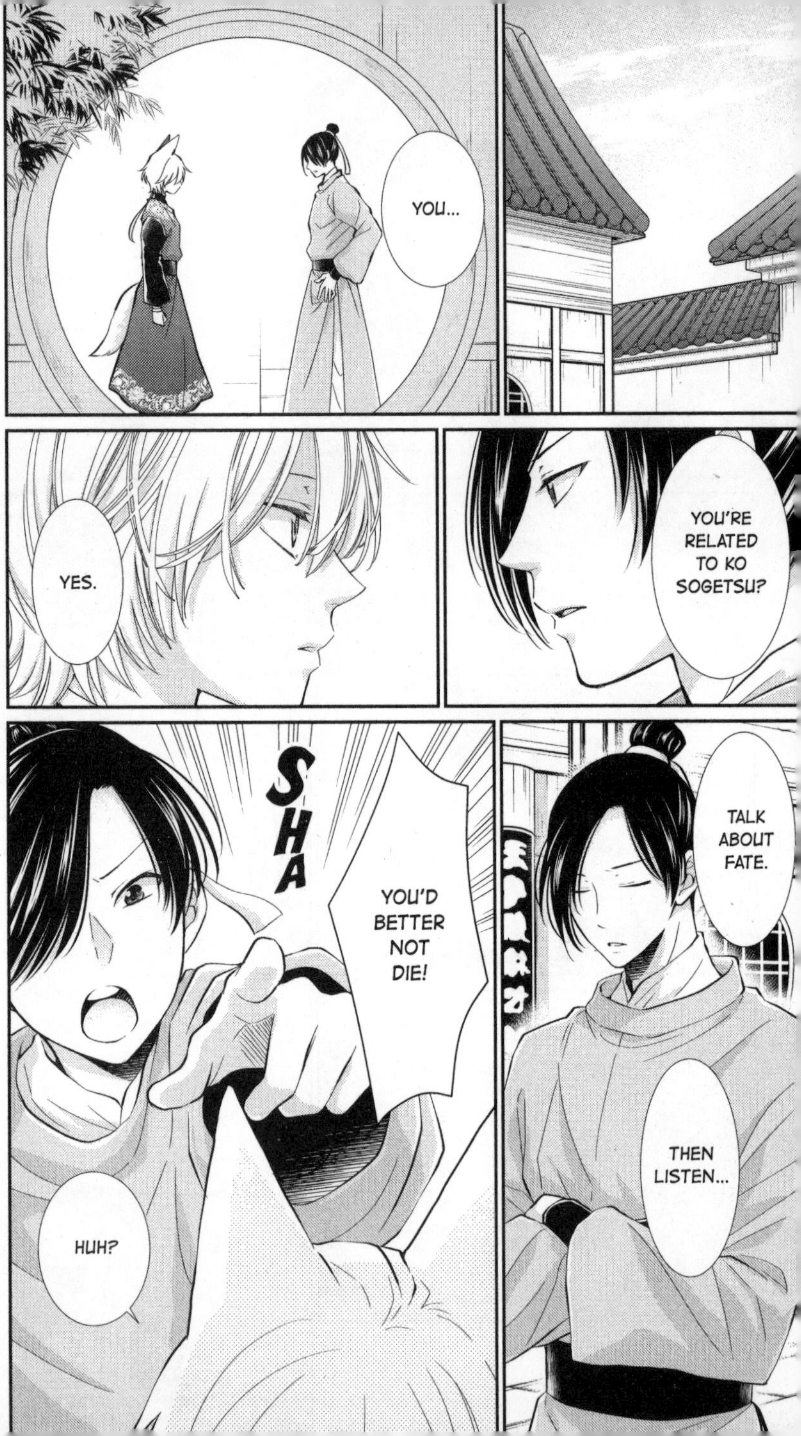
YOU...
YOU'RE RELATED TO KO SOGETSU?
YES.
TALK ABOUT FATE.
THEN LISTEN...
SHA
YOU'D BETTER NOT DIE!
HUH?

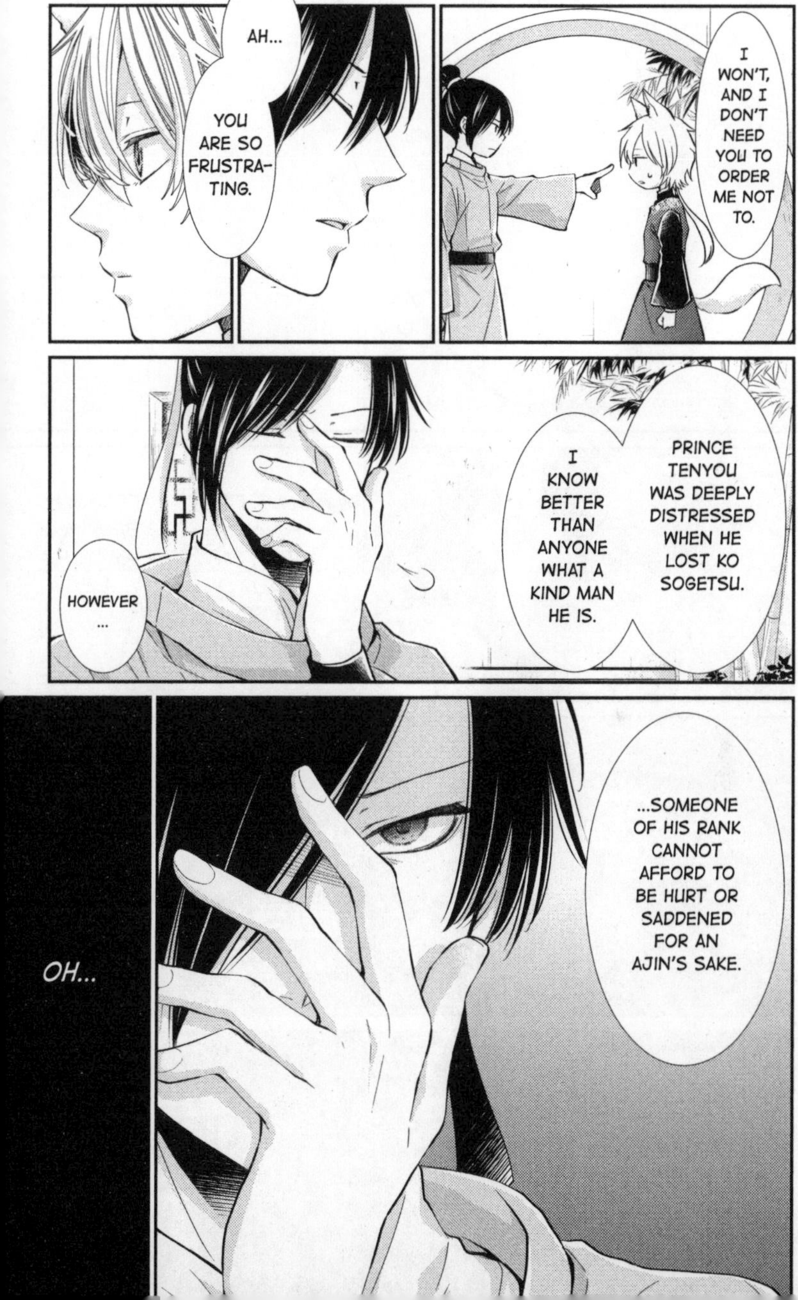
I WON'T, AND I DON'T NEED YOU TO ORDER ME NOT TO.
AH...
YOU ARE SO FRUSTRA-TING.
PRINCE TENYOU WAS DEEPLY DISTRESSED WHEN HE LOST KO SOGETSU.
I KNOW BETTER THAN ANYONE WHAT A KIND MAN HE IS.
HOWEVER ...
...SOMEONE OF HIS RANK CANNOT AFFORD TO BE HURT OR SADDENED FOR AN AJIN'S SAKE.
OH...

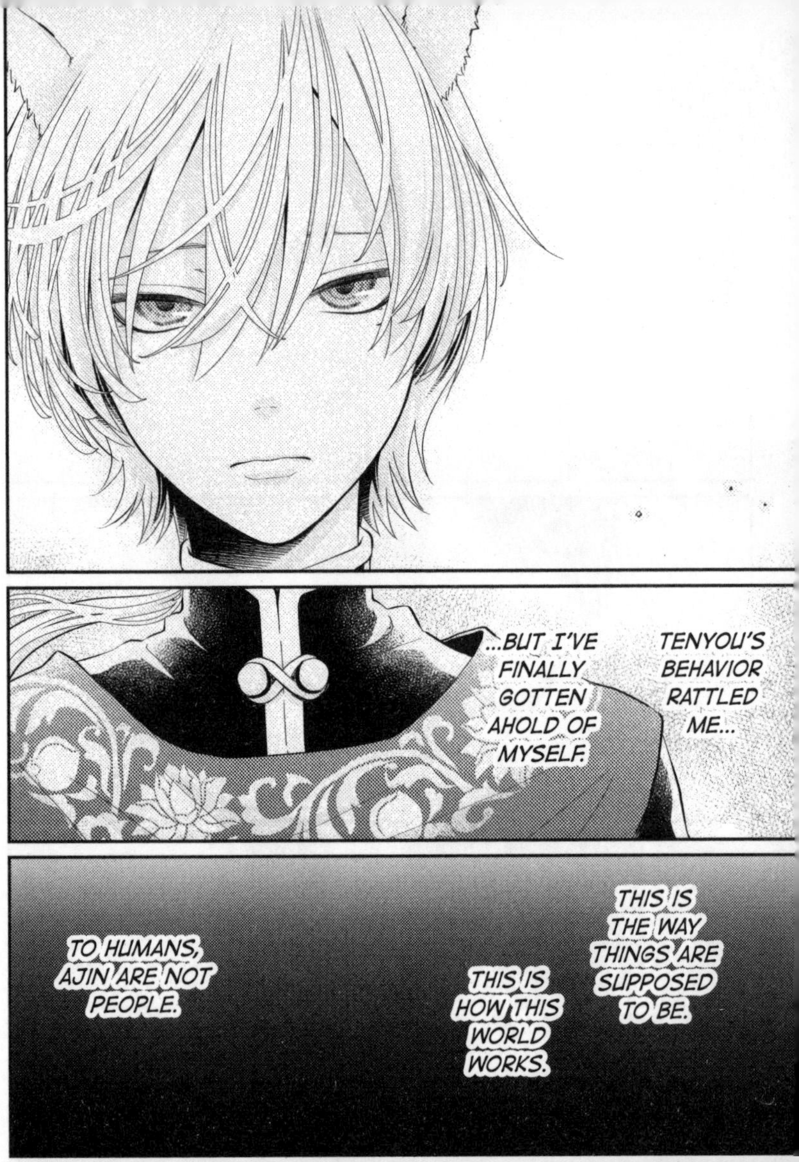
TENYOU'S BEHAVIOR RATTLED ME...
...BUT I'VE FINALLY GOTTEN AHOLD OF MYSELF.
THIS IS THE WAY THINGS ARE SUPPOSED TO BE.
THIS IS HOW THIS WORLD WORKS.
TO HUMANS, AJIN ARE NOT PEOPLE.

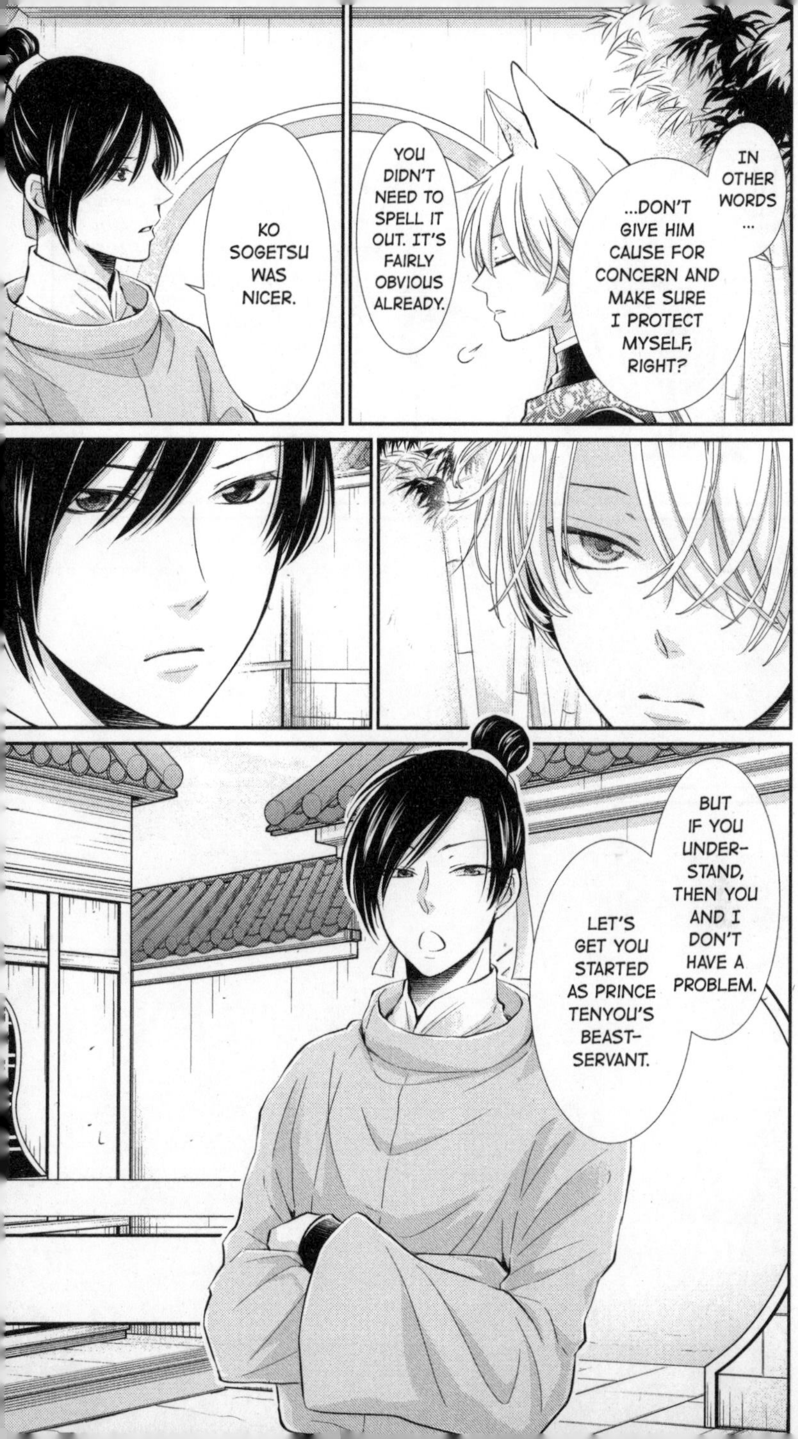
IN OTHER WORDS ...
...DON'T GIVE HIM CAUSE FOR CONCERN AND MAKE SURE I PROTECT MYSELF, RIGHT?
YOU DIDN'T NEED TO SPELL IT OUT. IT'S FAIRLY OBVIOUS ALREADY.
KO SOGETSU WAS NICER.
BUT IF YOU UNDER-STAND, THEN YOU AND I DON'T HAVE A PROBLEM.
LET'S GET YOU STARTED AS PRINCE TENYOU'S BEAST-SERVANT.

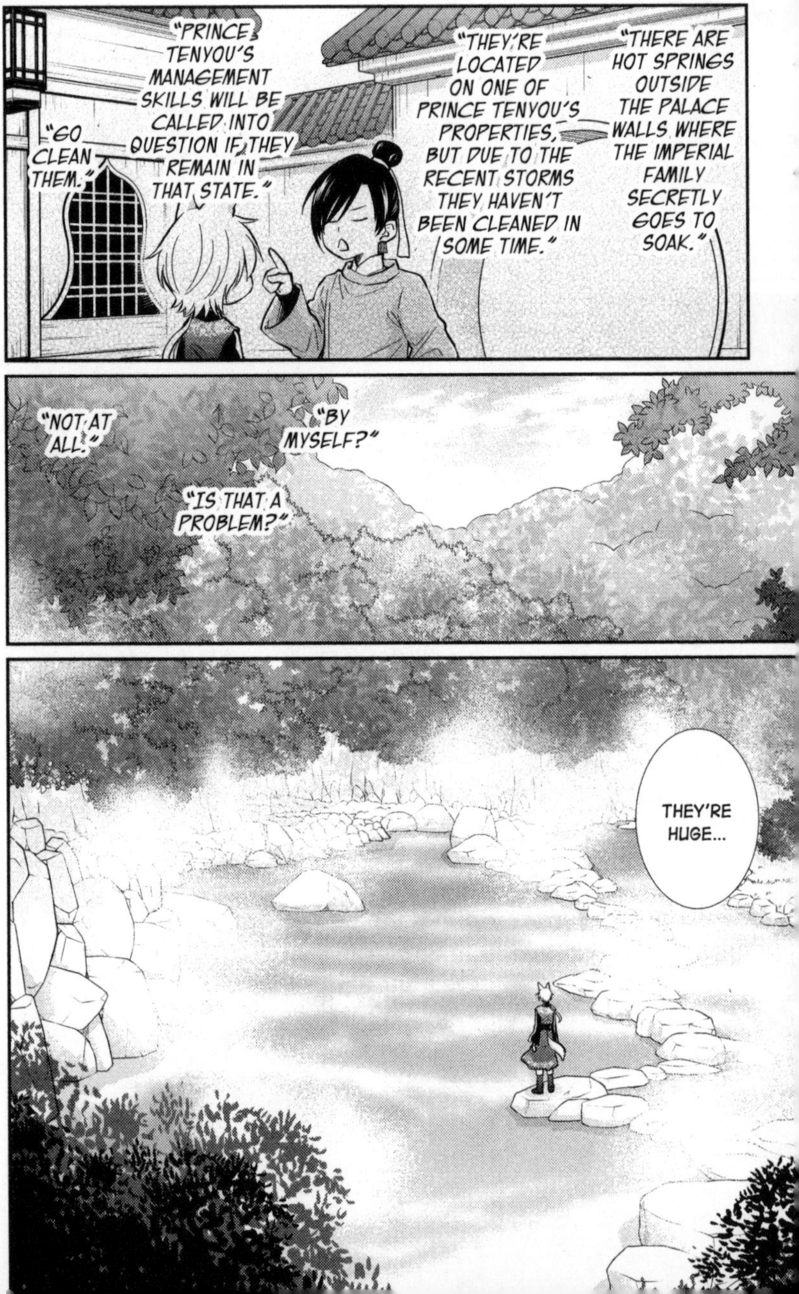
"THERE ARE HOT SPRINGS OUTSIDE THE PALACE WALLS WHERE THE IMPERIAL FAMILY SECRETLY GOES TO SOAK."
"THEY'RE LOCATED ON ONE OF PRINCE TENYOU'S PROPERTIES, BUT DUE TO THE RECENT STORMS THEY HAVEN'T BEEN CLEANED IN SOME TIME."
"PRINCE TENYOU'S MANAGEMENT SKILLS WILL BE CALLED INTO QUESTION IF THEY REMAIN IN THAT STATE."
"GO CLEAN THEM."
"BY MYSELF?"
"IS THAT A PROBLEM?"
"NOT AT ALL."
THEY'RE HUGE...

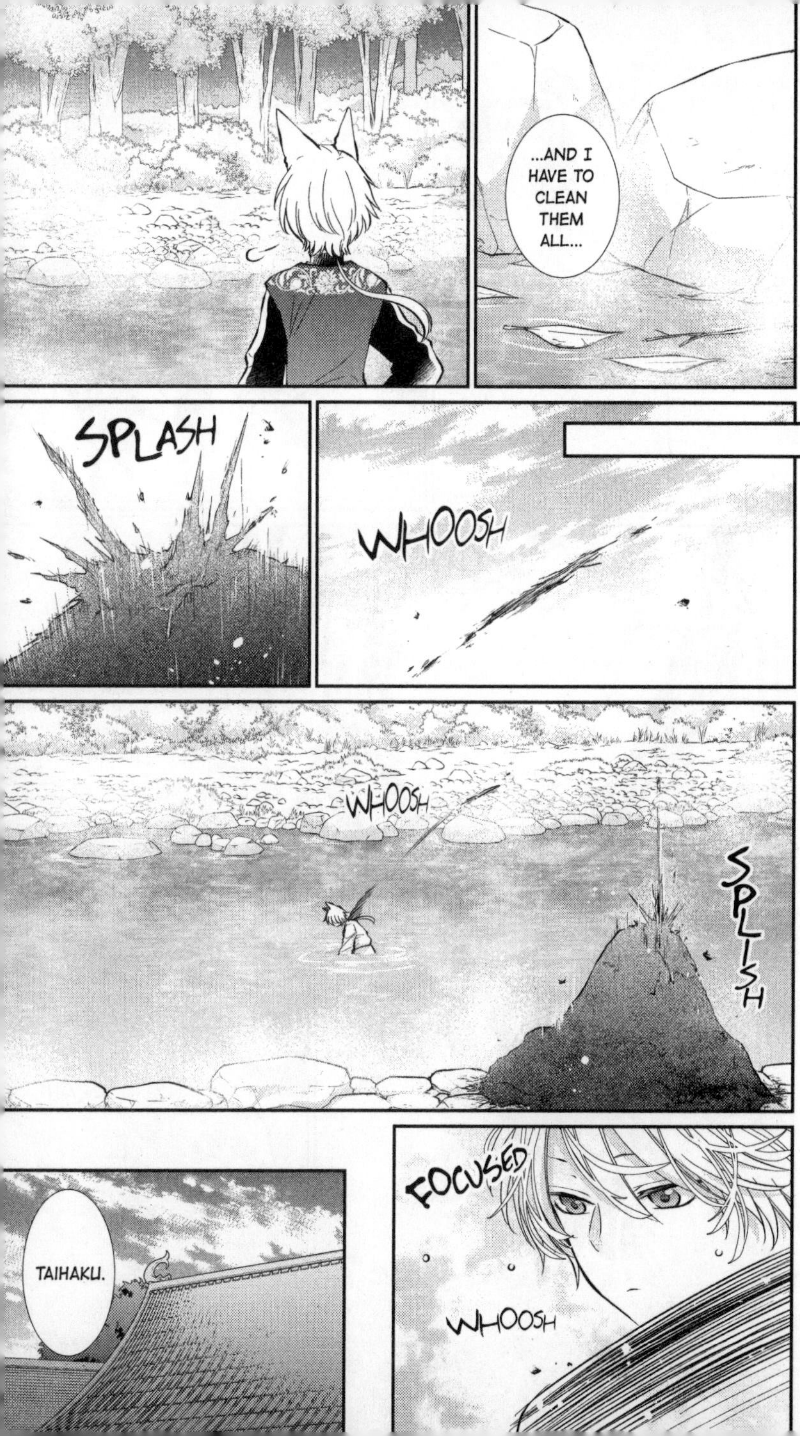
...AND I HAVE TO CLEAN THEM ALL...
WHOOSH
SPLASH
WHOOSH
SPLISH
FOCUSED
WHOOSH
TAIHAKU.

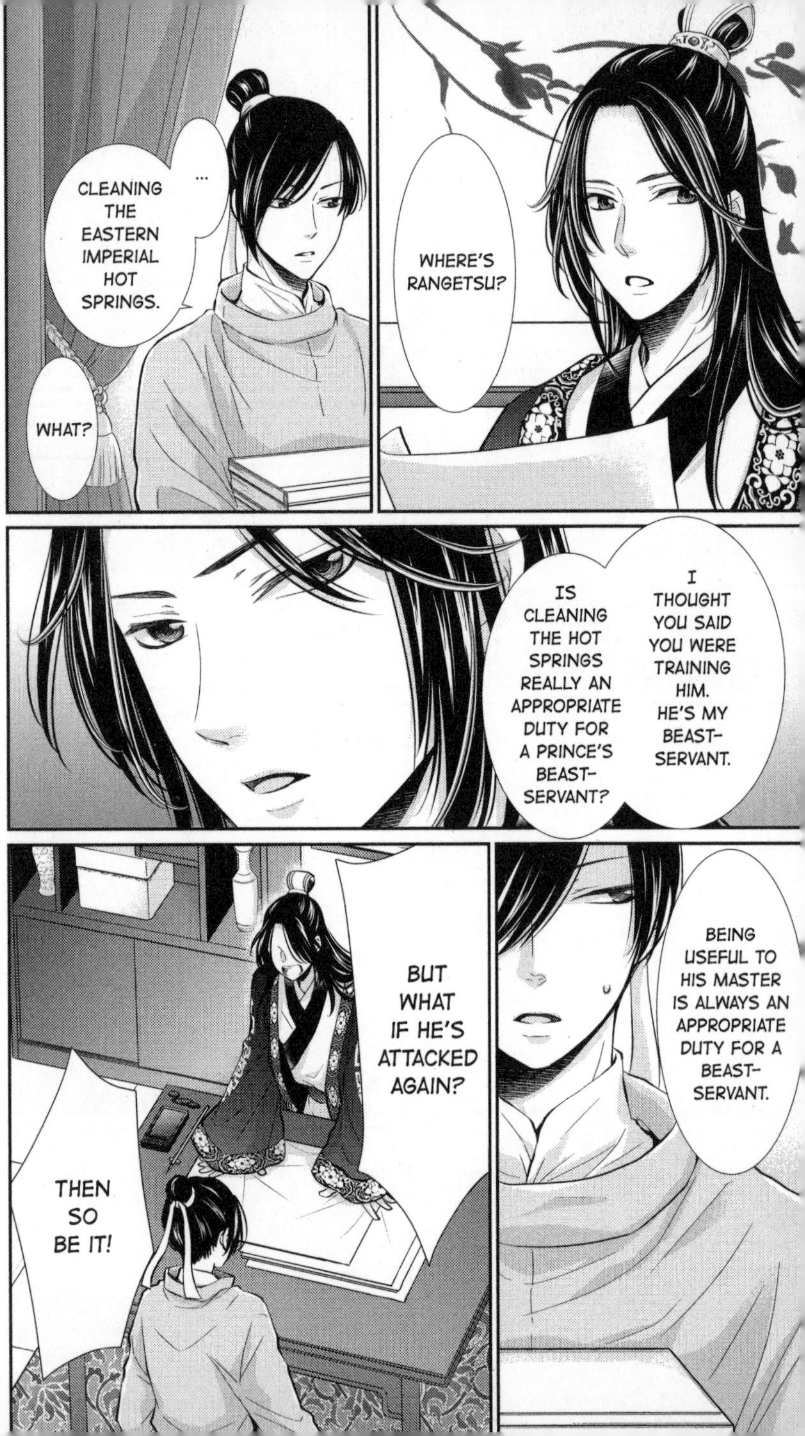
WHERE'S RANGETSU?
...
CLEANING THE EASTERN IMPERIAL HOT SPRINGS.
WHAT?
I THOUGHT YOU SAID YOU WERE TRAINING HIM. HE'S MY BEAST-SERVANT.
IS CLEANING THE HOT SPRINGS REALLY AN APPROPRIATE DUTY FOR A PRINCE'S BEAST-SERVANT?
BEING USEFUL TO HIS MASTER IS ALWAYS AN APPROPRIATE DUTY FOR A BEAST-SERVANT.
BUT WHAT IF HE'S ATTACKED AGAIN?
THEN SO BE IT!

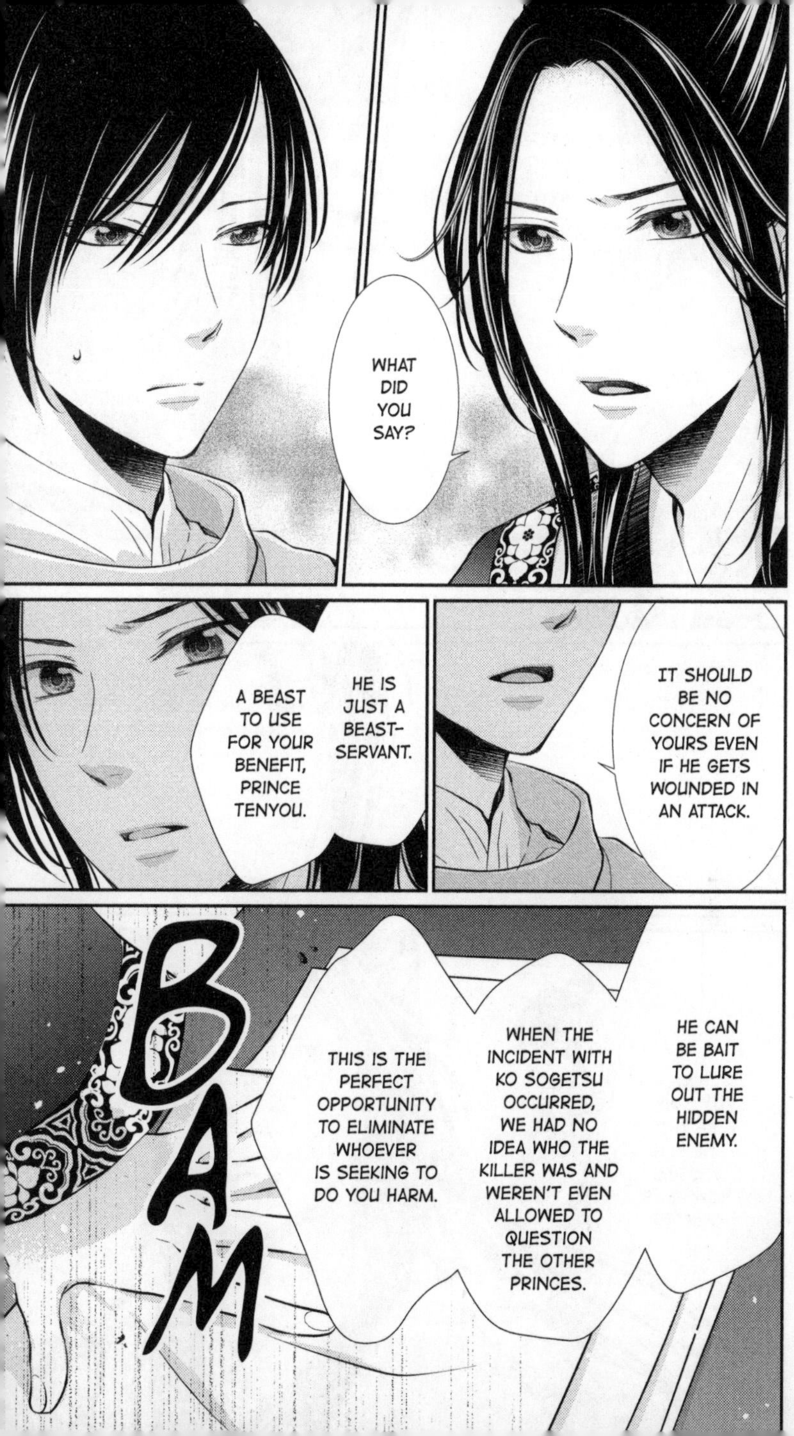
WHAT DID YOU SAY?
IT SHOULD BE NO CONCERN OF YOURS EVEN IF HE GETS WOUNDED IN AN ATTACK.
HE IS JUST A BEAST-SERVANT.
A BEAST TO USE FOR YOUR BENEFIT, PRINCE TENYOU.
HE CAN BE BAIT TO LURE OUT THE HIDDEN ENEMY.
WHEN THE INCIDENT WITH KO SOGETSU OCCURRED, WE HAD NO IDEA WHO THE KILLER WAS AND WEREN'T EVEN ALLOWED TO QUESTION THE OTHER PRINCES.
THIS IS THE PERFECT OPPORTUNITY TO ELIMINATE WHOEVER IS SEEKING TO DO YOU HARM.
BAM

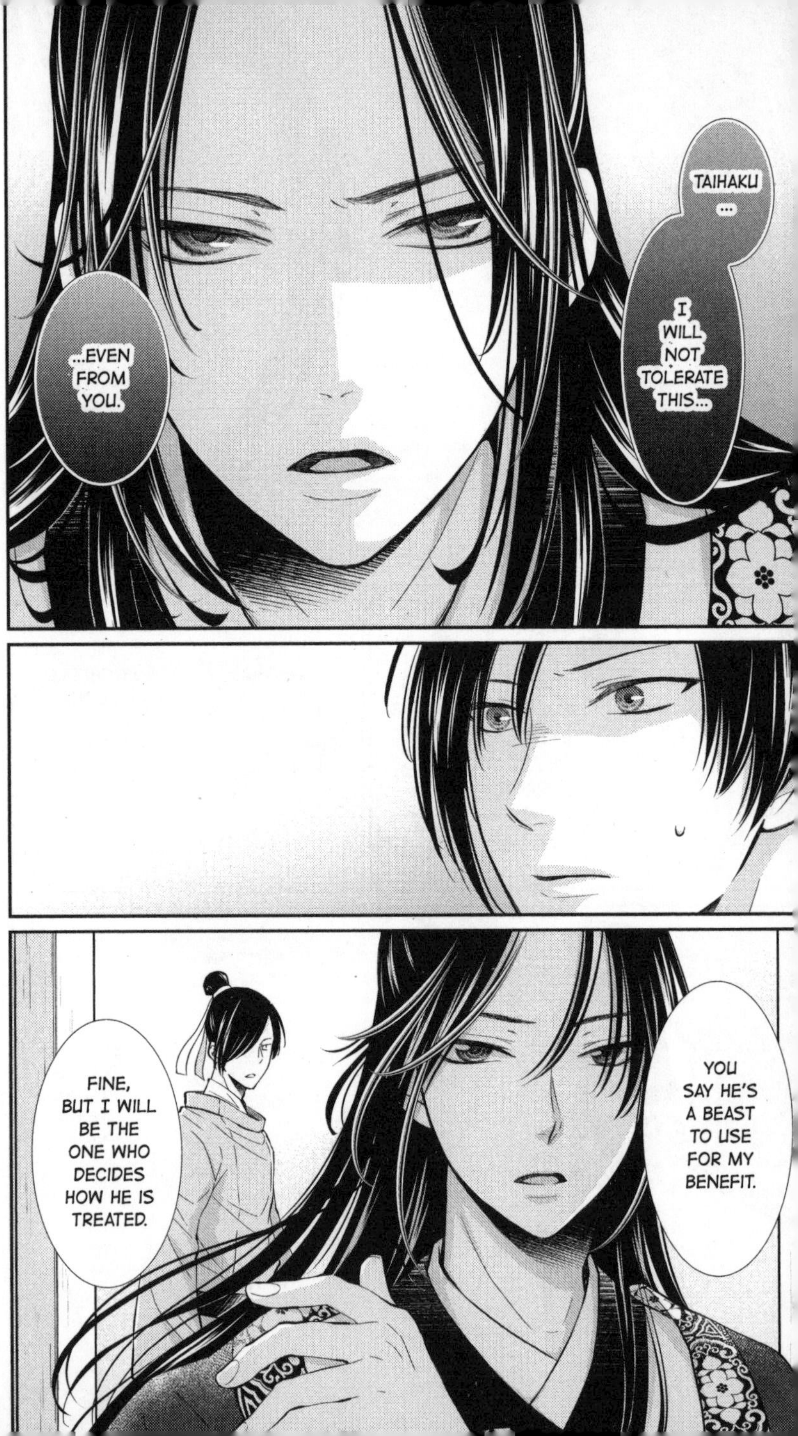
TAIHAKU ...
I WILL NOT TOLERATE THIS...
...EVEN FROM YOU.
YOU SAY HE'S A BEAST TO USE FOR MY BENEFIT.
FINE, BUT I WILL BE THE ONE WHO DECIDES HOW HE IS TREATED.

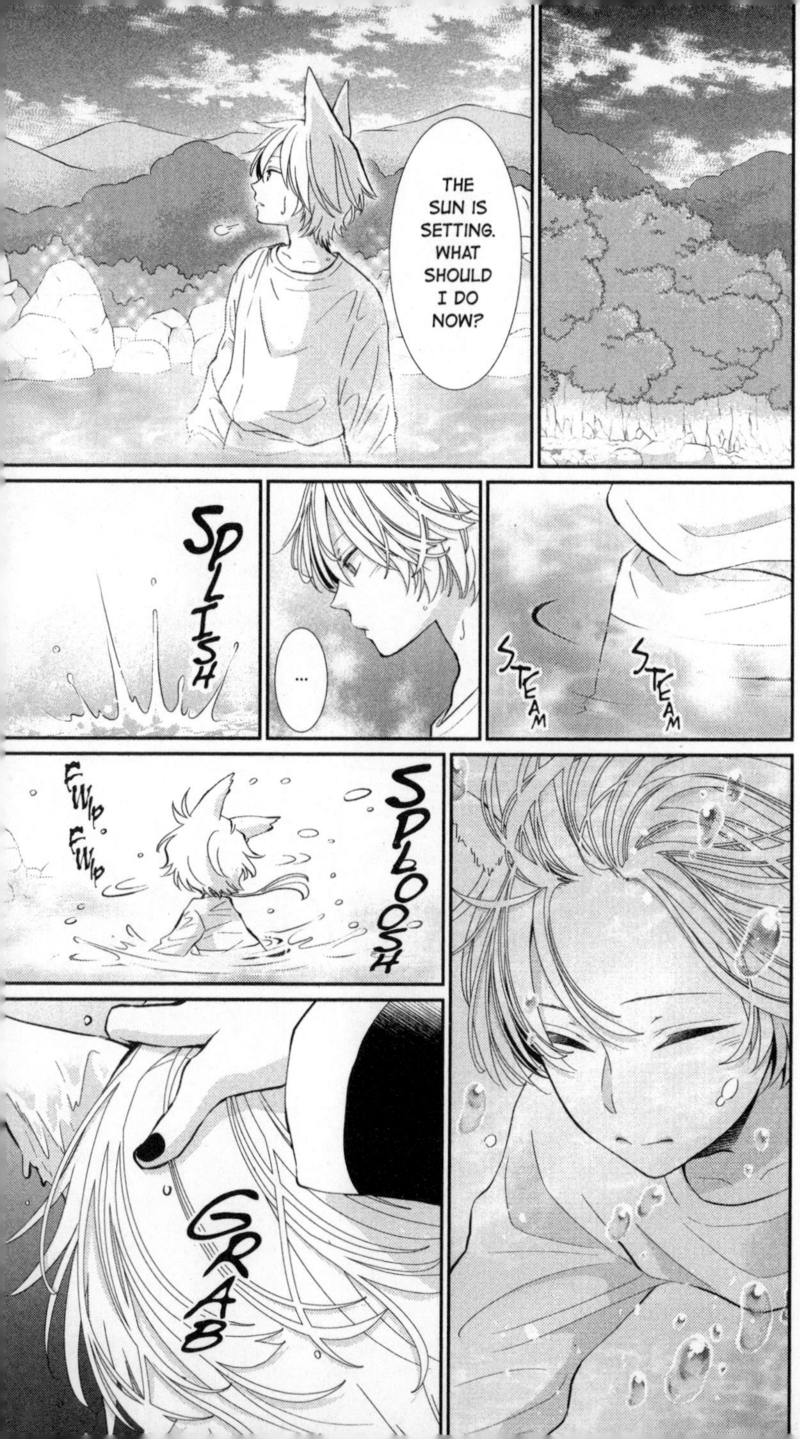
THE SUN IS SETTING. WHAT SHOULD I DO NOW?
STEAM
STEAM
...
SPLISH
SPLOOSH
FWIP FWIP
GRAB

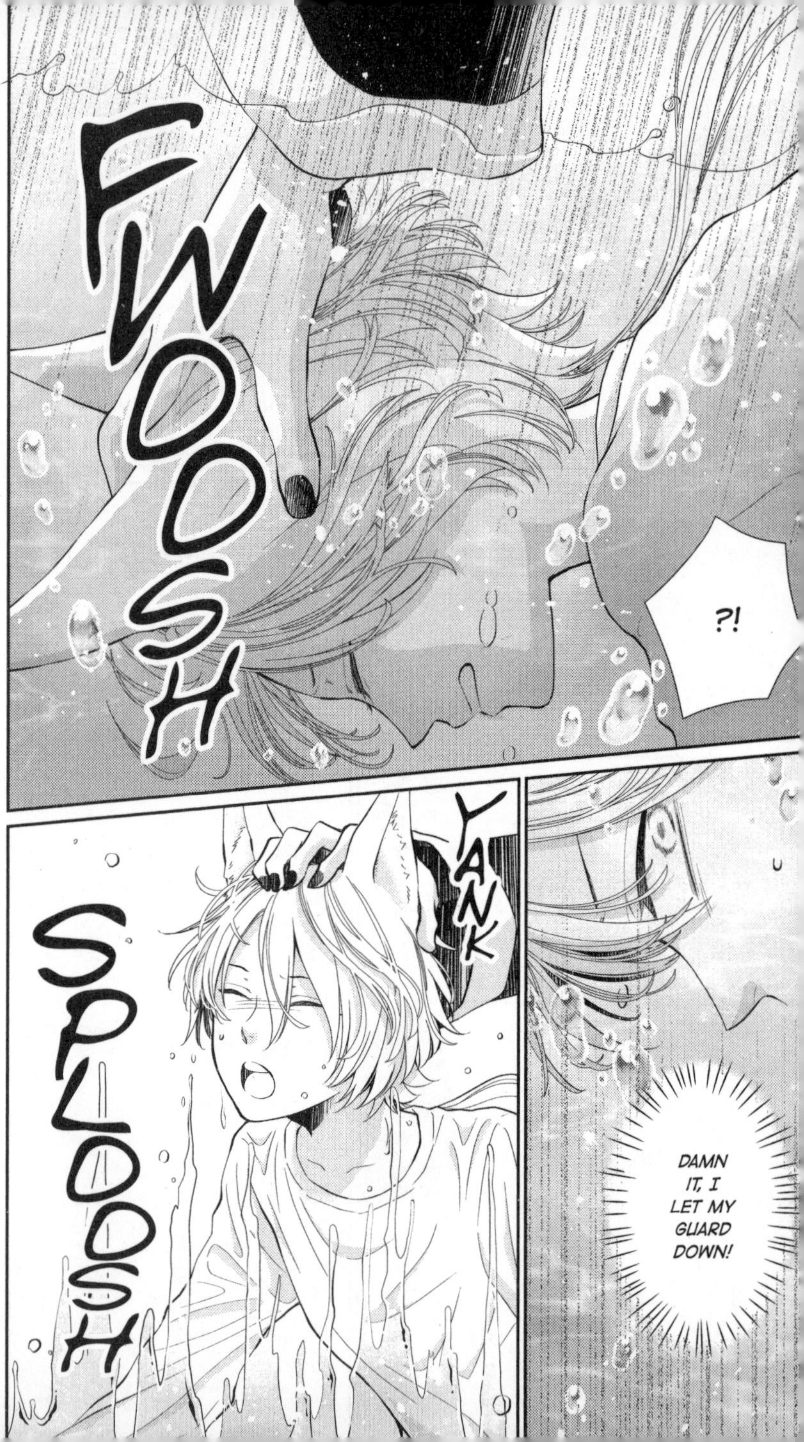
FWOOSH
?!
DAMN IT, I LET MY GUARD DOWN!
YANK
SPLOOSH

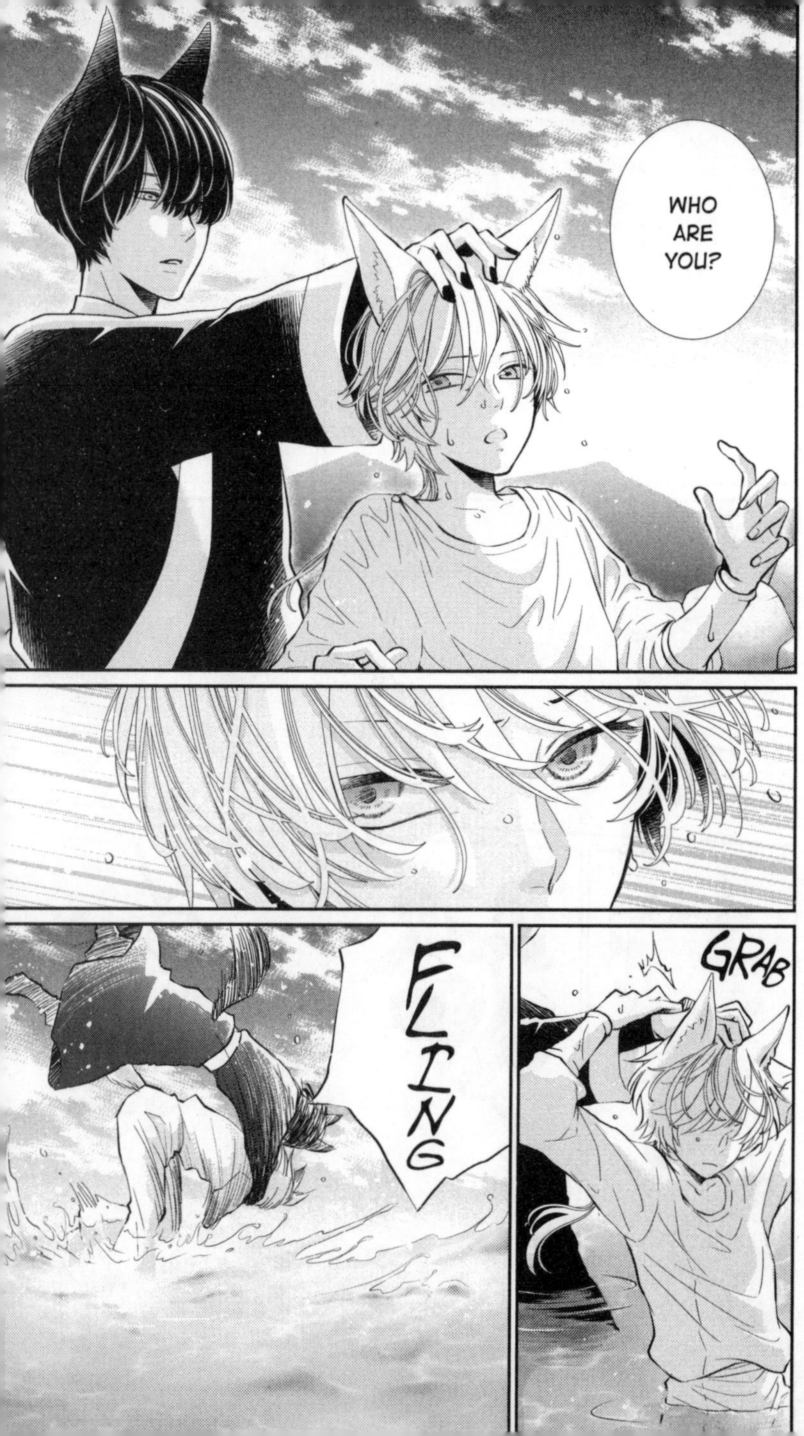
WHO ARE YOU?
GRAB
FLING

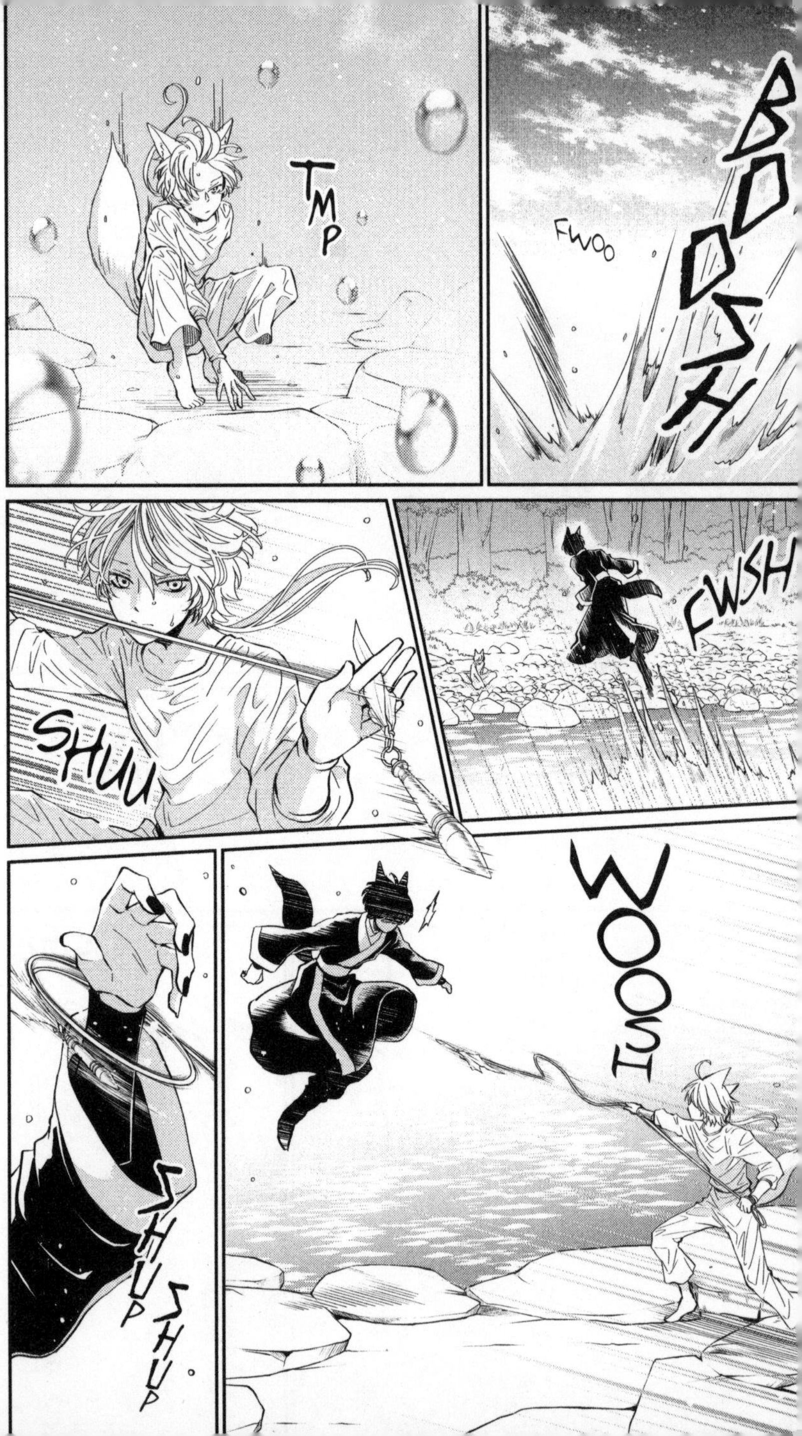
BOOSH
FWOO
TMP
FWSH
SHUU
WOOSH
SHUP
SHUP

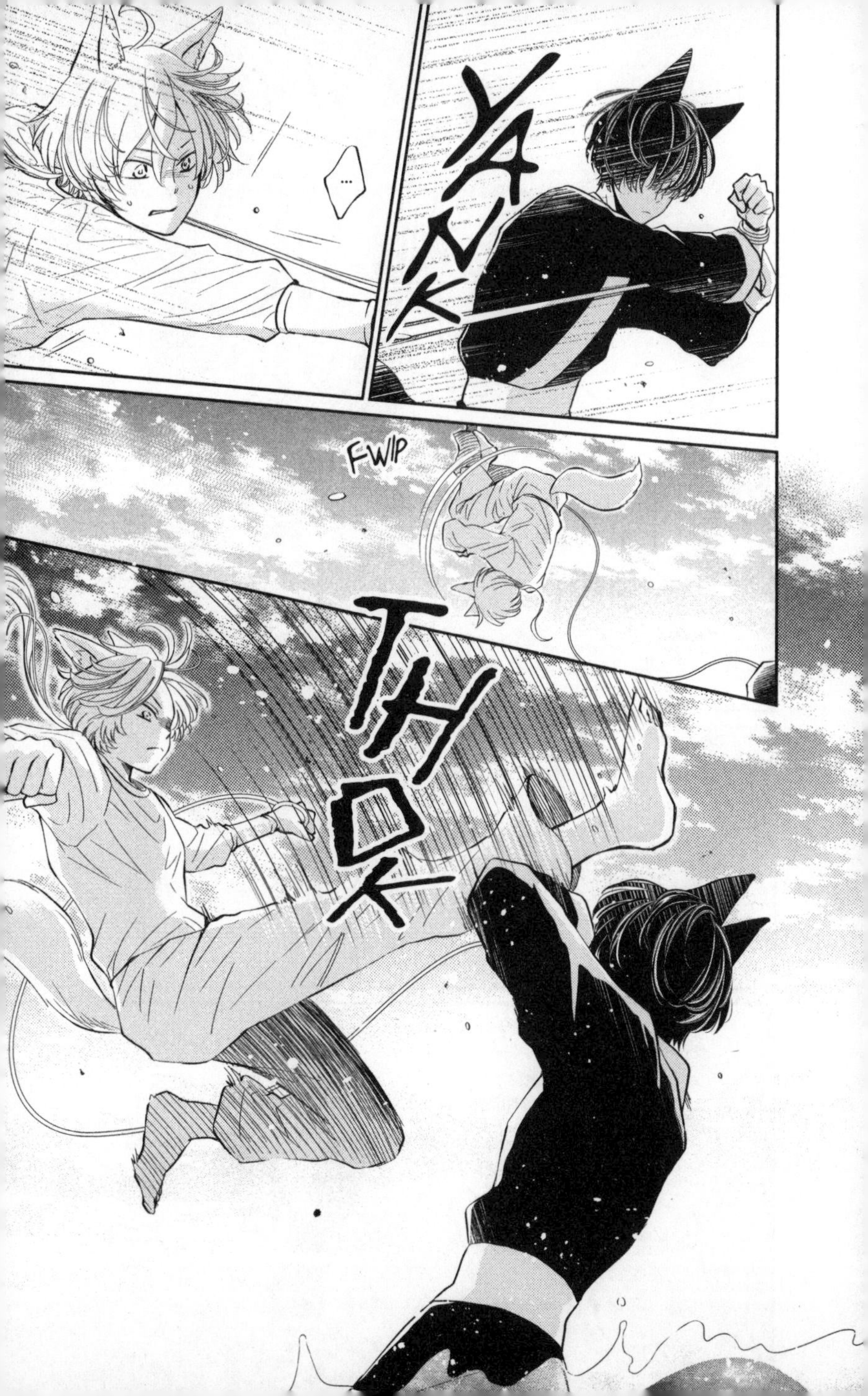
YANK
...
FWIP
THOK

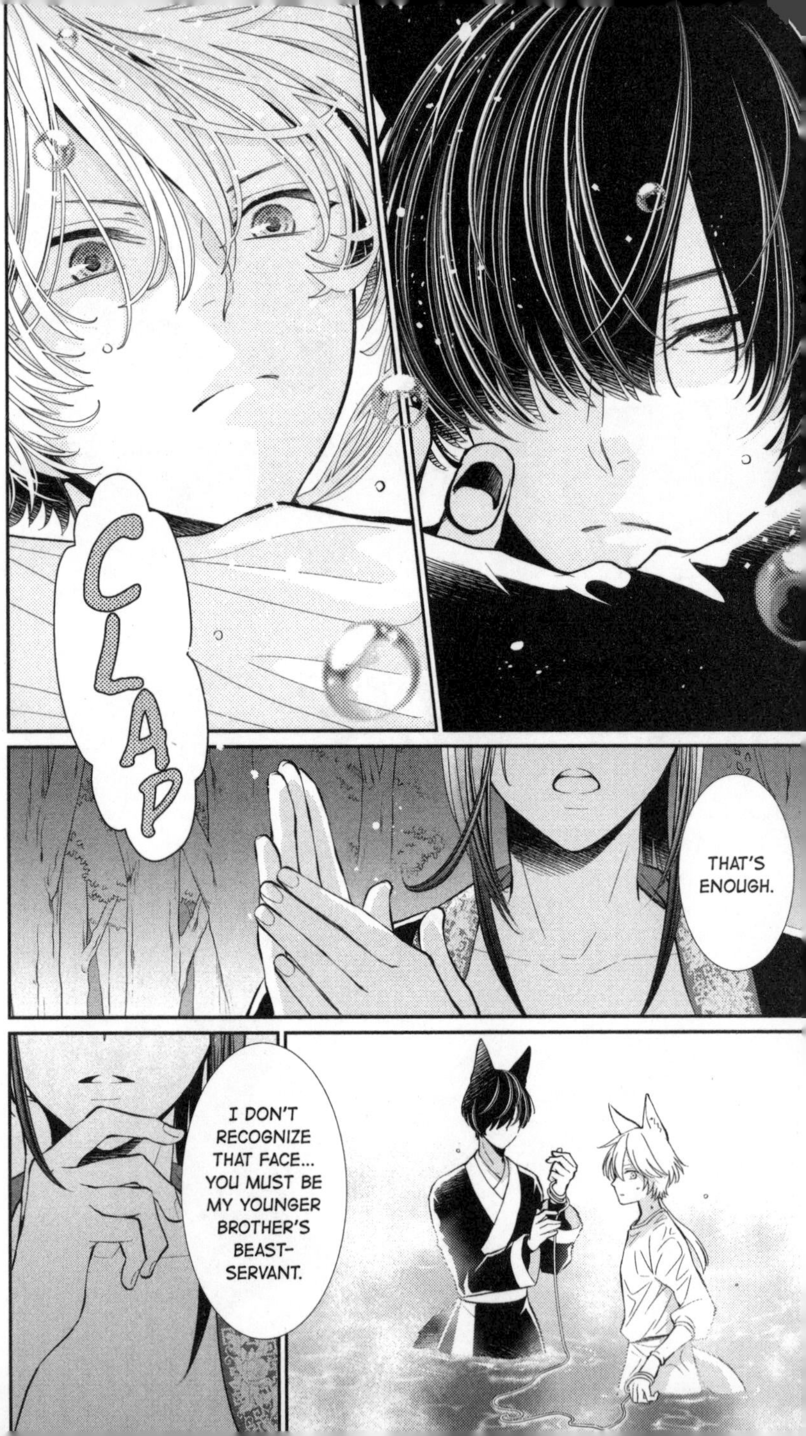
CLAP
THAT'S ENOUGH.
I DON'T RECOGNIZE THAT FACE... YOU MUST BE MY YOUNGER BROTHER'S BEAST-SERVANT.

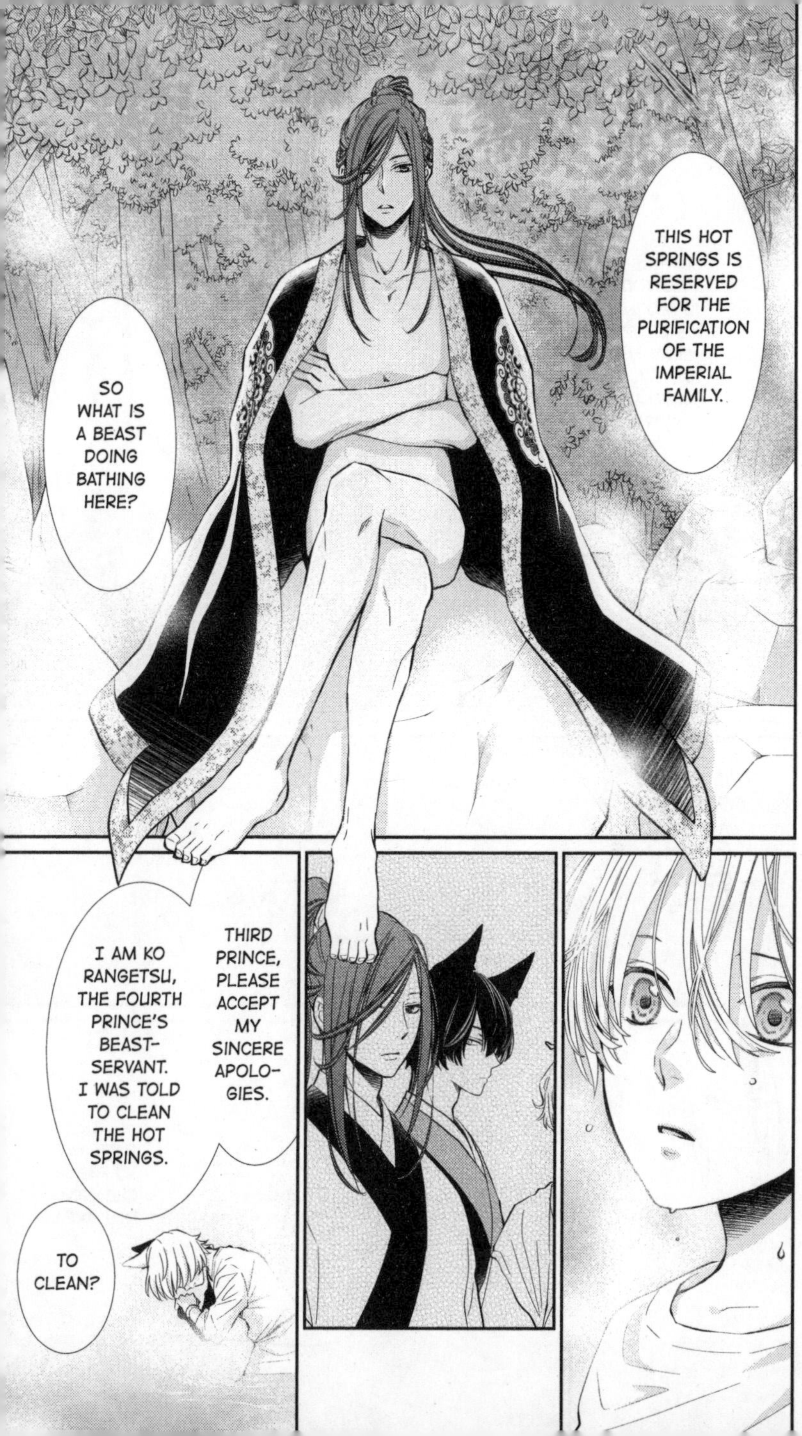
THIS HOT SPRINGS IS RESERVED FOR THE PURIFICATION OF THE IMPERIAL FAMILY.
SO WHAT IS A BEAST DOING BATHING HERE?
THIRD PRINCE, PLEASE ACCEPT MY SINCERE APOLOGIES.
I AM KO RANGETSU, THE FOURTH PRINCE'S BEAST-SERVANT. I WAS TOLD TO CLEAN THE HOT SPRINGS.
TO CLEAN?

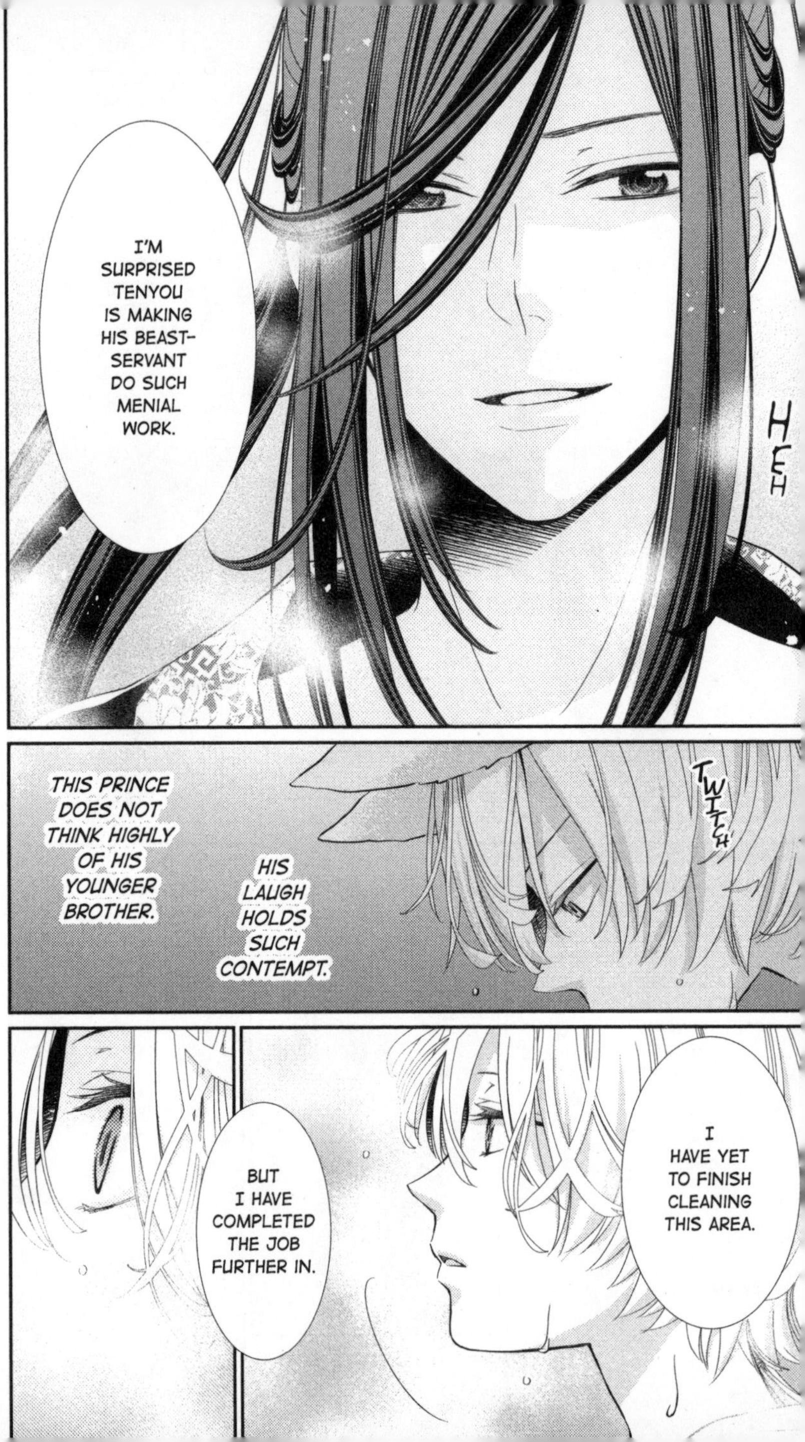
HEH
I'M SURPRISED TENYOU IS MAKING HIS BEAST-SERVANT DO SUCH MENIAL WORK.
TWITCH
HIS LAUGH HOLDS SUCH CONTEMPT.
THIS PRINCE DOES NOT THINK HIGHLY OF HIS YOUNGER BROTHER.
I HAVE YET TO FINISH CLEANING THIS AREA.
BUT I HAVE COMPLETED THE JOB FURTHER IN.

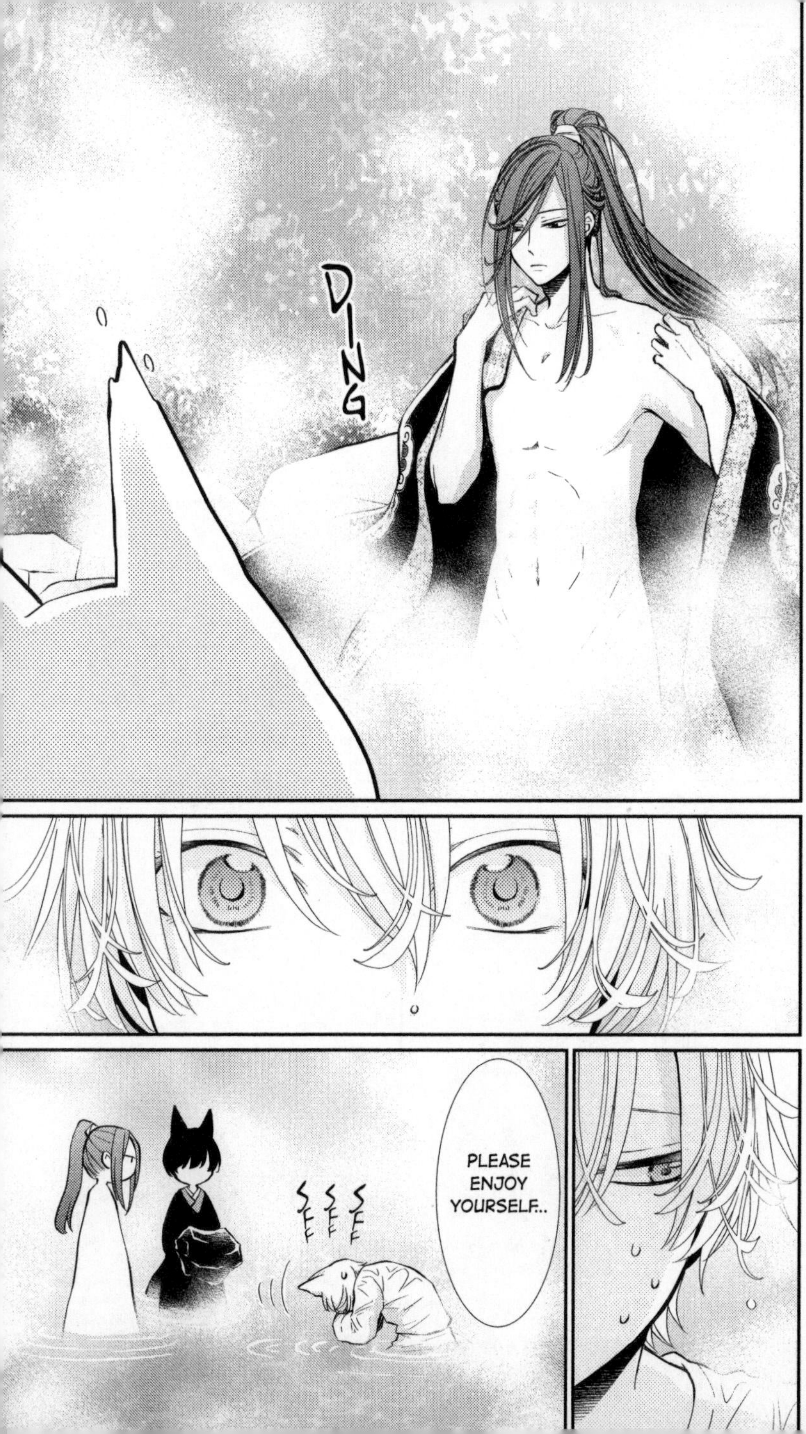
DING
PLEASE ENJOY YOURSELF...
SSS
FFF
FFF

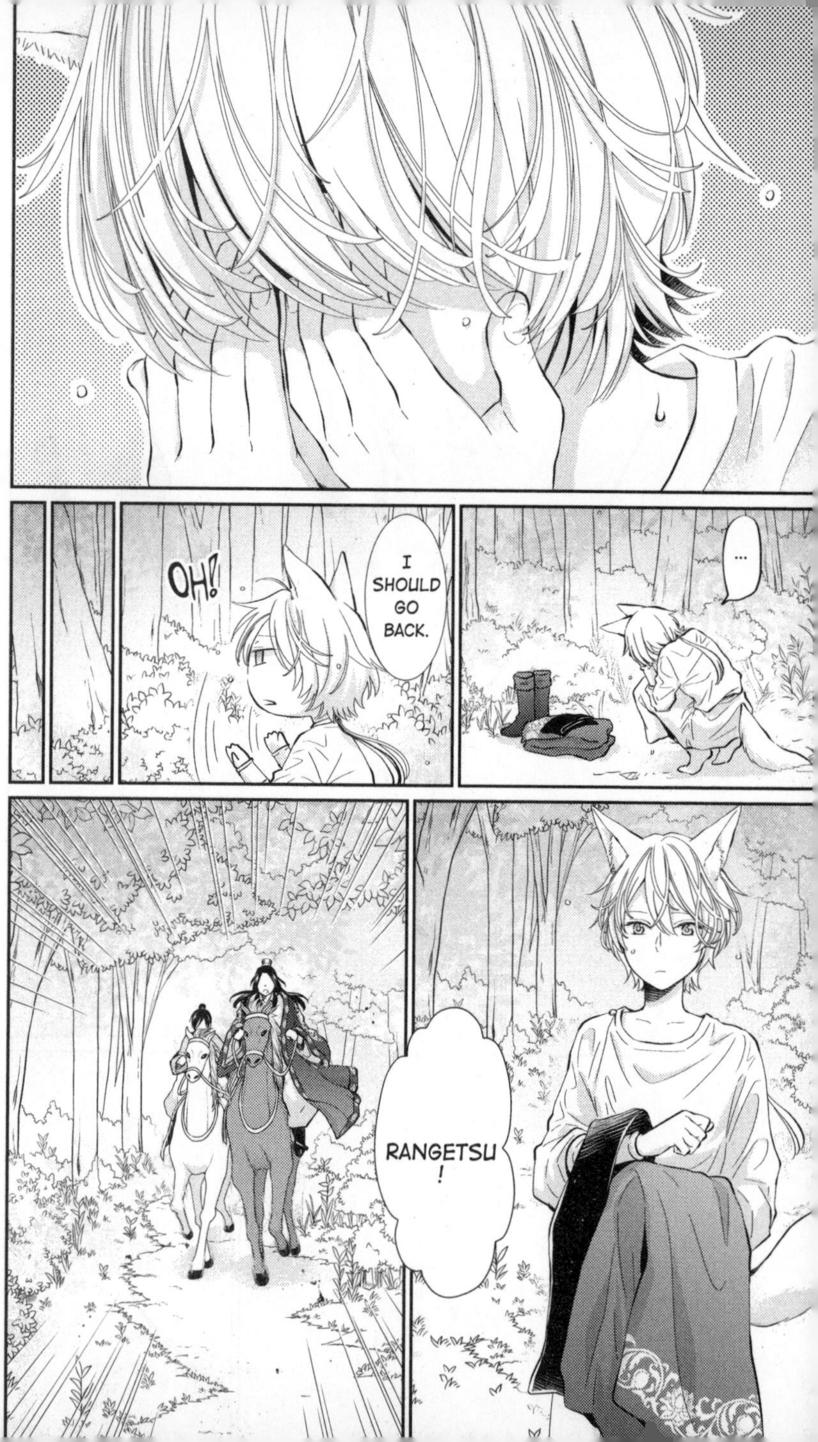
...
I SHOULD GO BACK.
OH!?
RANGETSU!

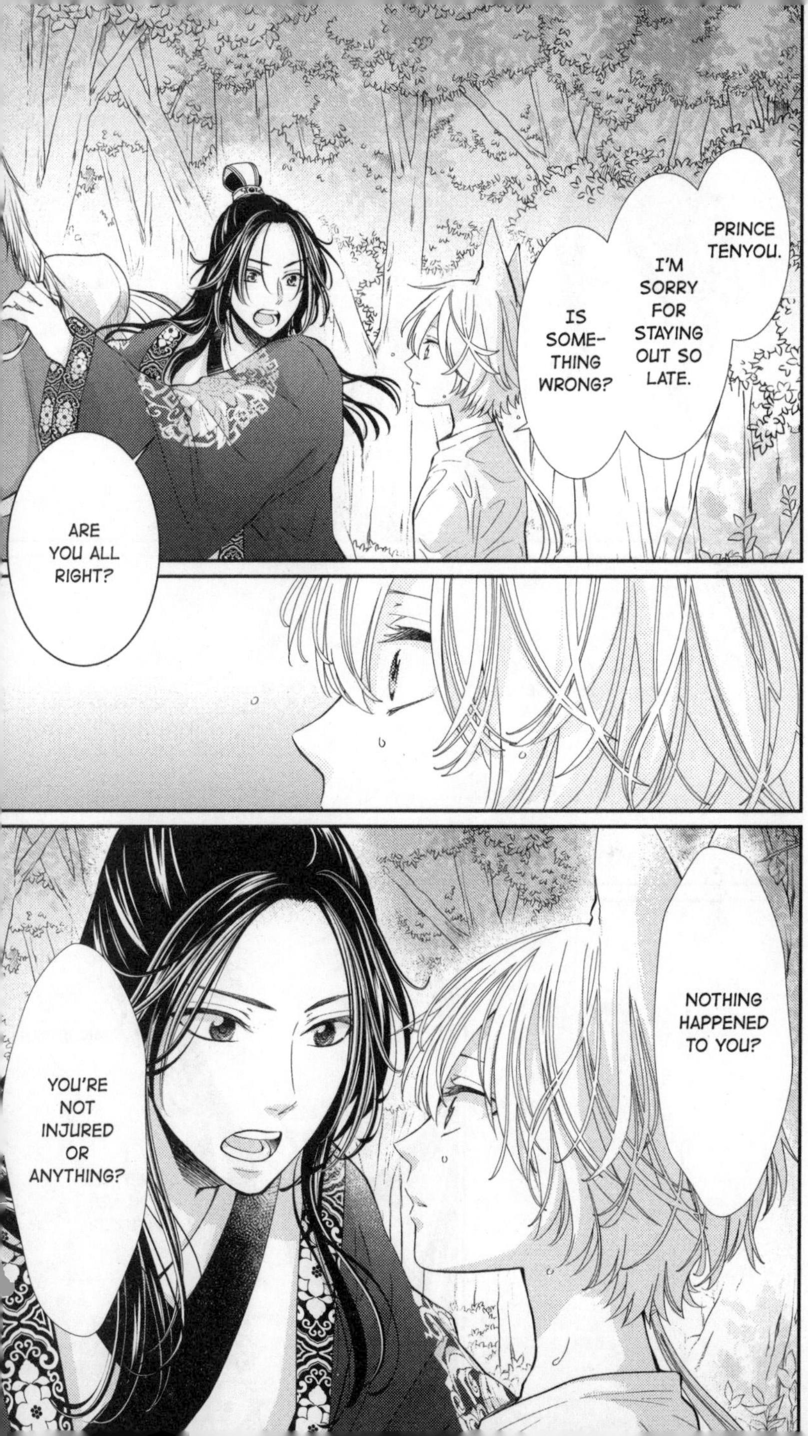
PRINCE TENYOU.
I'M SORRY FOR STAYING OUT SO LATE.
IS SOME-THING WRONG?
ARE YOU ALL RIGHT?
NOTHING HAPPENED TO YOU?
YOU'RE NOT INJURED OR ANYTHING?

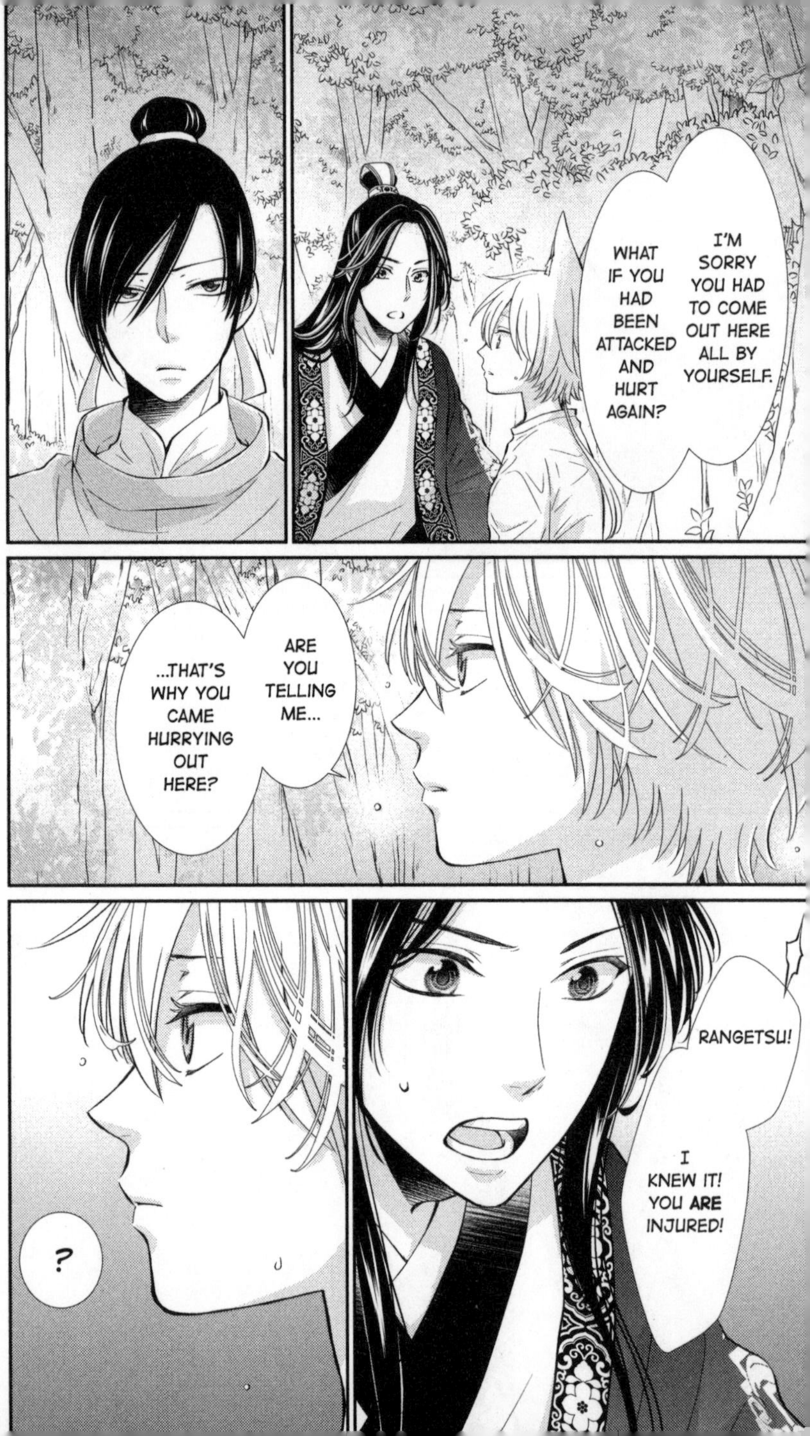
I'M SORRY YOU HAD TO COME OUT HERE ALL BY YOURSELF.
WHAT IF YOU HAD BEEN ATTACKED AND HURT AGAIN?
ARE YOU TELLING ME...
...THAT'S WHY YOU CAME HURRYING OUT HERE?
RANGETSU!
I KNEW IT! YOU **ARE** INJURED!
?

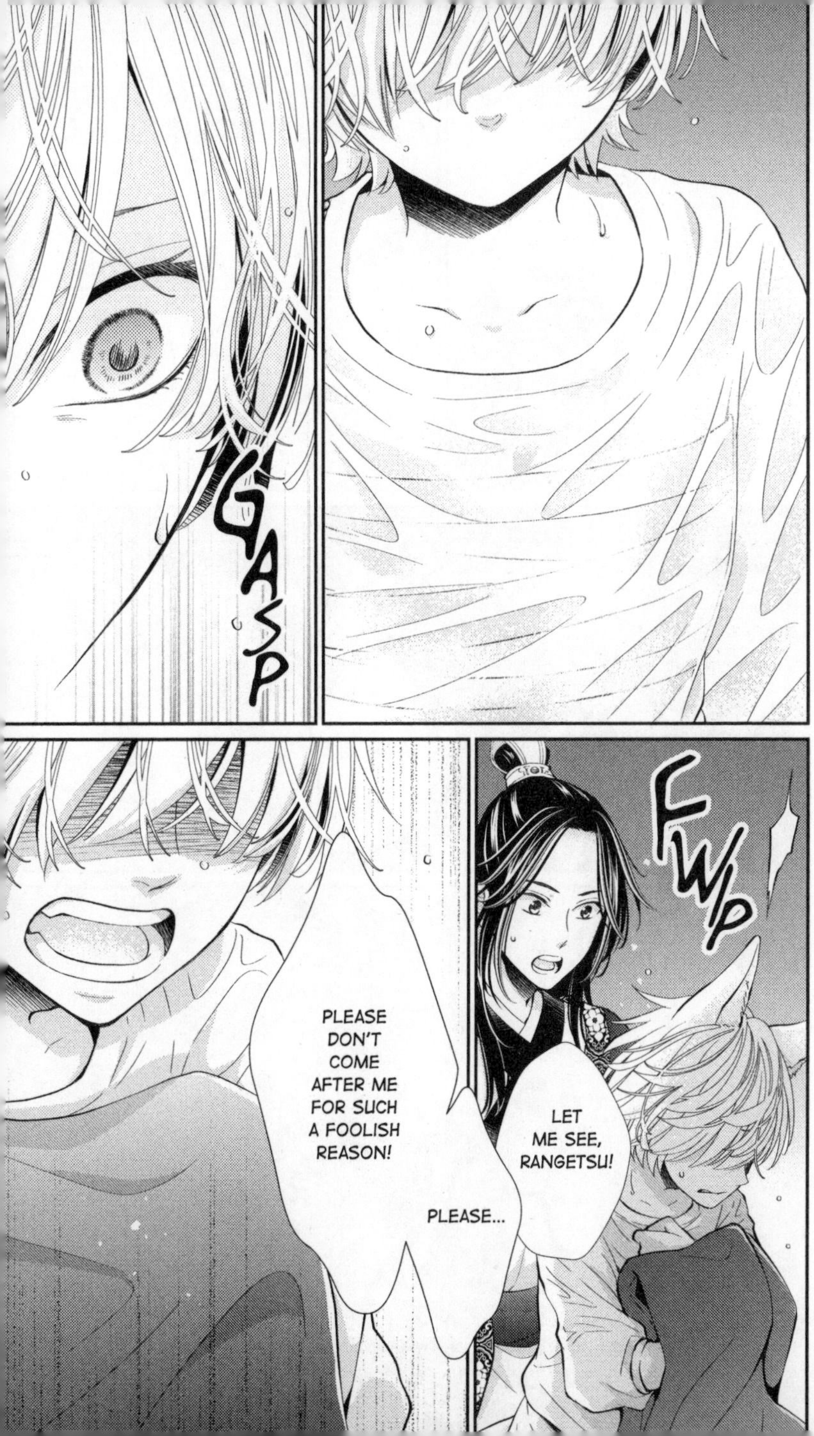
GASP
FWIP
!
LET ME SEE, RANGETSU!
PLEASE DON'T COME AFTER ME FOR SUCH A FOOLISH REASON!
PLEASE...

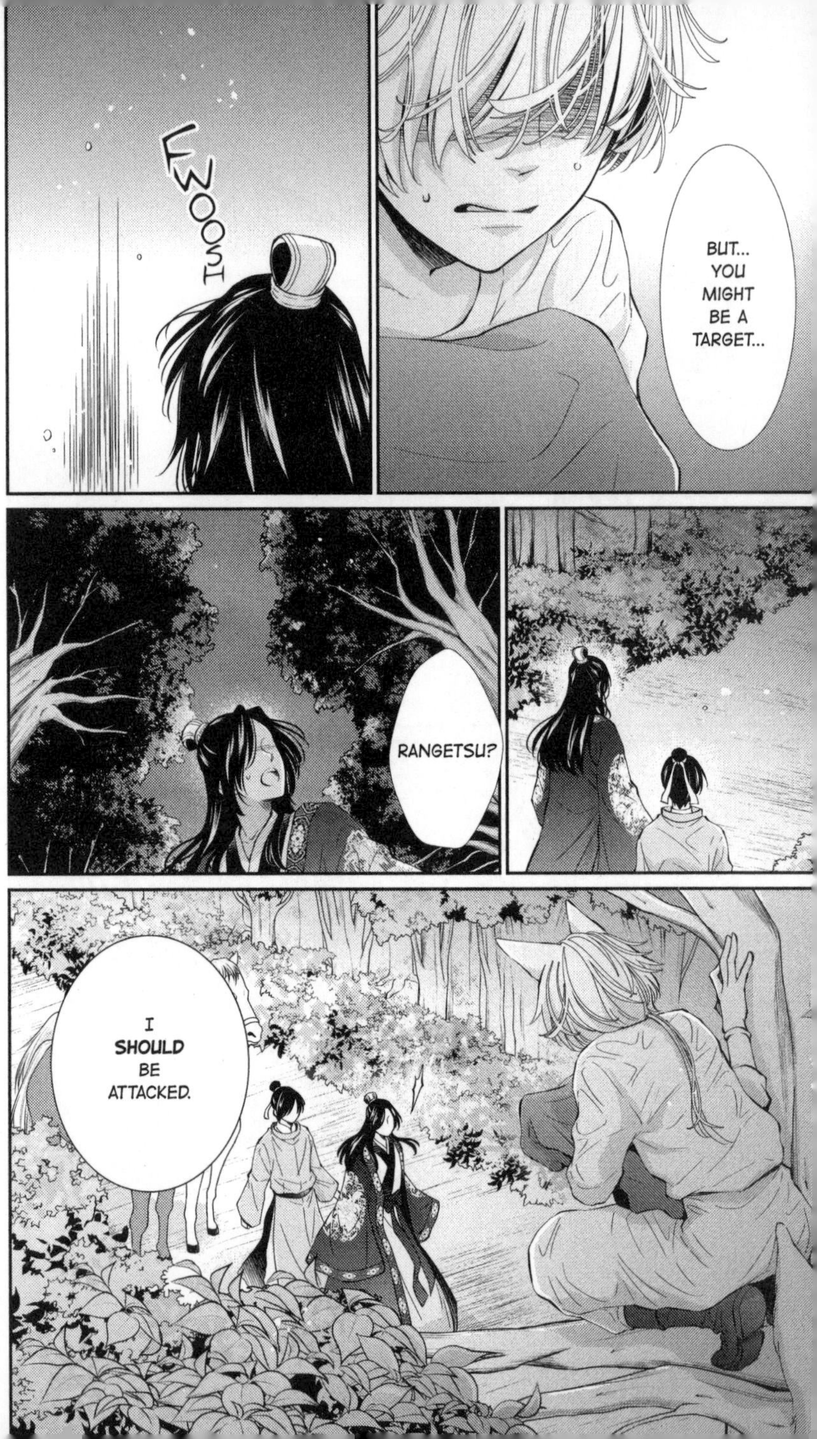
BUT... YOU MIGHT BE A TARGET...
FWOOSH
RANGETSU?
I **SHOULD** BE ATTACKED.

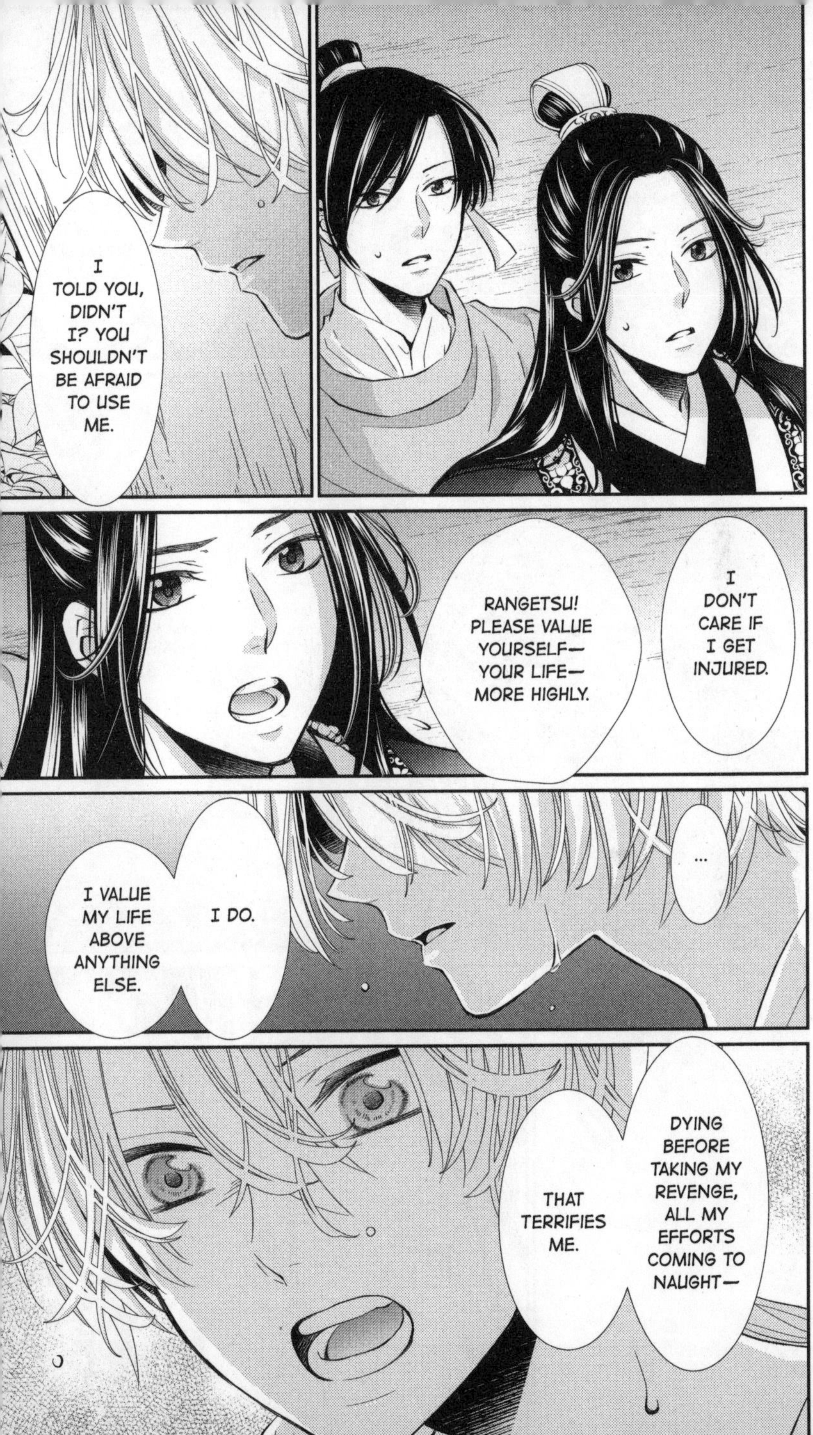
I TOLD YOU, DIDN'T I? YOU SHOULDN'T BE AFRAID TO USE ME.
I DON'T CARE IF I GET INJURED.
RANGETSU! PLEASE VALUE YOURSELF— YOUR LIFE— MORE HIGHLY.
...
I DO.
I VALUE MY LIFE ABOVE ANYTHING ELSE.
DYING BEFORE TAKING MY REVENGE, ALL MY EFFORTS COMING TO NAUGHT—
THAT TERRIFIES ME.

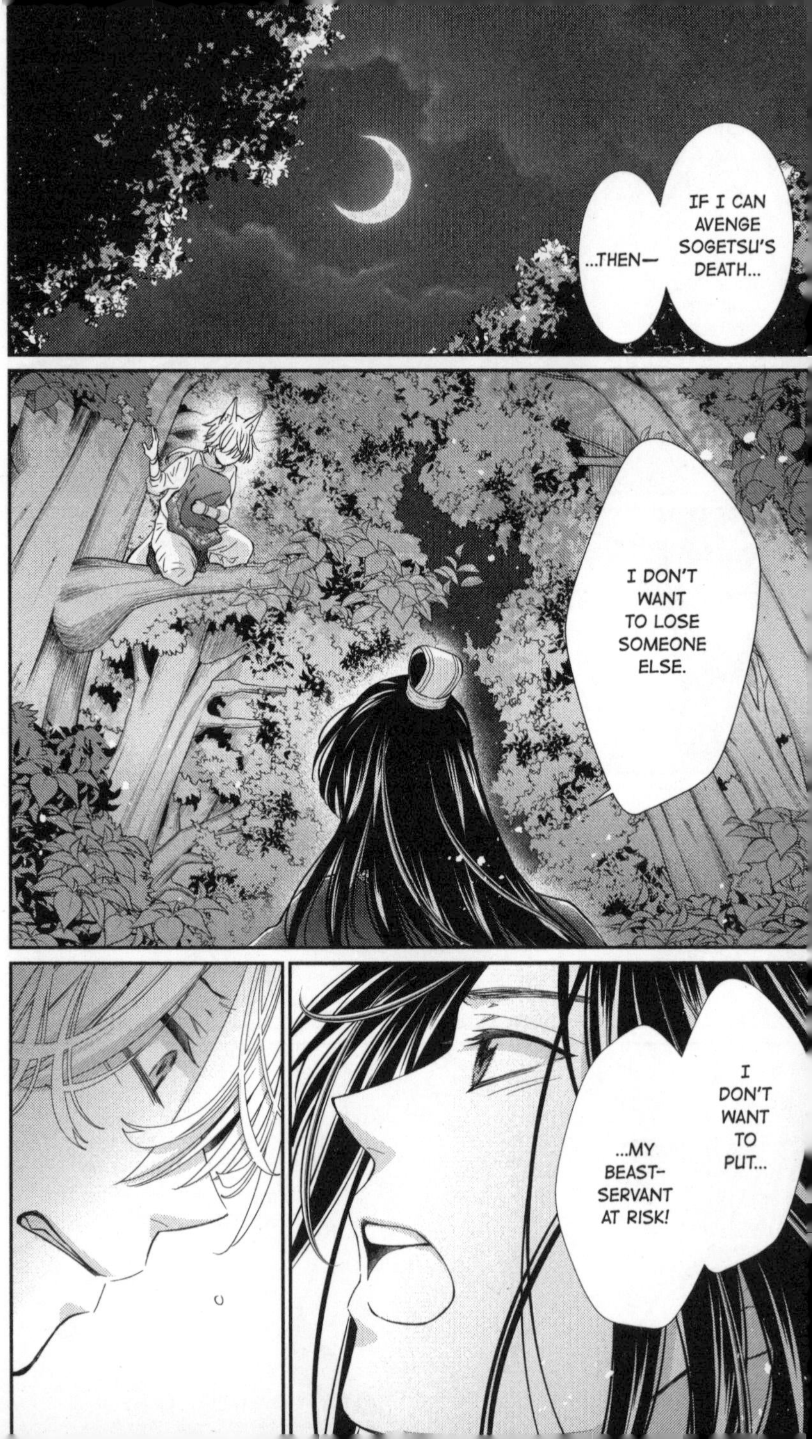
IF I CAN AVENGE SOGETSU'S DEATH...
...THEN—
I DON'T WANT TO LOSE SOMEONE ELSE.
I DON'T WANT TO PUT...
...MY BEAST-SERVANT AT RISK!

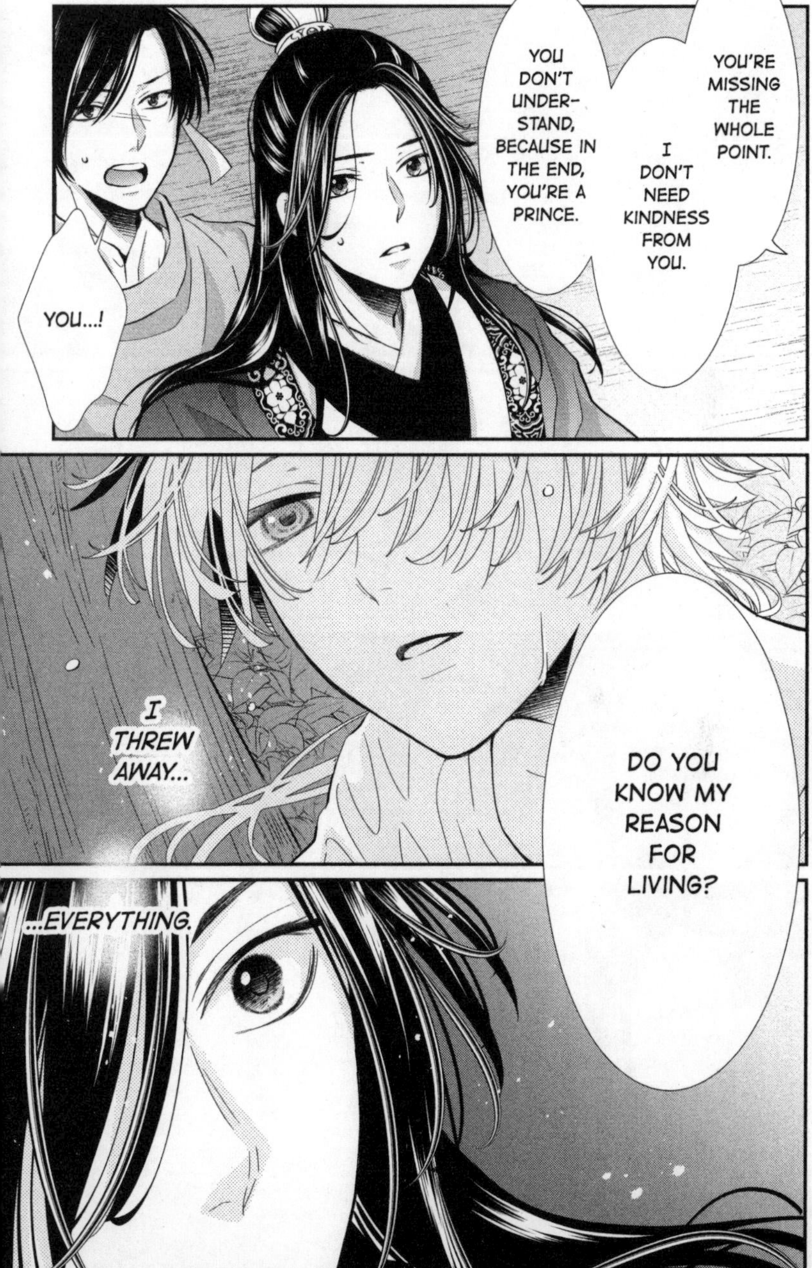
YOU'RE MISSING THE WHOLE POINT.
I DON'T NEED KINDNESS FROM YOU.
YOU DON'T UNDER-STAND, BECAUSE IN THE END, YOU'RE A PRINCE.
YOU...!
DO YOU KNOW MY REASON FOR LIVING?
I THREW AWAY...
...EVERYTHING.

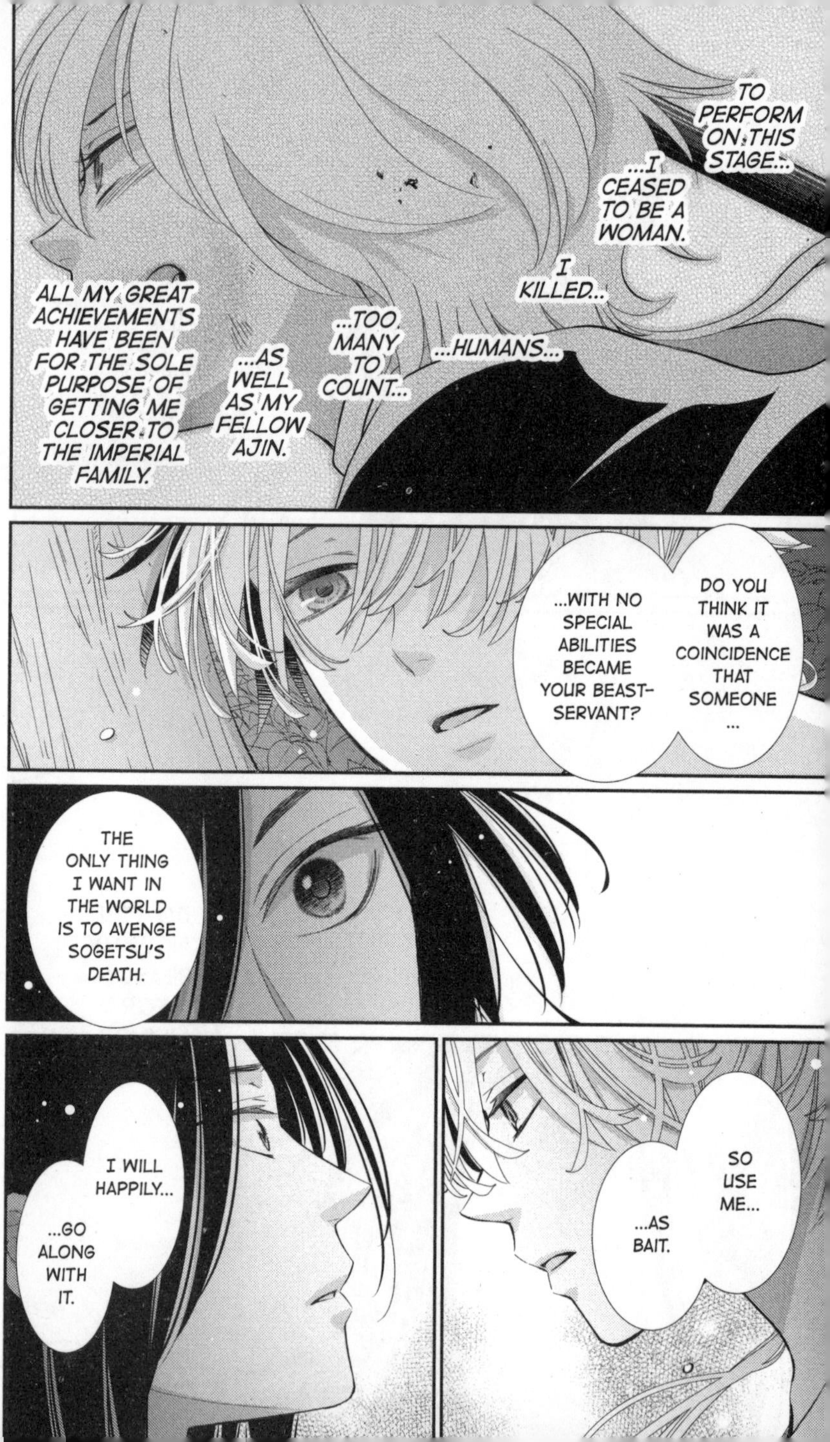
TO PERFORM ON THIS STAGE...
...I CEASED TO BE A WOMAN.
I KILLED...
...HUMANS...
...TOO MANY TO COUNT...
...AS WELL AS MY FELLOW AJIN.
ALL MY GREAT ACHIEVEMENTS HAVE BEEN FOR THE SOLE PURPOSE OF GETTING ME CLOSER TO THE IMPERIAL FAMILY.
DO YOU THINK IT WAS A COINCIDENCE THAT SOMEONE ...
...WITH NO SPECIAL ABILITIES BECAME YOUR BEAST-SERVANT?
THE ONLY THING I WANT IN THE WORLD IS TO AVENGE SOGETSU'S DEATH.
SO USE ME...
...AS BAIT.
I WILL HAPPILY...
...GO ALONG WITH IT.

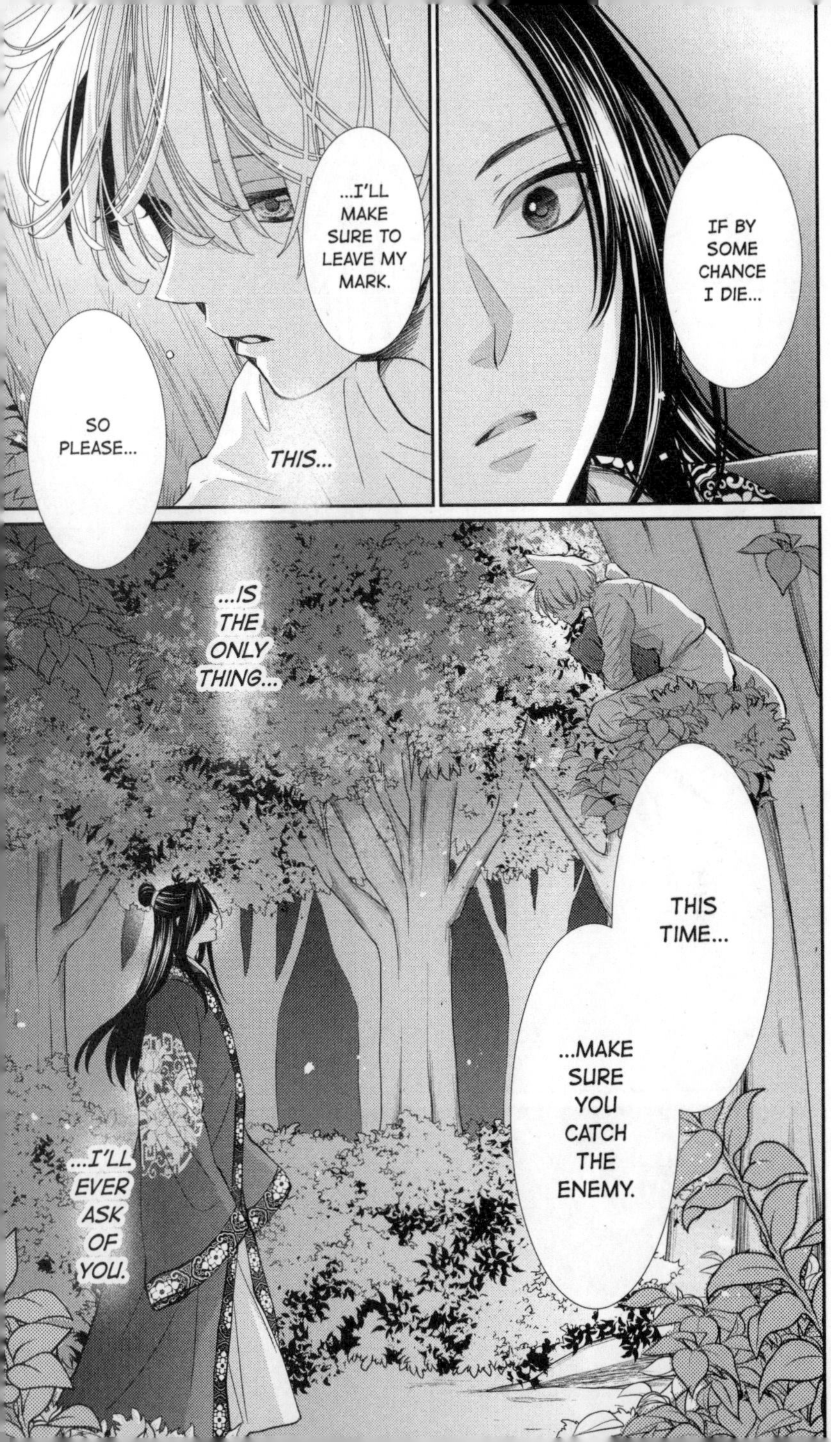
IF BY SOME CHANCE I DIE...
...I'LL MAKE SURE TO LEAVE MY MARK.
SO PLEASE...
THIS...
THIS TIME...
...MAKE SURE YOU CATCH THE ENEMY.
...IS THE ONLY THING...
...I'LL EVER ASK OF YOU.

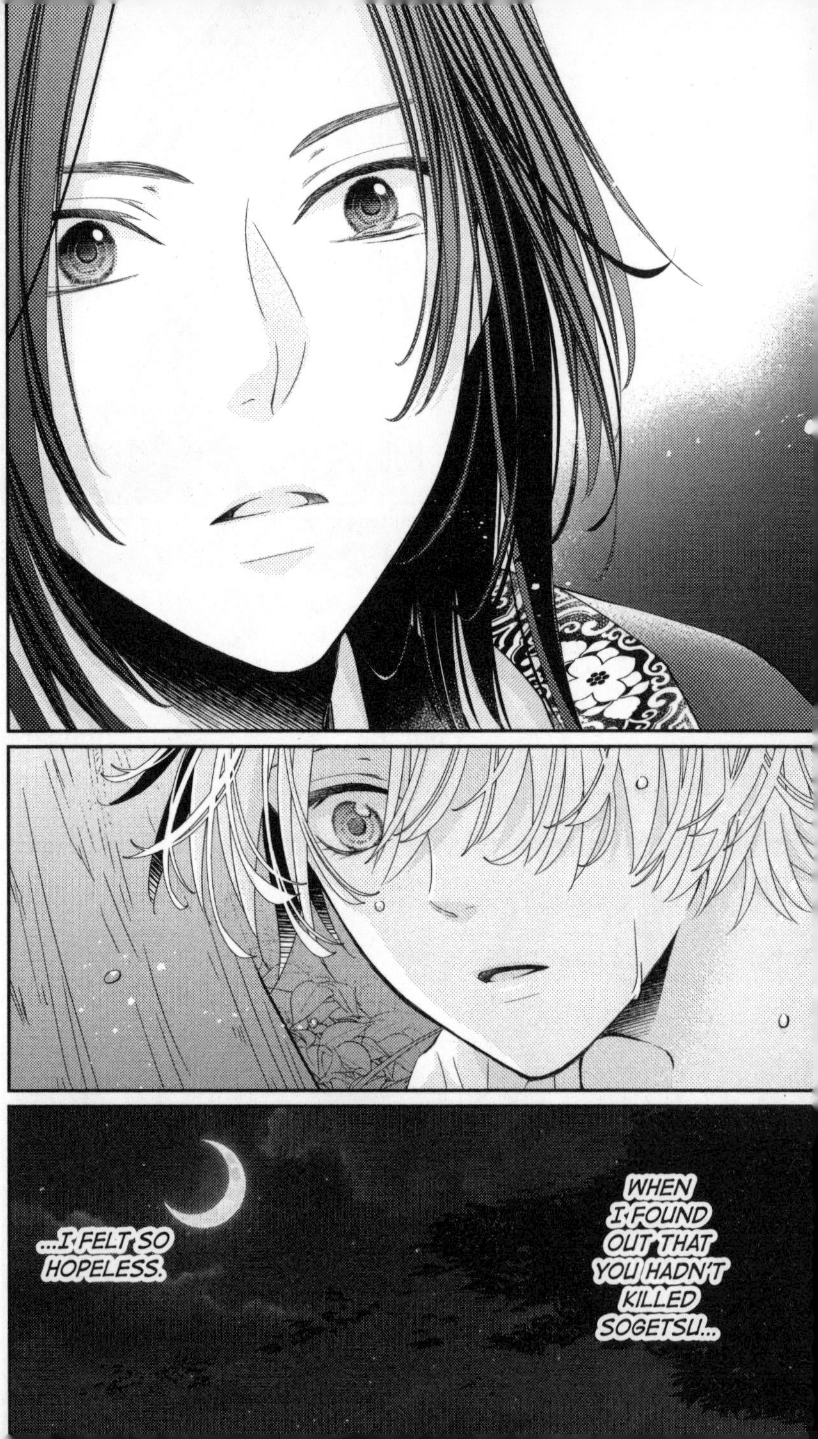
WHEN I FOUND OUT THAT YOU HADN'T KILLED SOGETSU...
...I FELT SO HOPELESS.

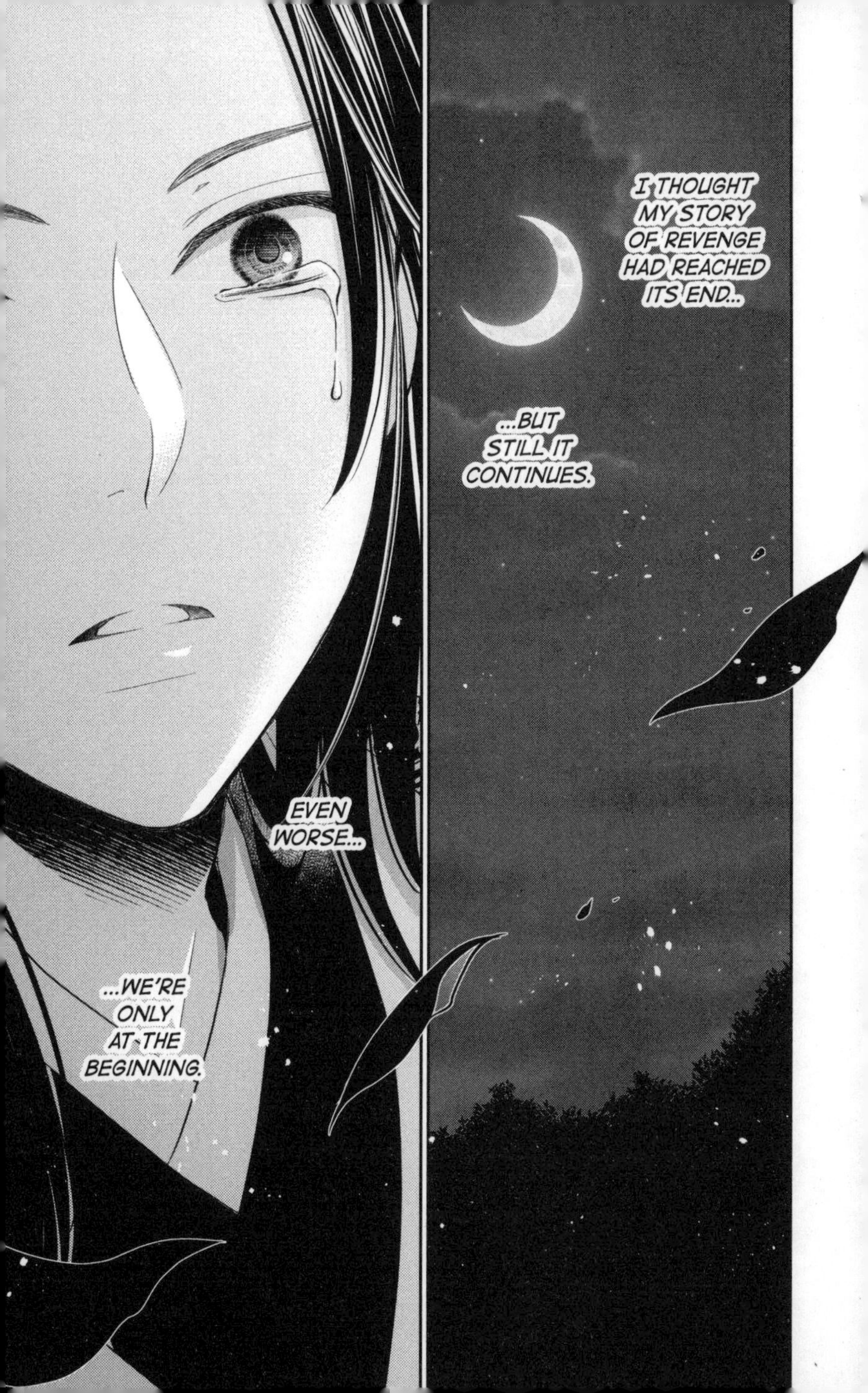
I THOUGHT MY STORY OF REVENGE HAD REACHED ITS END...
...BUT STILL IT CONTINUES.
EVEN WORSE...
...WE'RE ONLY AT THE BEGINNING.

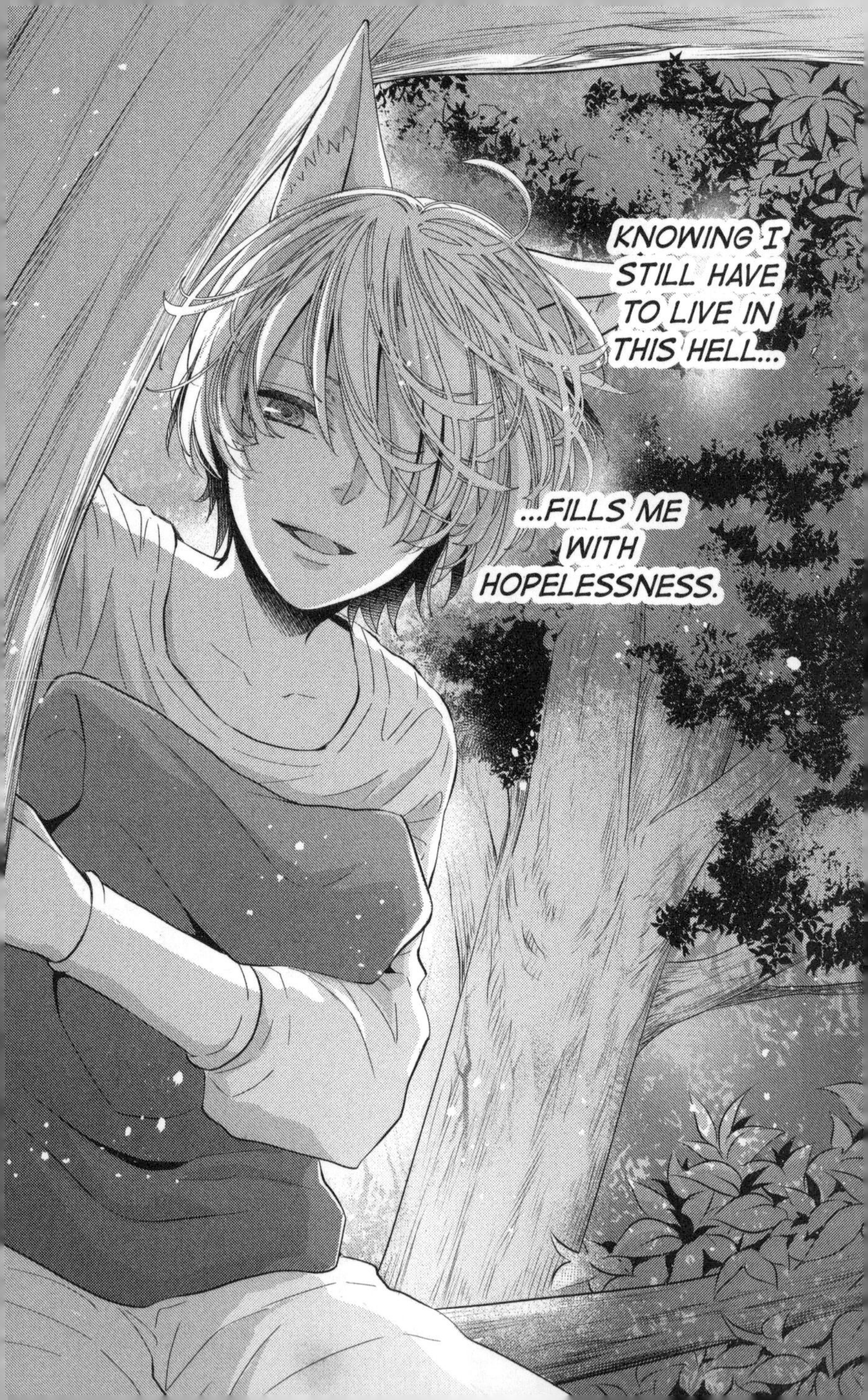
KNOWING I STILL HAVE TO LIVE IN THIS HELL...
...FILLS ME WITH HOPELESSNESS.

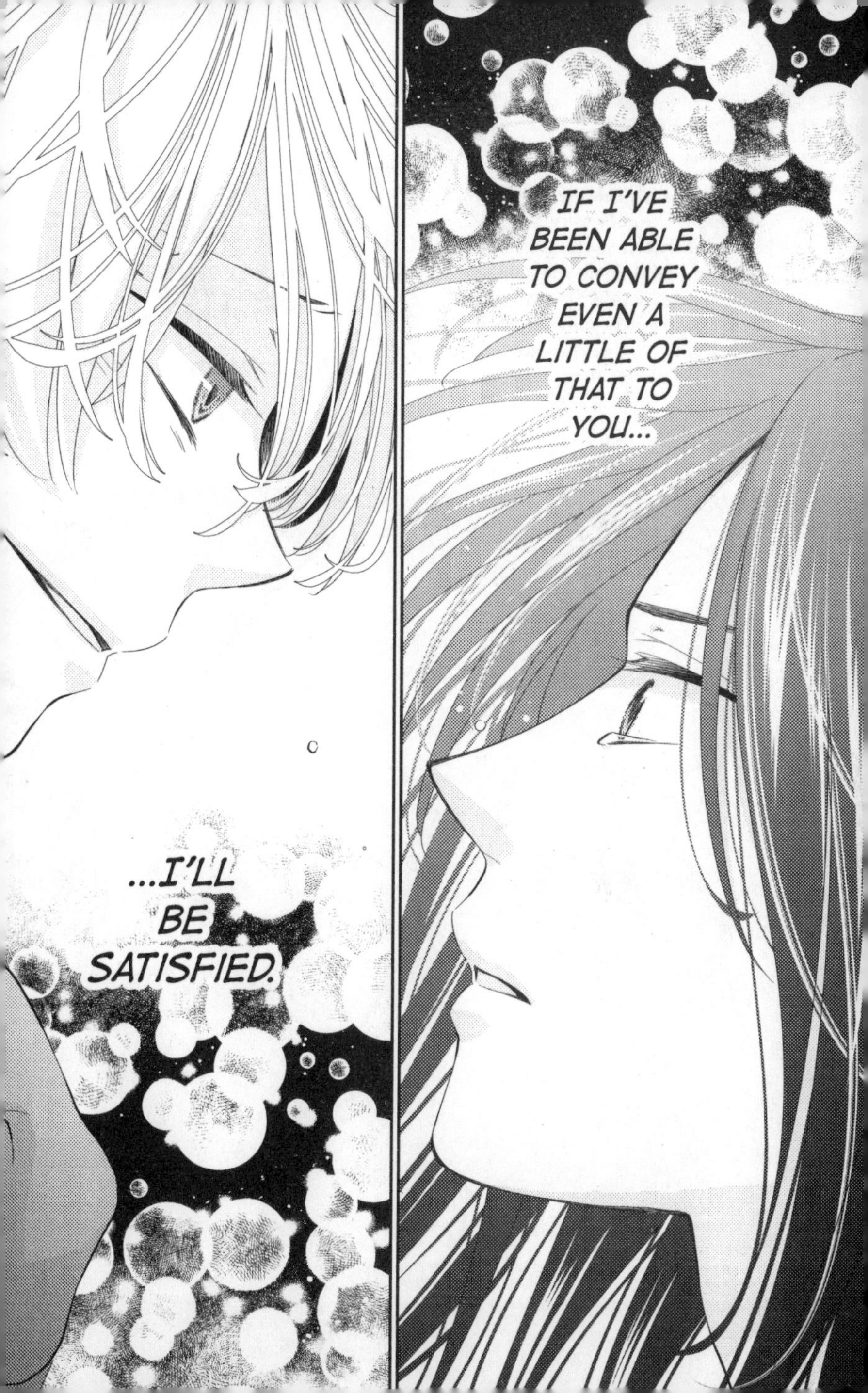
IF I'VE BEEN ABLE TO CONVEY EVEN A LITTLE OF THAT TO YOU...
...I'LL BE SATISFIED.

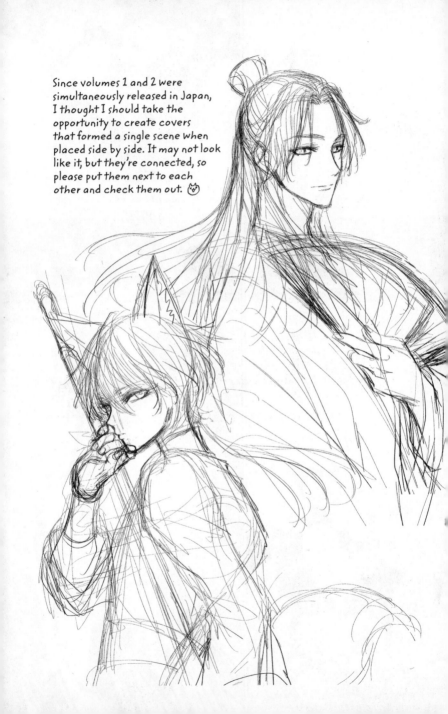

Since volumes 1 and 2 were simultaneously released in Japan, I thought I should take the opportunity to create covers that formed a single scene when placed side by side. It may not look like it, but they're connected, so please put them next to each other and check them out. 🐱

# Chapter 3

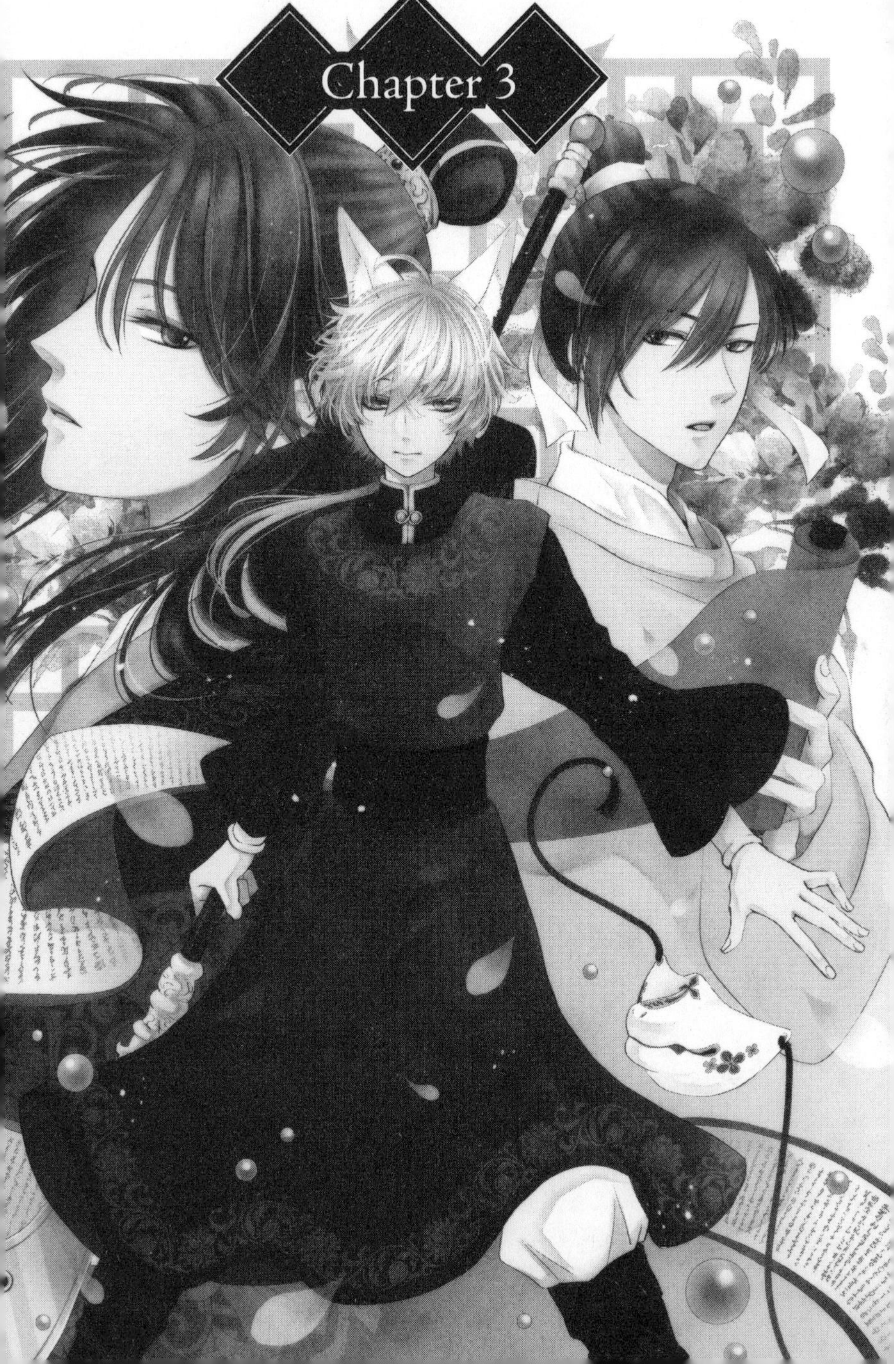

THE KING'S Beast

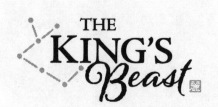

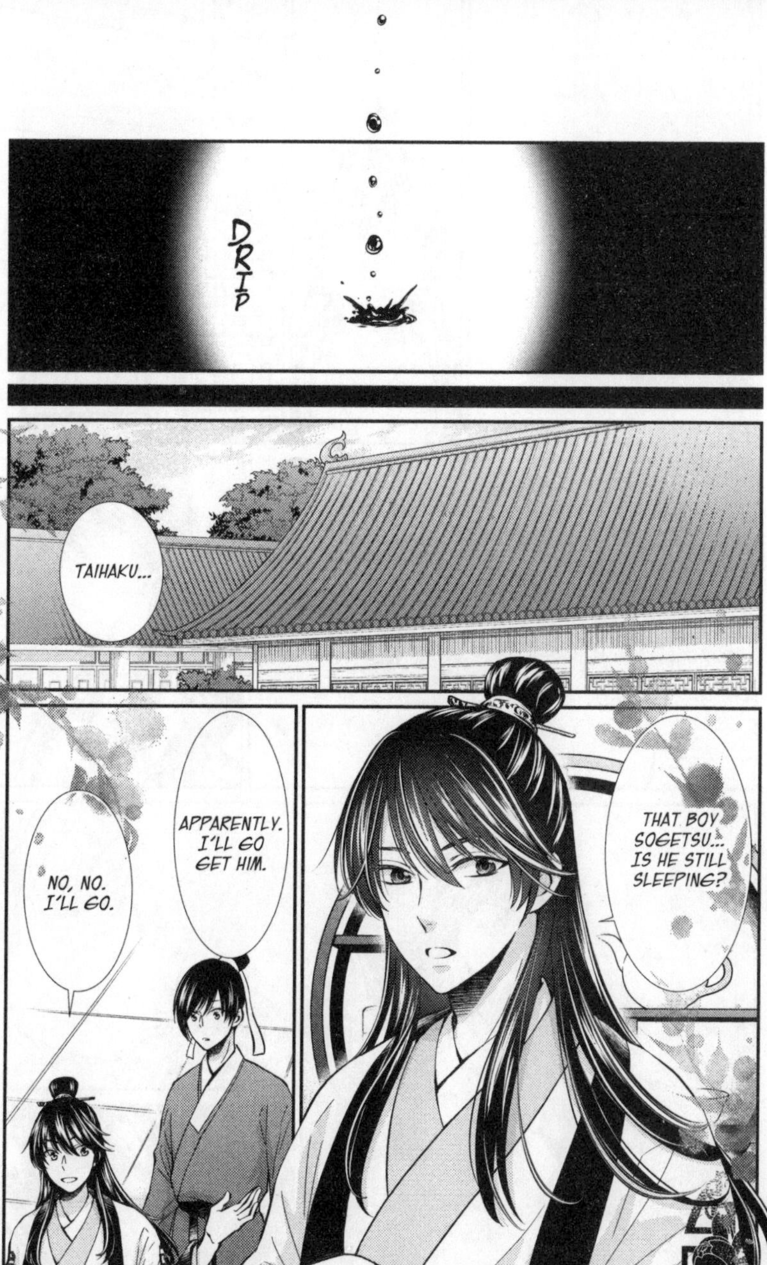
DRIP
TAIHAKU...
THAT BOY SOGETSU... IS HE STILL SLEEPING?
APPARENTLY. I'LL GO GET HIM.
NO, NO. I'LL GO.

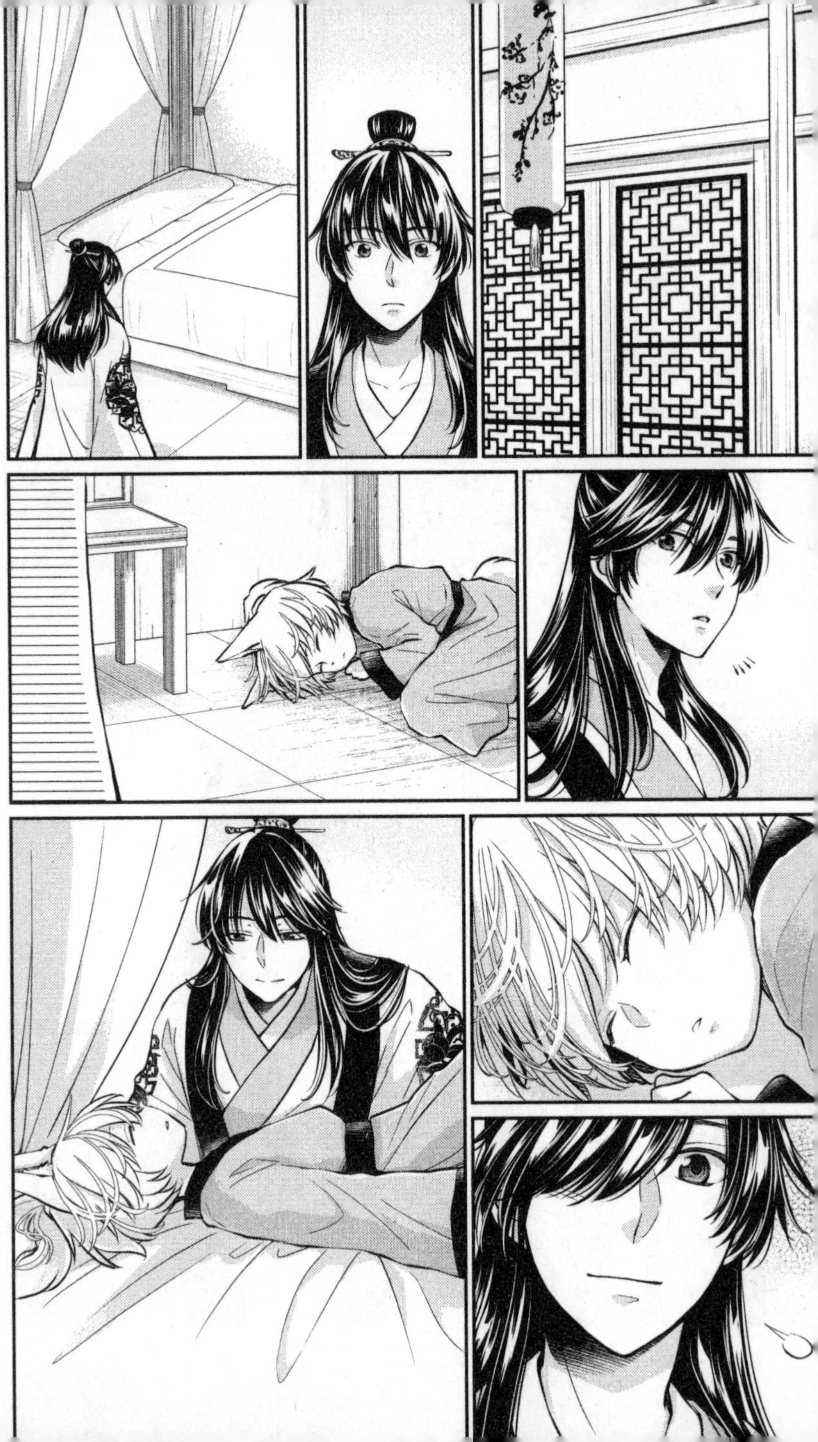

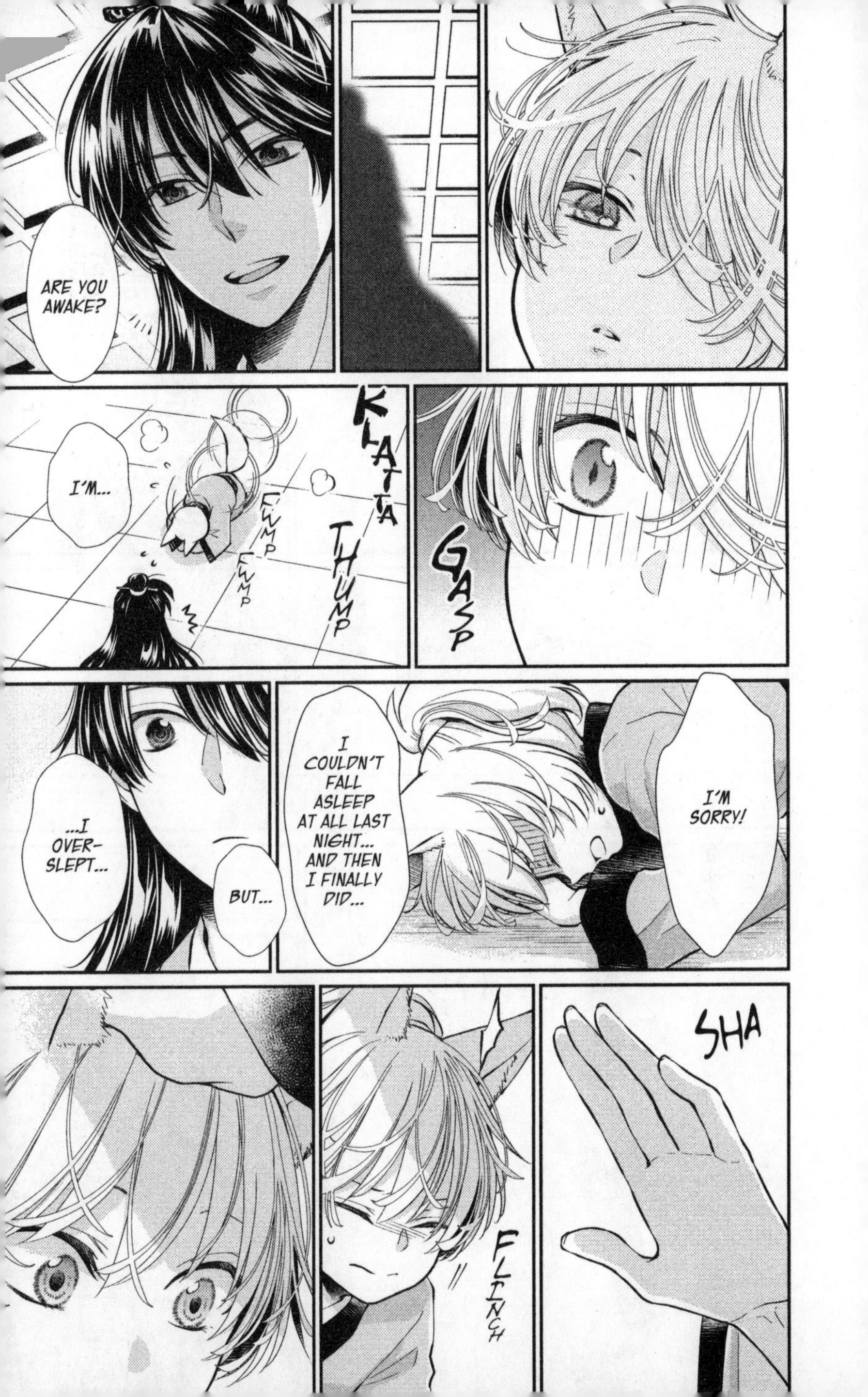
ARE YOU AWAKE?
GASP
KLATTA
THUMP
FWMP FWMP
I'M...
I'M SORRY!
I COULDN'T FALL ASLEEP AT ALL LAST NIGHT... AND THEN I FINALLY DID...
...I OVERSLEPT...
BUT...
SHA
FLINCH

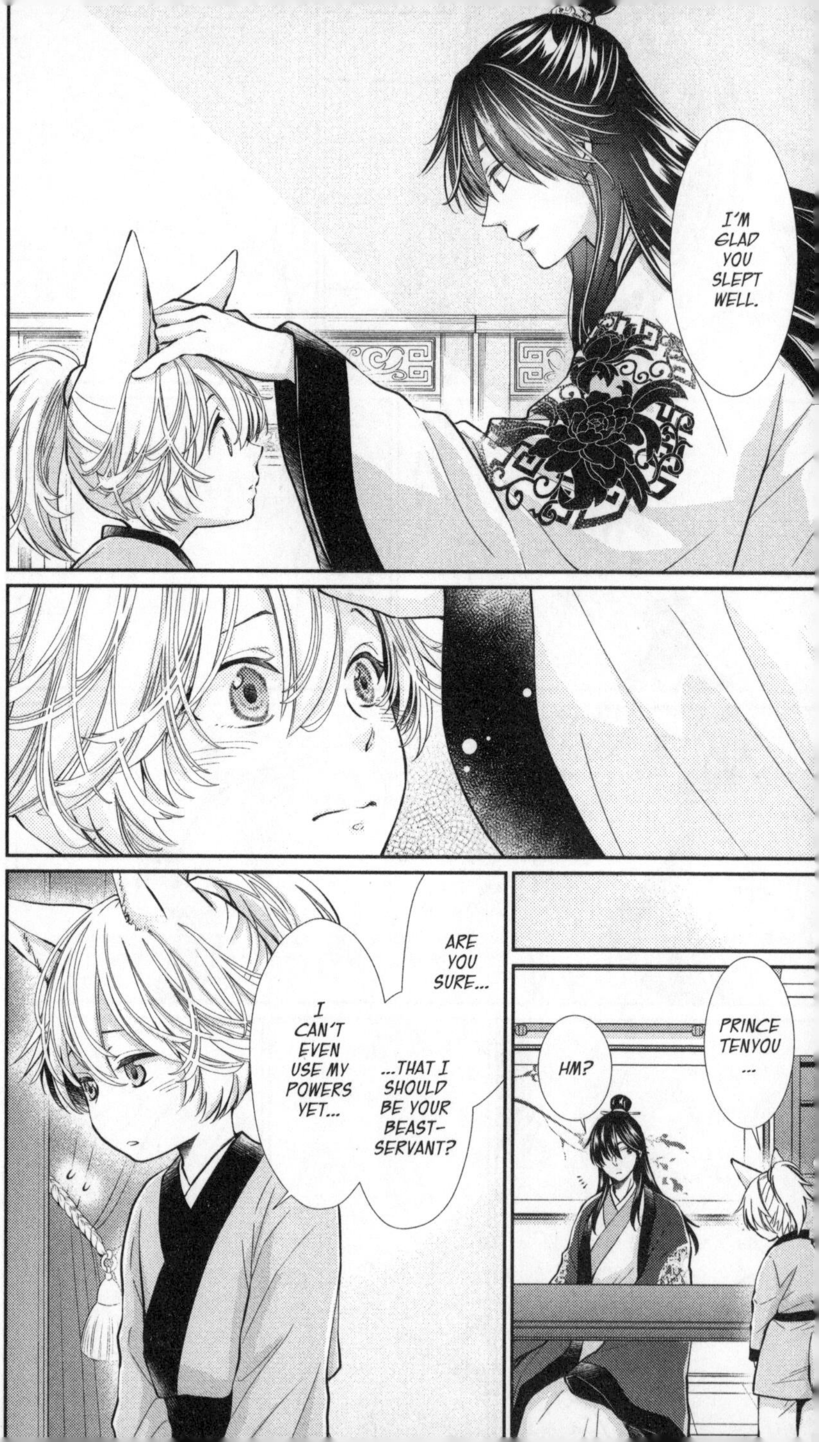
I'M GLAD YOU SLEPT WELL.
PRINCE TENYOU ...
HM?
ARE YOU SURE...
...THAT I SHOULD BE YOUR BEAST-SERVANT?
I CAN'T EVEN USE MY POWERS YET...

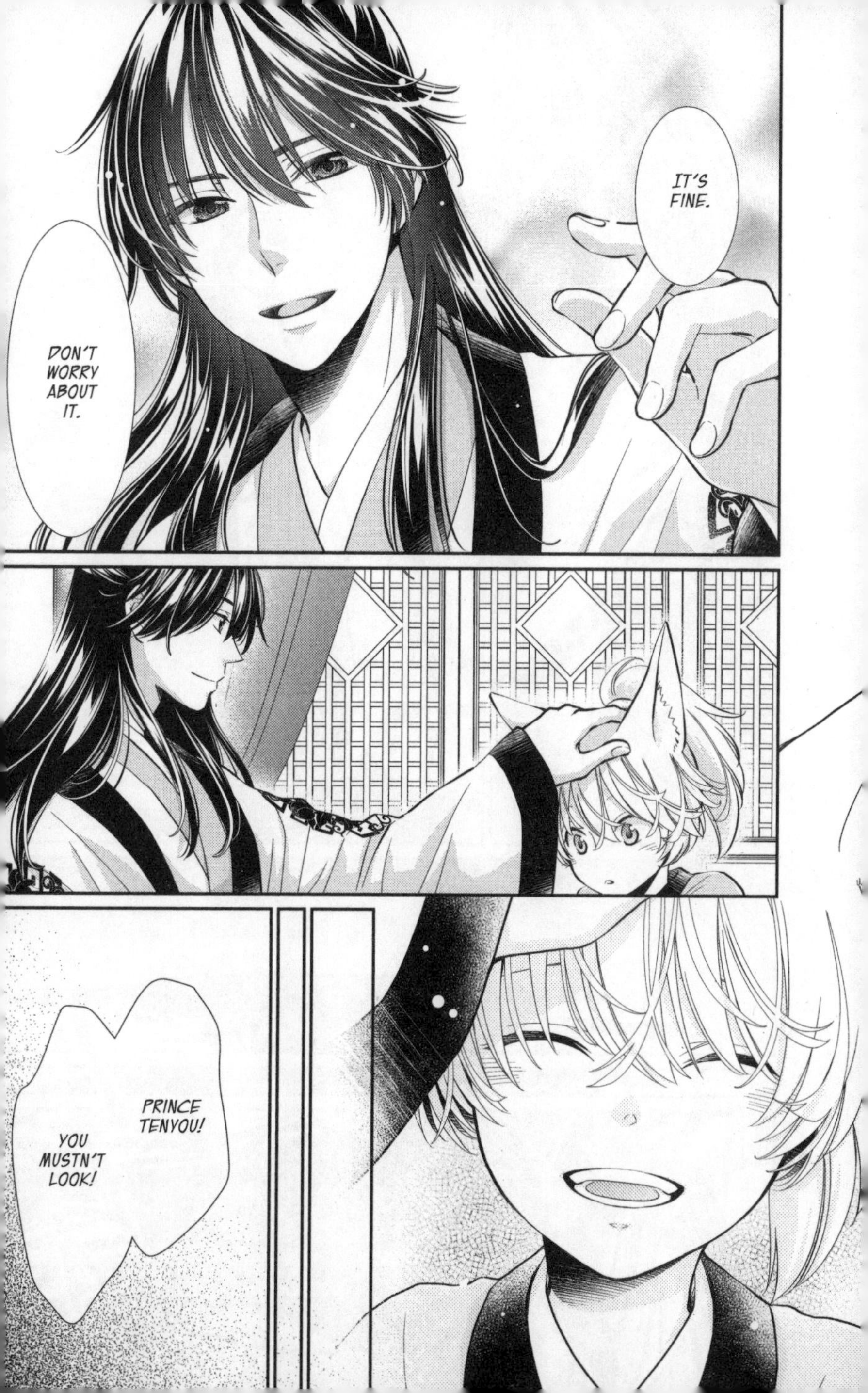
IT'S FINE.
DON'T WORRY ABOUT IT.
PRINCE TENYOU! YOU MUSTN'T LOOK!

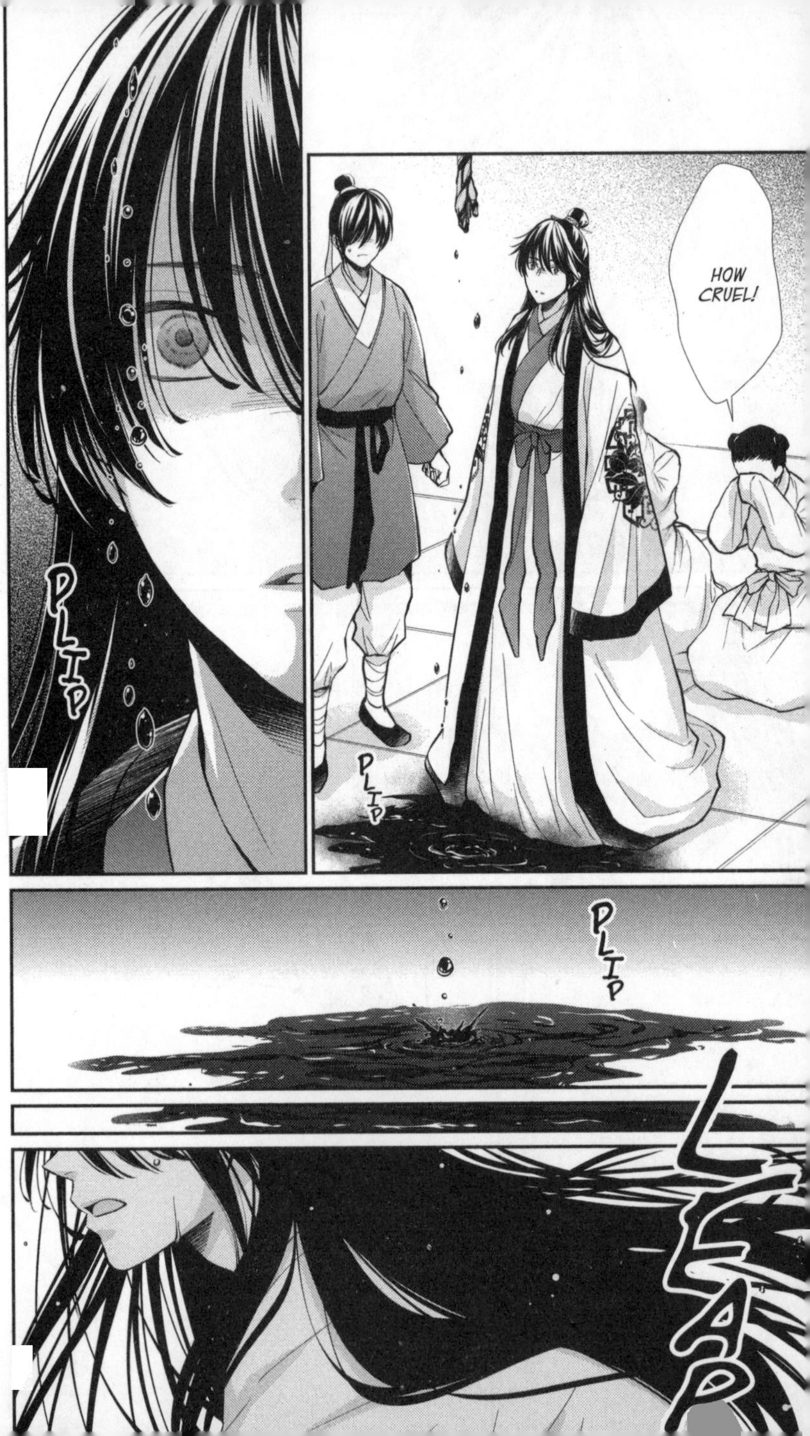
HOW CRUEL!
PLIP
PLIP
PLIP
LEAP

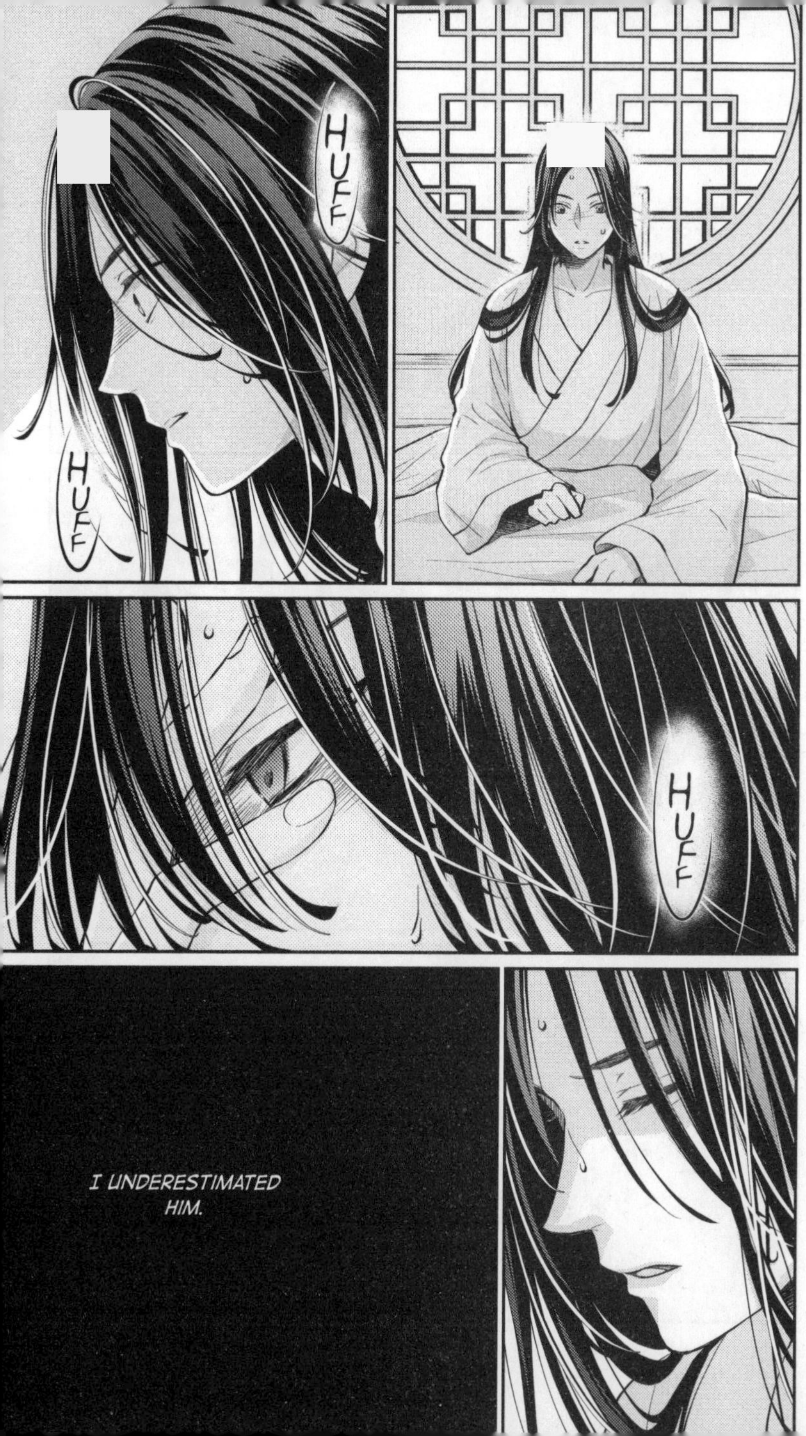
HUFF
HUFF
HUFF
I UNDERESTIMATED HIM.

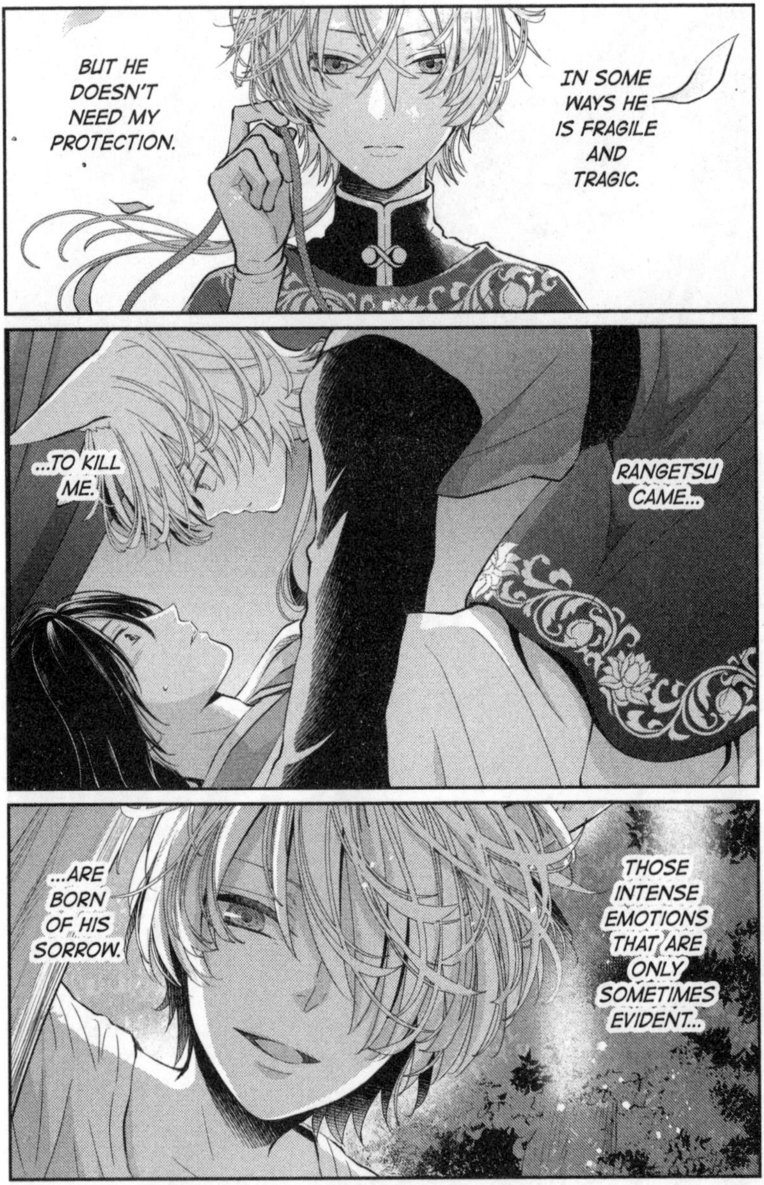
IN SOME WAYS HE IS FRAGILE AND TRAGIC.
BUT HE DOESN'T NEED MY PROTECTION.
RANGETSU CAME...
...TO KILL ME.
THOSE INTENSE EMOTIONS THAT ARE ONLY SOMETIMES EVIDENT...
...ARE BORN OF HIS SORROW.

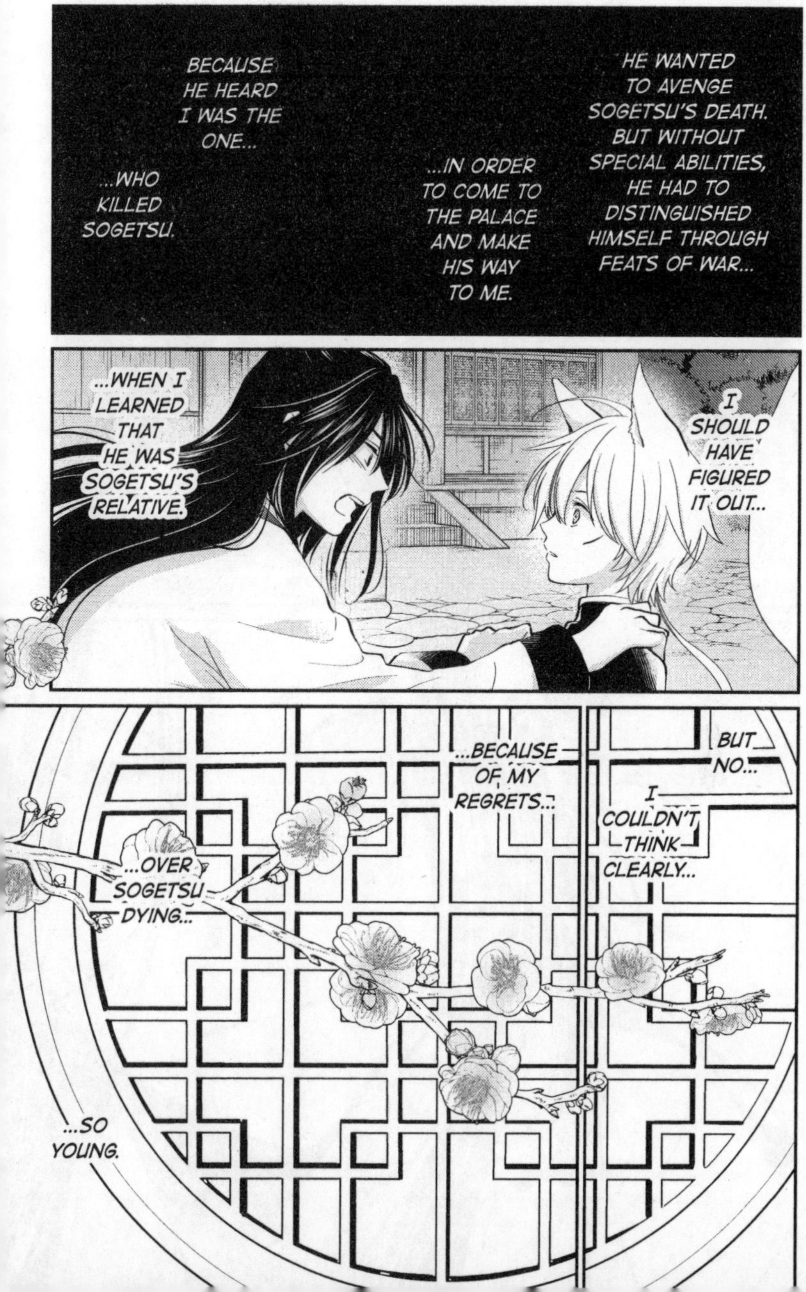
HE WANTED TO AVENGE SOGETSU'S DEATH. BUT WITHOUT SPECIAL ABILITIES, HE HAD TO DISTINGUISHED HIMSELF THROUGH FEATS OF WAR...
...IN ORDER TO COME TO THE PALACE AND MAKE HIS WAY TO ME.
BECAUSE HE HEARD I WAS THE ONE...
...WHO KILLED SOGETSU.
I SHOULD HAVE FIGURED IT OUT...
...WHEN I LEARNED THAT HE WAS SOGETSU'S RELATIVE.
BUT NO...
I COULDN'T THINK CLEARLY...
...BECAUSE OF MY REGRETS...
...OVER SOGETSU DYING...
...SO YOUNG.

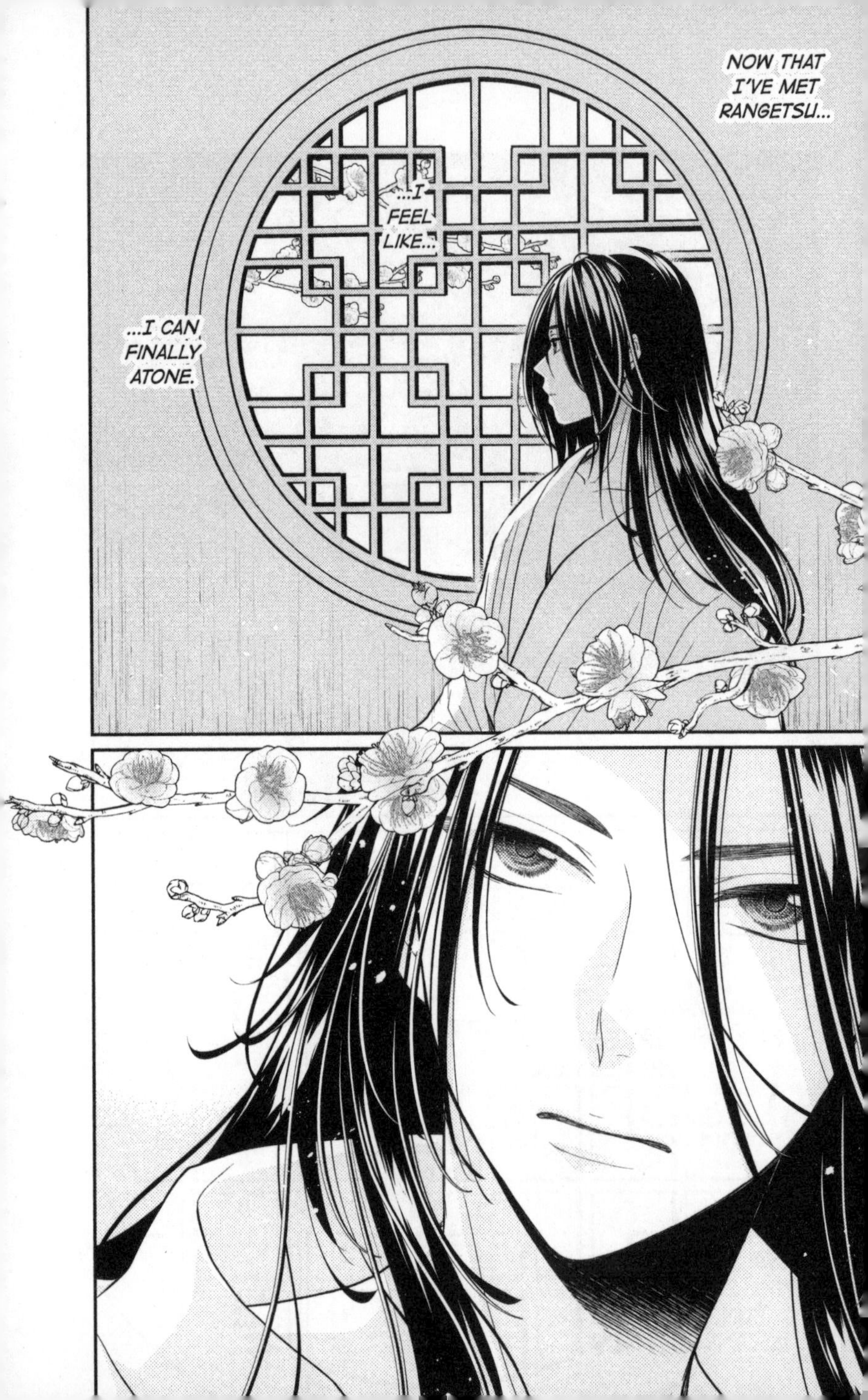
NOW THAT I'VE MET RANGETSU...
...I FEEL LIKE...
...I CAN FINALLY ATONE.

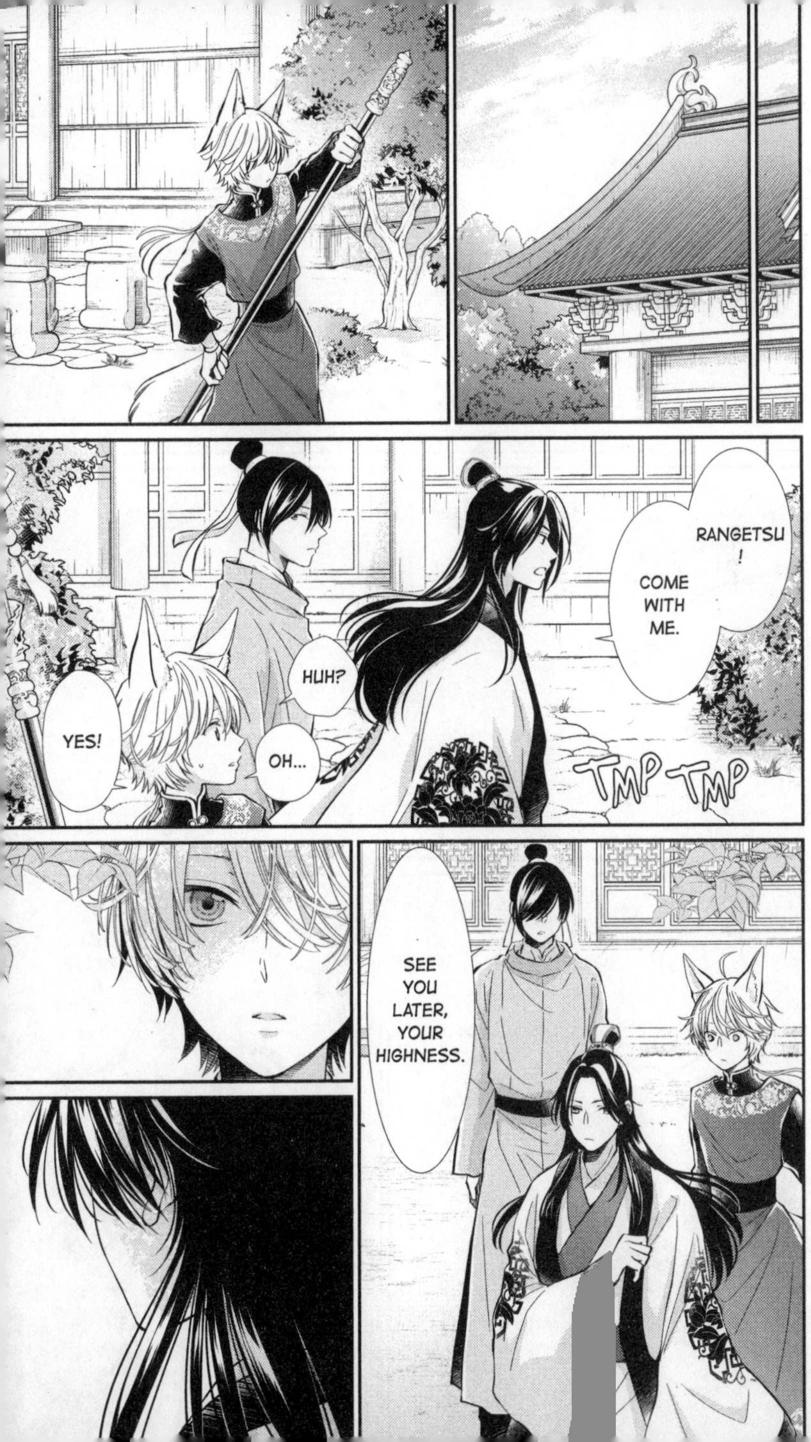
RANGETSU!
COME WITH ME.
TMP TMP
HUH?
OH...
YES!
SEE YOU LATER, YOUR HIGHNESS.

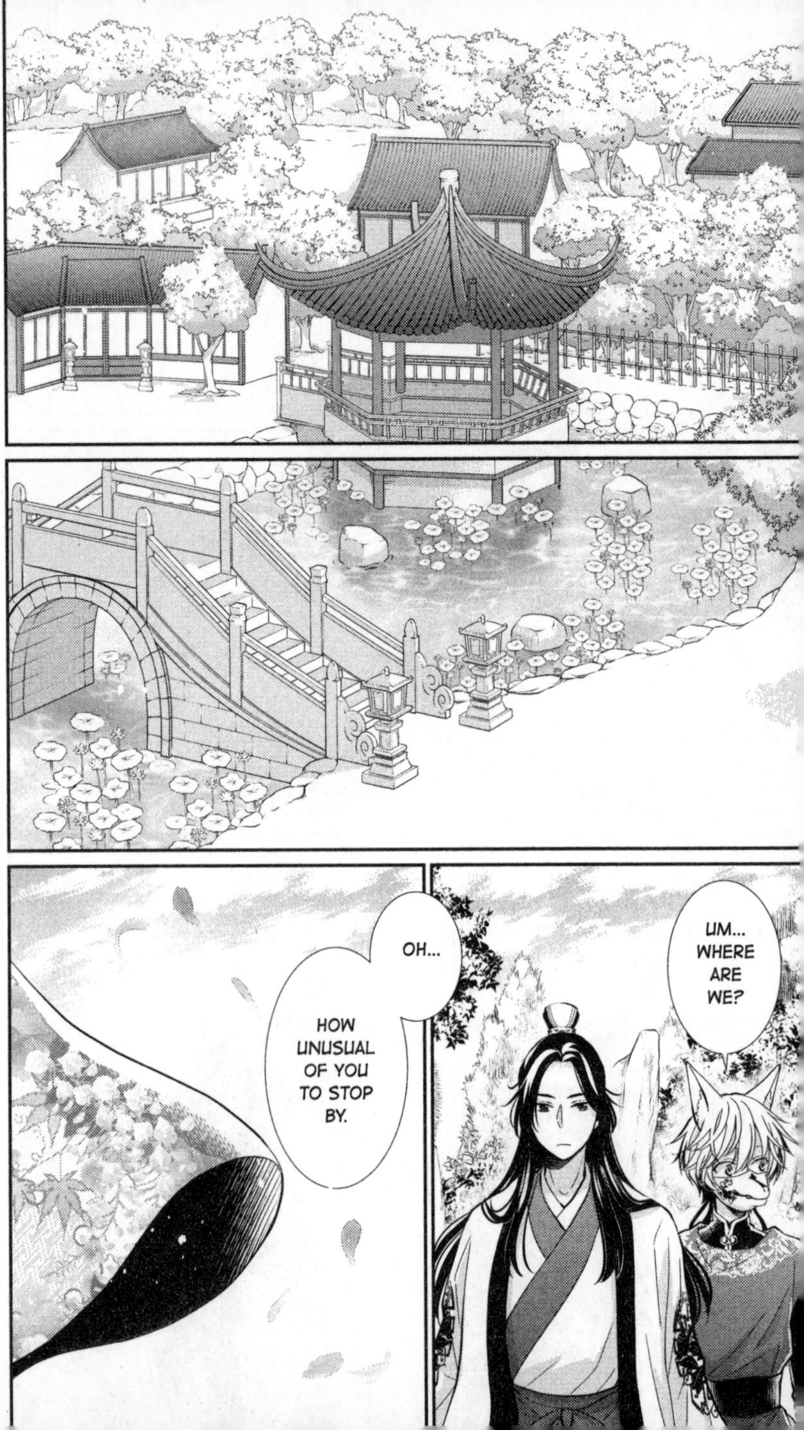
UM... WHERE ARE WE?
OH...
HOW UNUSUAL OF YOU TO STOP BY.

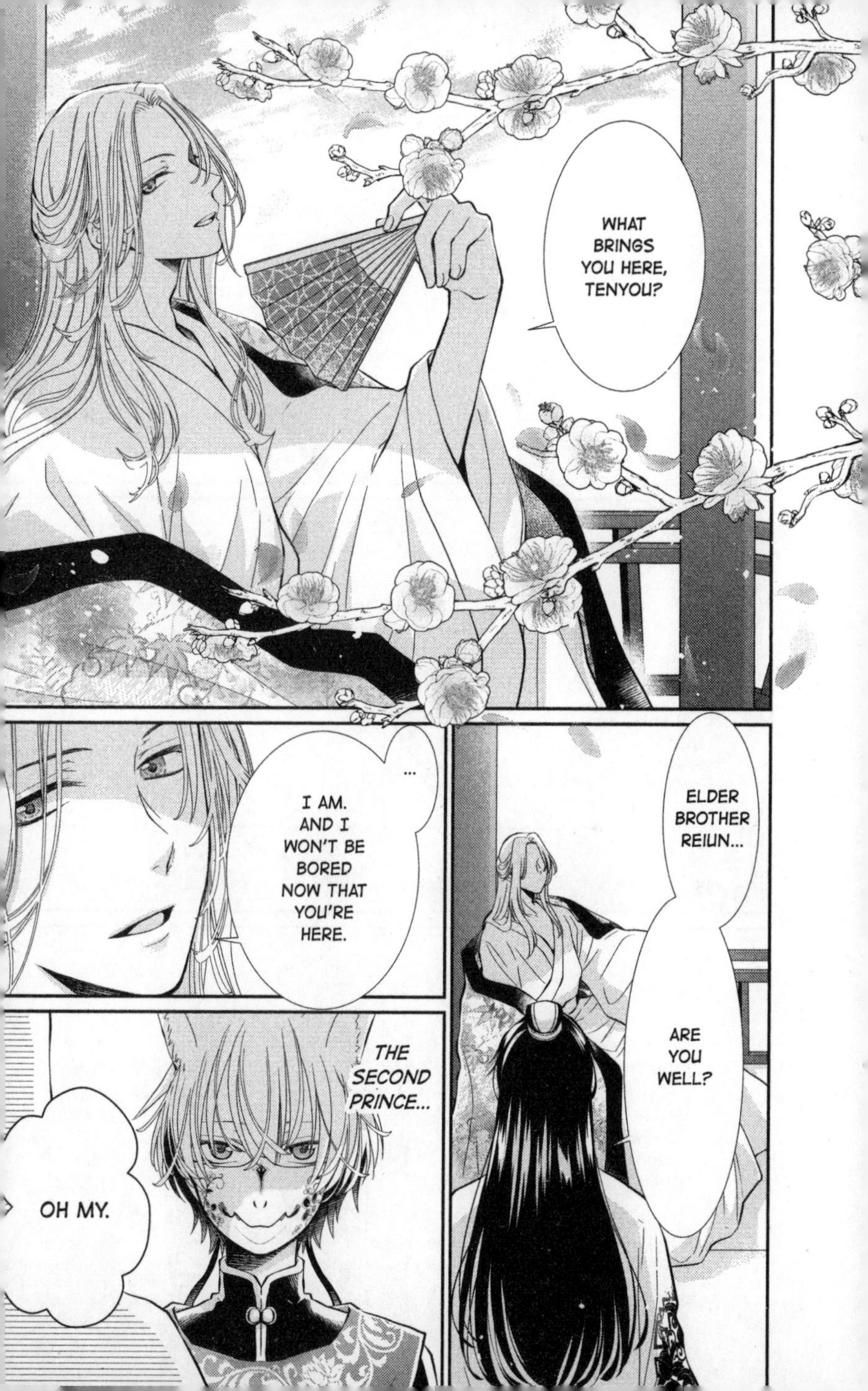
WHAT BRINGS YOU HERE, TENYOU?
ELDER BROTHER REIUN...
ARE YOU WELL?
...
I AM. AND I WON'T BE BORED NOW THAT YOU'RE HERE.
THE SECOND PRINCE...
OH MY.

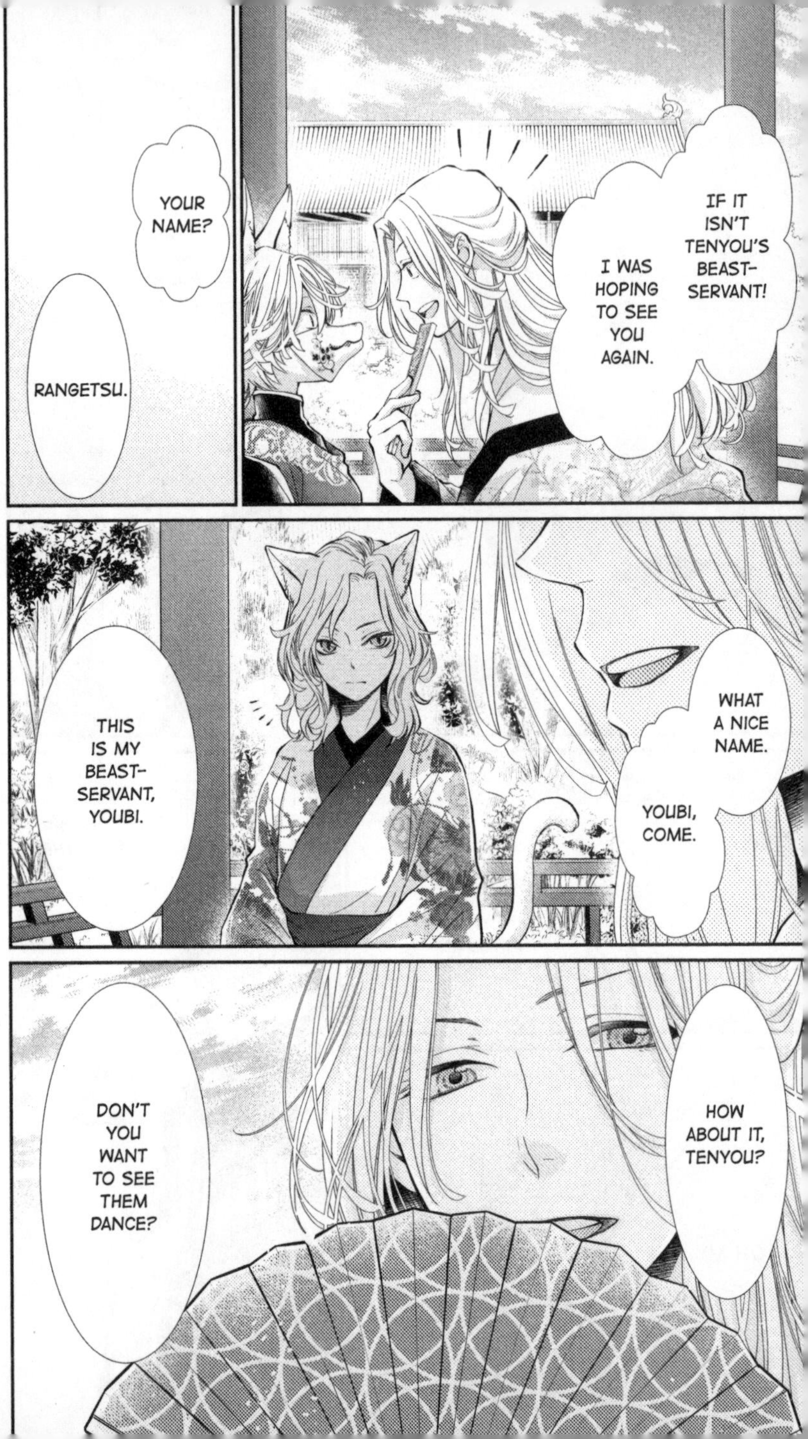
IF IT ISN'T TENYOU'S BEAST-SERVANT!
I WAS HOPING TO SEE YOU AGAIN.
YOUR NAME?
RANGETSU.
WHAT A NICE NAME.
YOUBI, COME.
THIS IS MY BEAST-SERVANT, YOUBI.
HOW ABOUT IT, TENYOU?
DON'T YOU WANT TO SEE THEM DANCE?

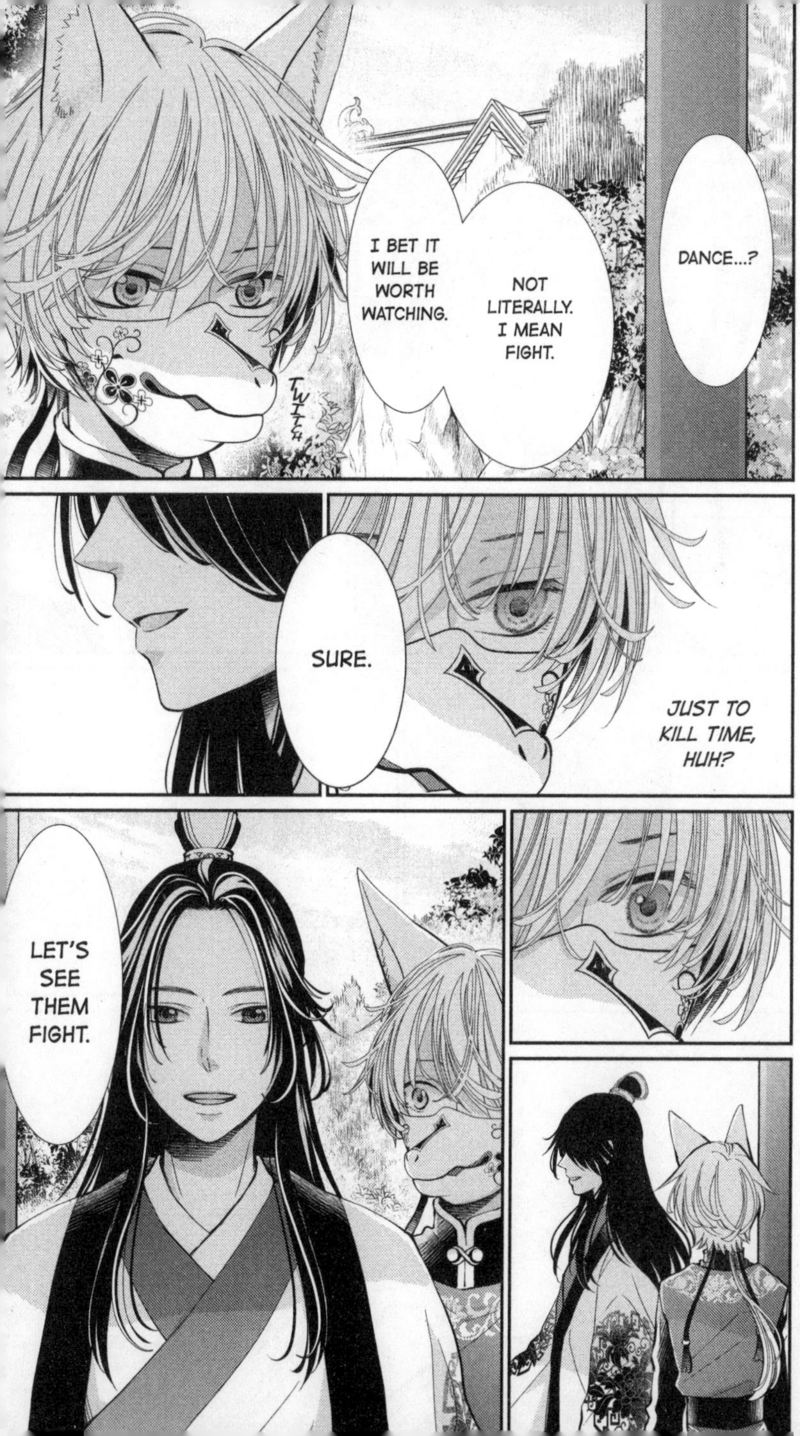
DANCE...?
NOT LITERALLY. I MEAN FIGHT.
I BET IT WILL BE WORTH WATCHING.
TWITCH
JUST TO KILL TIME, HUH?
SURE.
LET'S SEE THEM FIGHT.

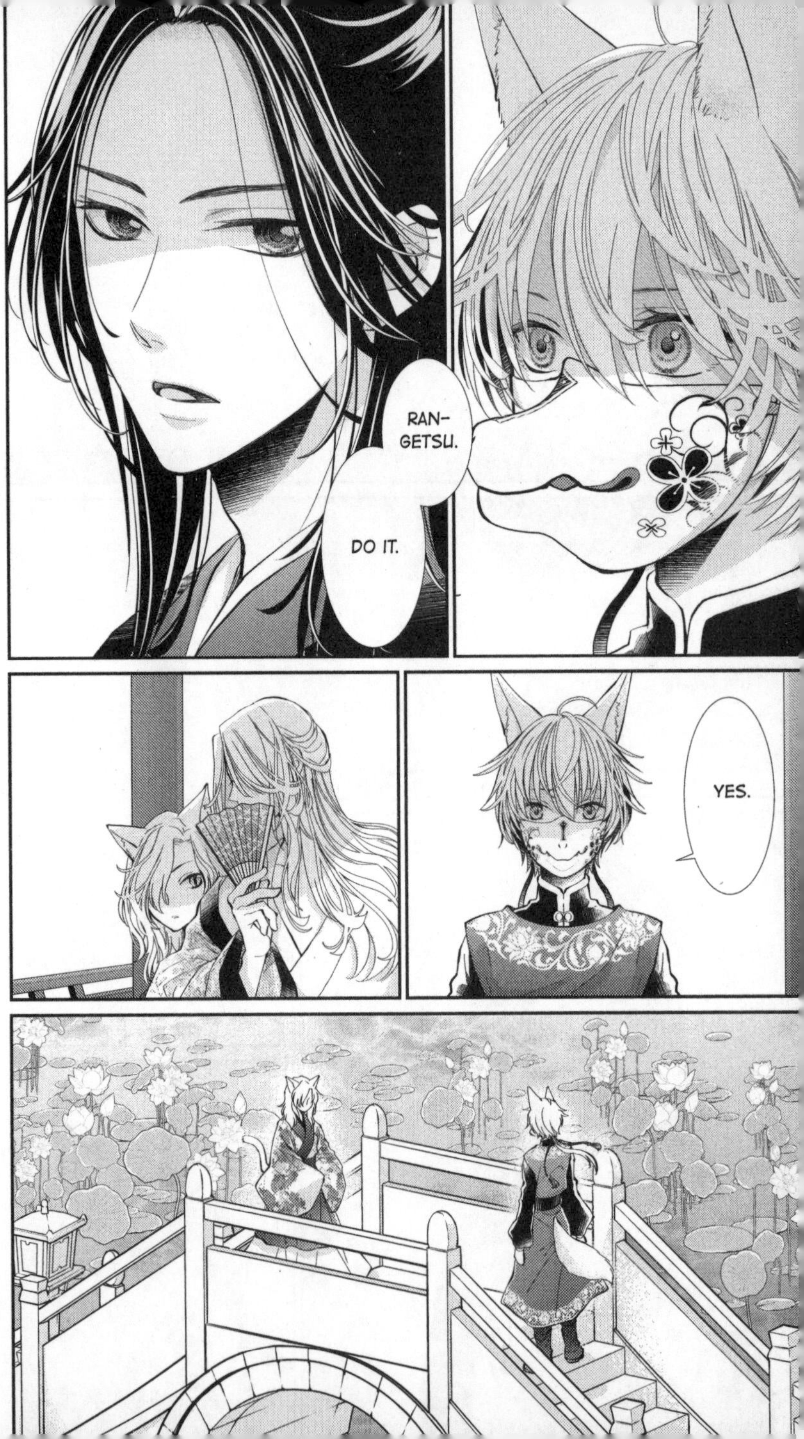
RAN-GETSU.
DO IT.
YES.

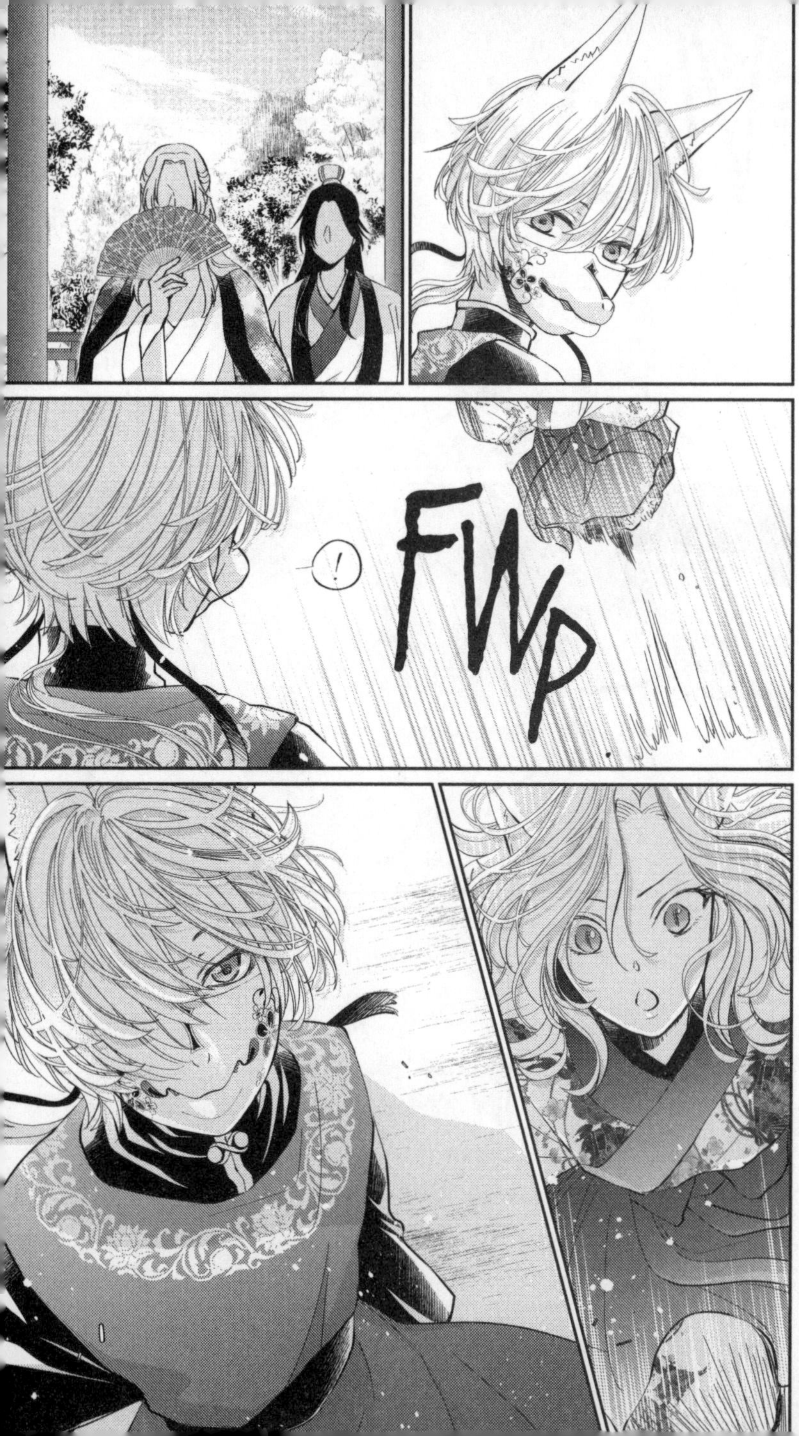
FWP
!

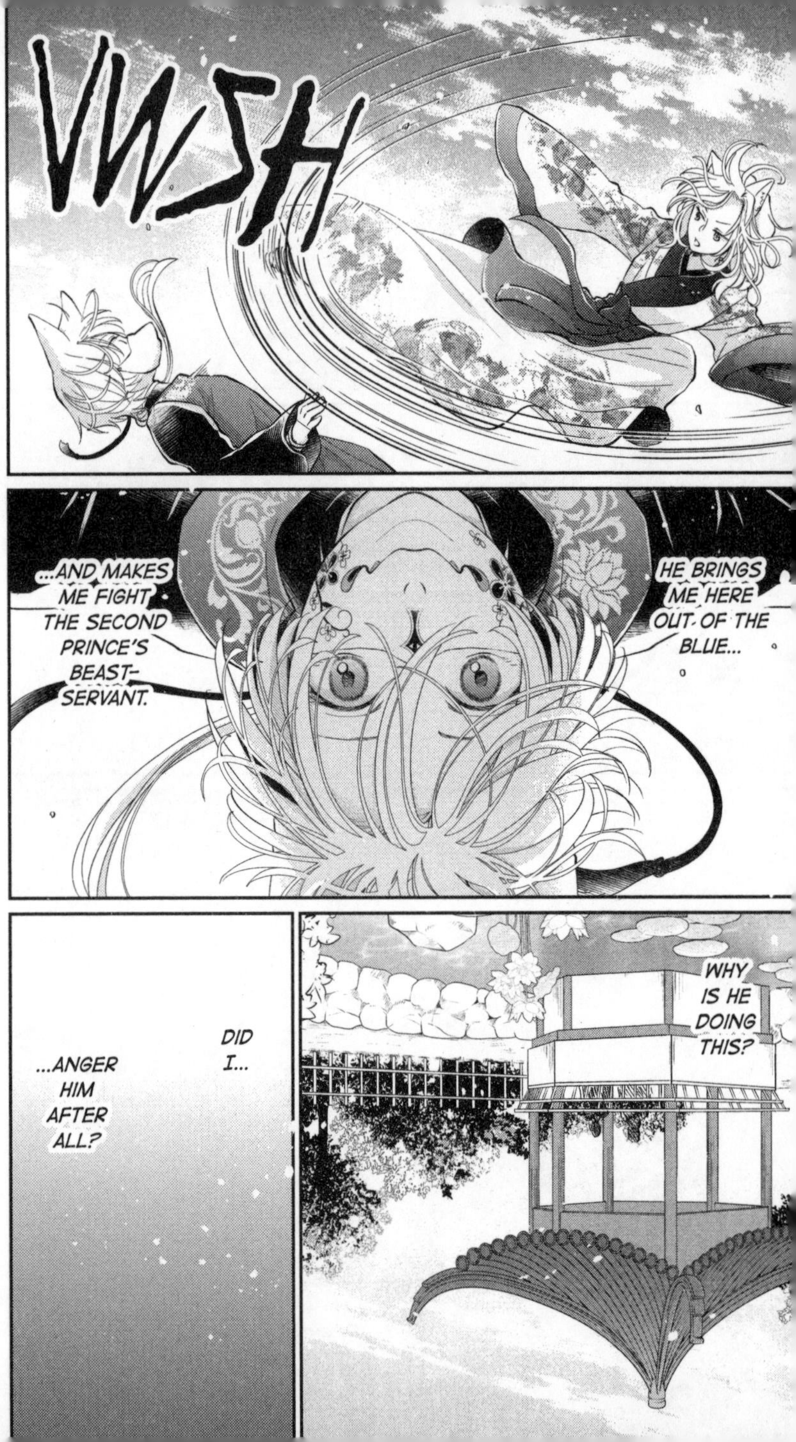
VWSH
HE BRINGS ME HERE OUT OF THE BLUE...
...AND MAKES ME FIGHT THE SECOND PRINCE'S BEAST-SERVANT.
WHY IS HE DOING THIS?
DID I...
...ANGER HIM AFTER ALL?

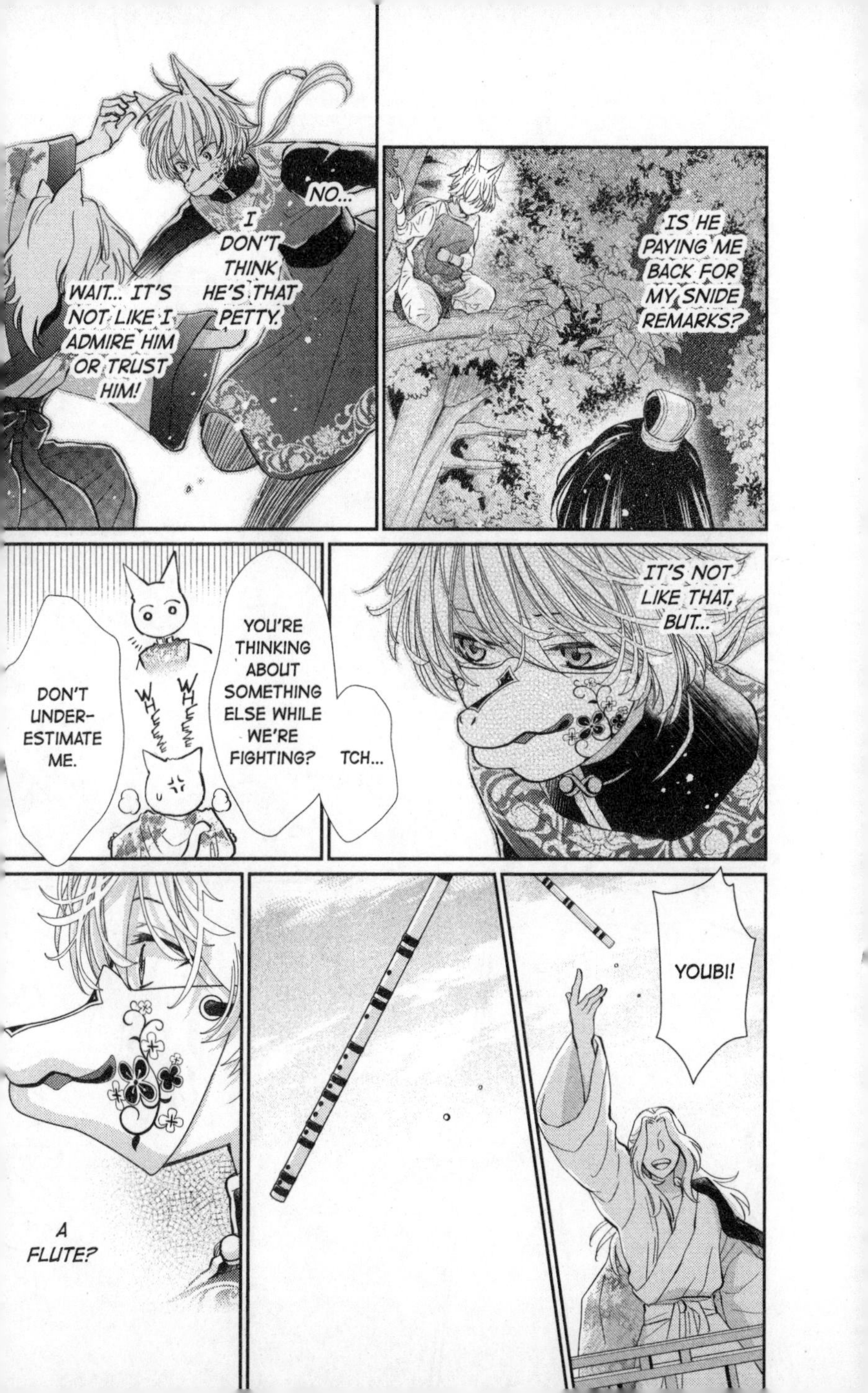
IS HE PAYING ME BACK FOR MY SNIDE REMARKS?
NO...
I DON'T THINK HE'S THAT PETTY.
WAIT... IT'S NOT LIKE I ADMIRE HIM OR TRUST HIM!
IT'S NOT LIKE THAT, BUT...
TCH...
YOU'RE THINKING ABOUT SOMETHING ELSE WHILE WE'RE FIGHTING?
WHEEZE
WHEEZE
DON'T UNDER-ESTIMATE ME.
YOUBI!
A FLUTE?

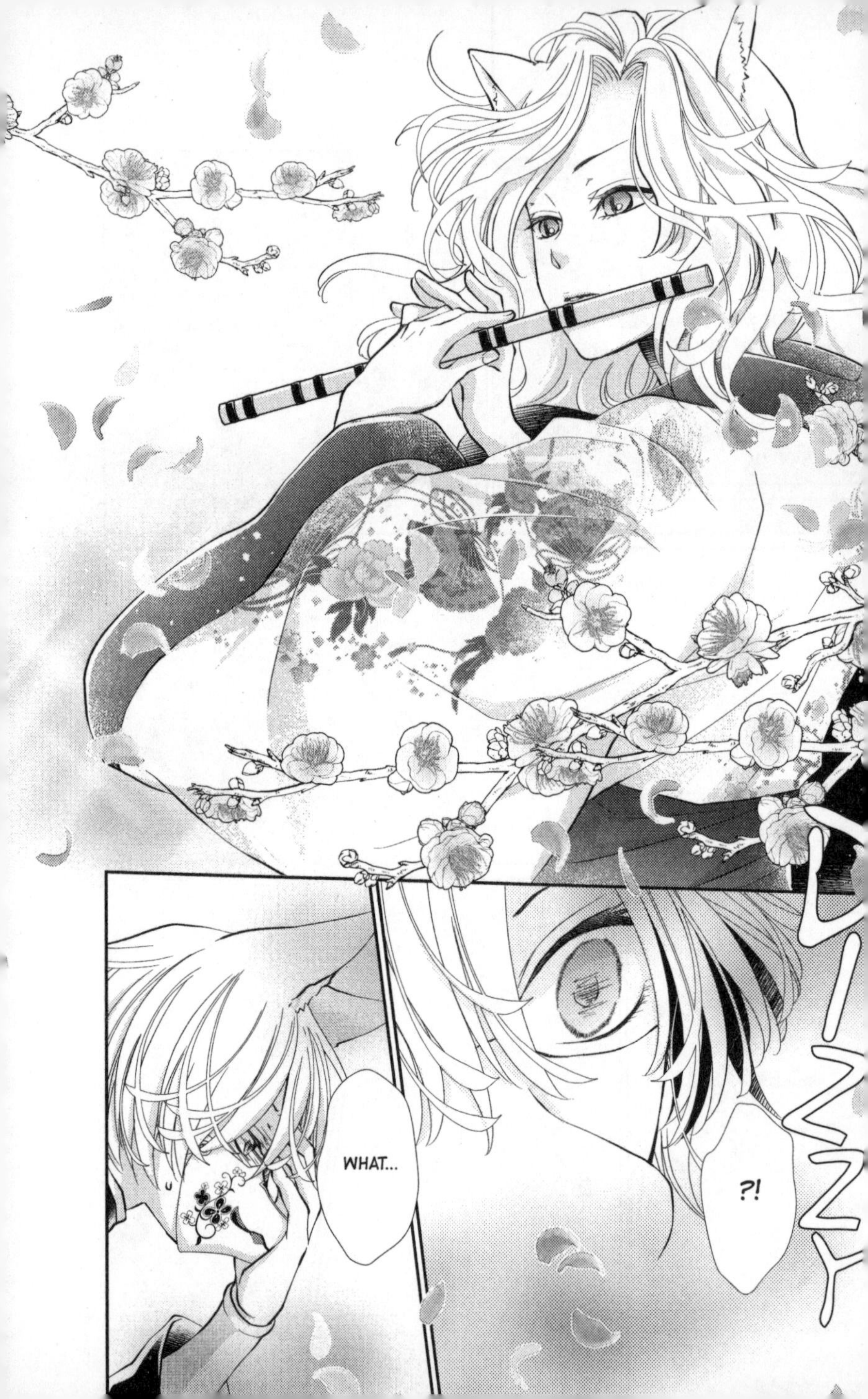
?!
WHAT...

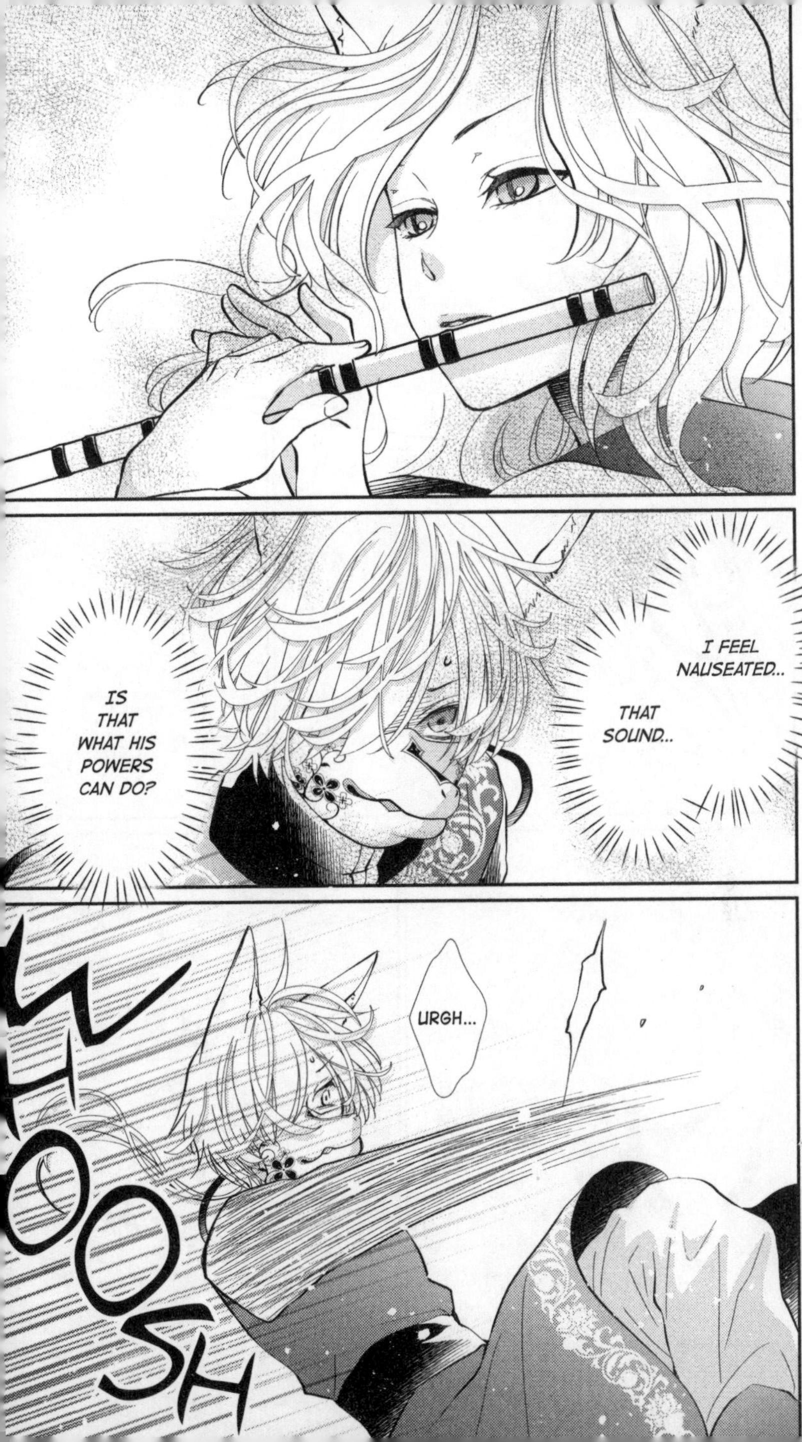
I FEEL NAUSEATED...
THAT SOUND...
IS THAT WHAT HIS POWERS CAN DO?
URGH...
WHOOSH

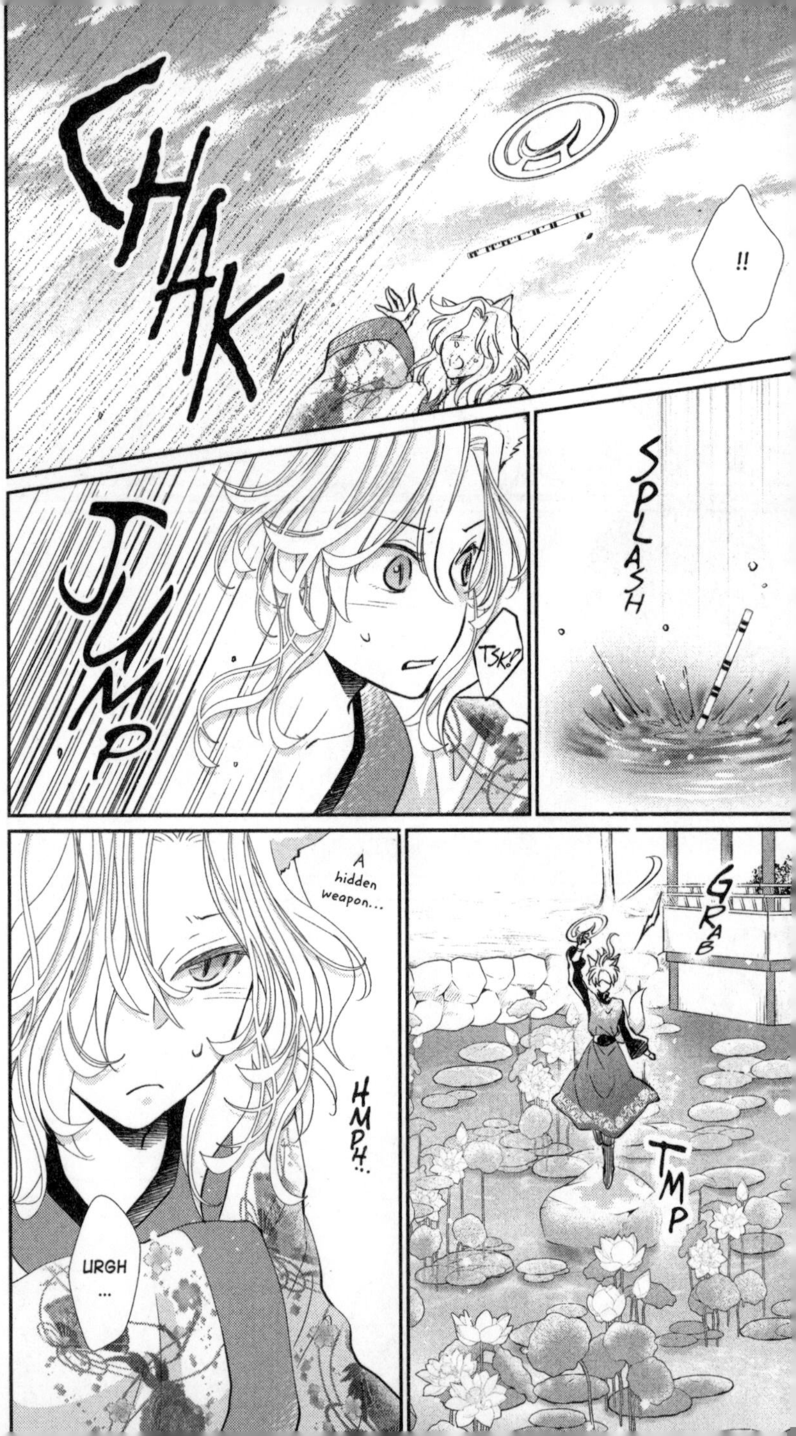
!!
CHAK
SPLASH
TSK!?
JUMP
GRAB
TMP
A hidden weapon...
HMPH...
URGH
...

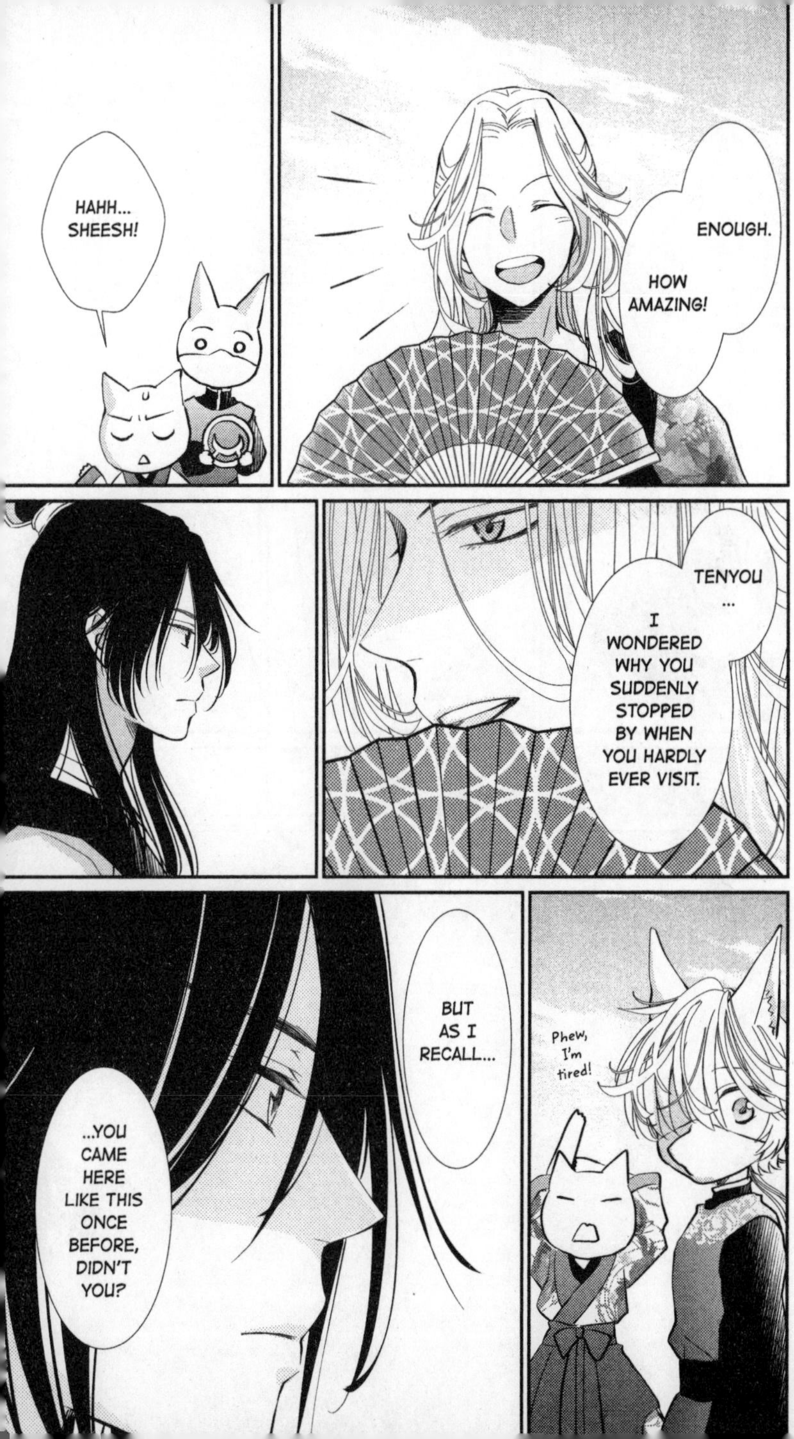
ENOUGH.
HOW AMAZING!
HAHH... SHEESH!
TENYOU ...
I WONDERED WHY YOU SUDDENLY STOPPED BY WHEN YOU HARDLY EVER VISIT.
Phew, I'm tired!
BUT AS I RECALL...
...YOU CAME HERE LIKE THIS ONCE BEFORE, DIDN'T YOU?

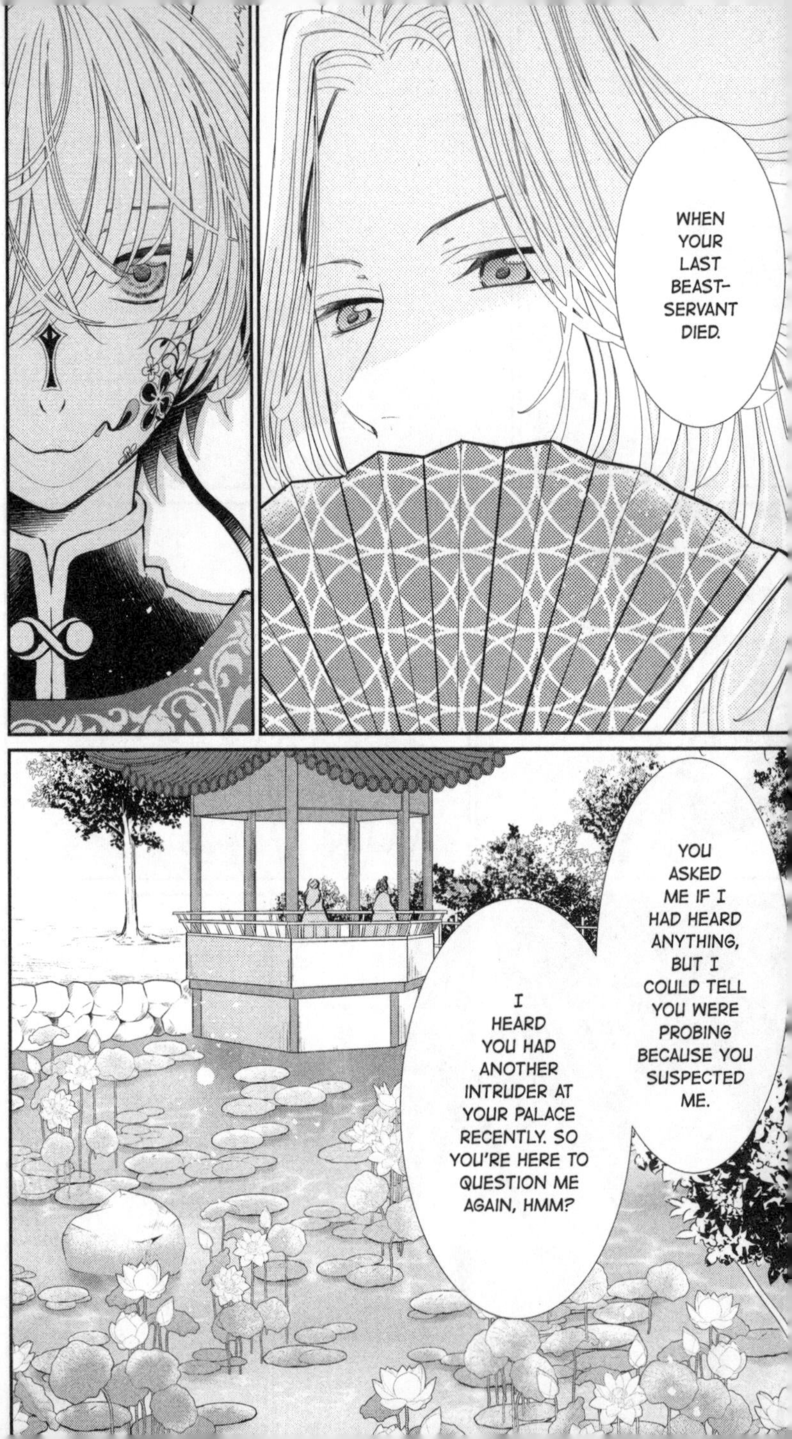
WHEN YOUR LAST BEAST-SERVANT DIED.
YOU ASKED ME IF I HAD HEARD ANYTHING, BUT I COULD TELL YOU WERE PROBING BECAUSE YOU SUSPECTED ME.
I HEARD YOU HAD ANOTHER INTRUDER AT YOUR PALACE RECENTLY. SO YOU'RE HERE TO QUESTION ME AGAIN, HMM?

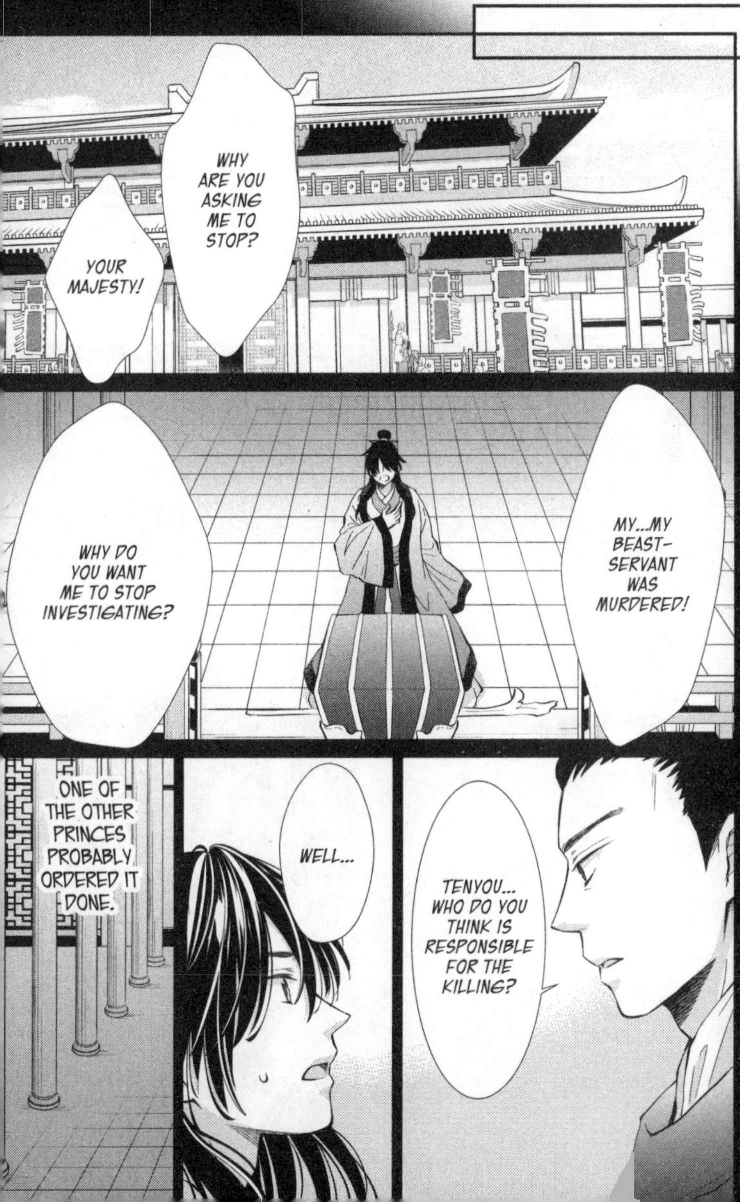
WHY ARE YOU ASKING ME TO STOP?
YOUR MAJESTY!
MY...MY BEAST-SERVANT WAS MURDERED!
WHY DO YOU WANT ME TO STOP INVESTIGATING?
TENYOU... WHO DO YOU THINK IS RESPONSIBLE FOR THE KILLING?
WELL...
ONE OF THE OTHER PRINCES PROBABLY ORDERED IT DONE.

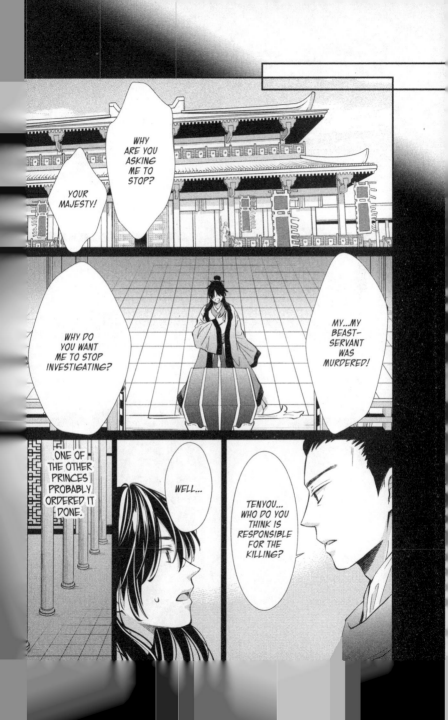

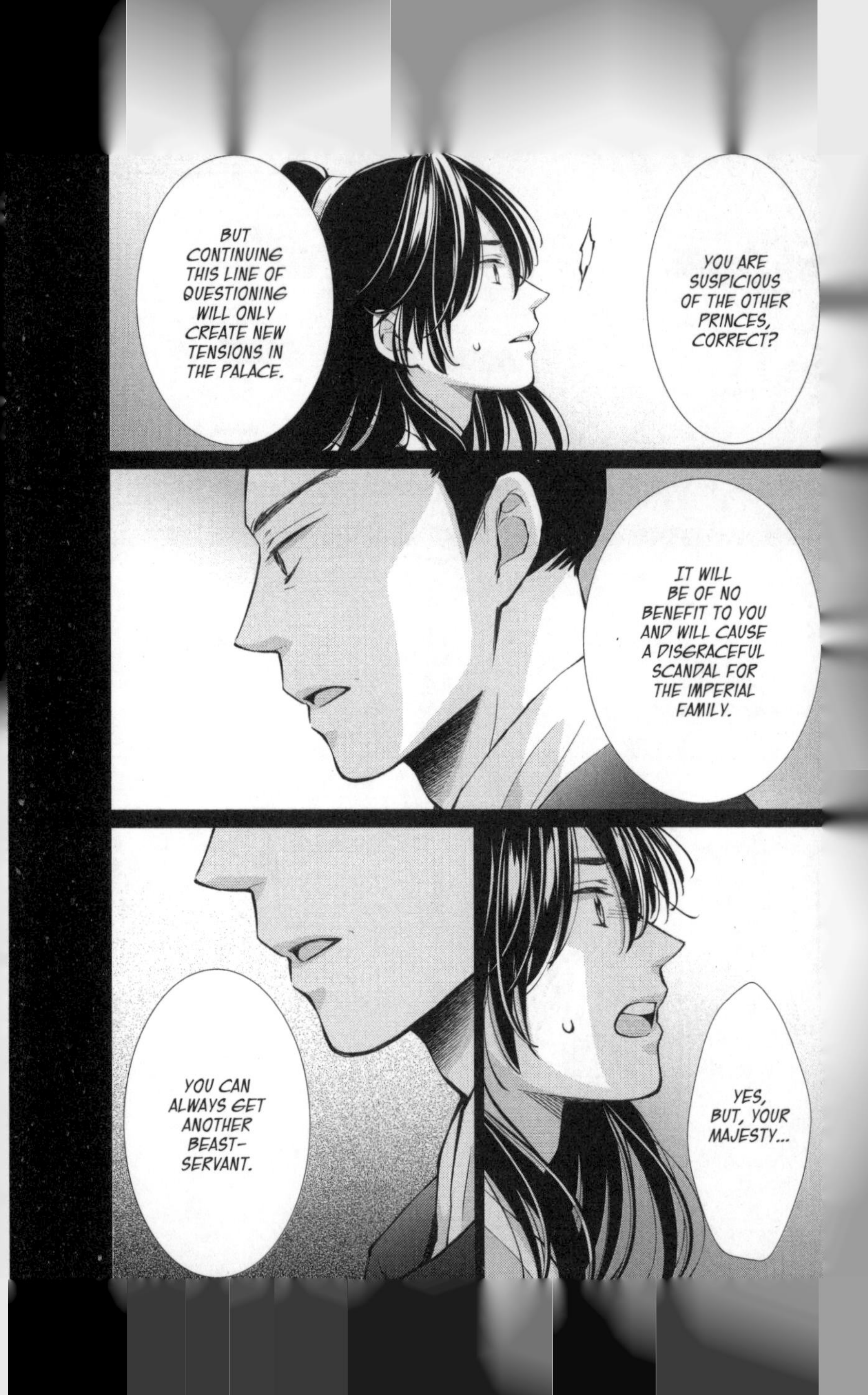
YOU ARE SUSPICIOUS OF THE OTHER PRINCES, CORRECT?
BUT CONTINUING THIS LINE OF QUESTIONING WILL ONLY CREATE NEW TENSIONS IN THE PALACE.
IT WILL BE OF NO BENEFIT TO YOU AND WILL CAUSE A DISGRACEFUL SCANDAL FOR THE IMPERIAL FAMILY.
YES, BUT, YOUR MAJESTY...
YOU CAN ALWAYS GET ANOTHER BEAST-SERVANT.

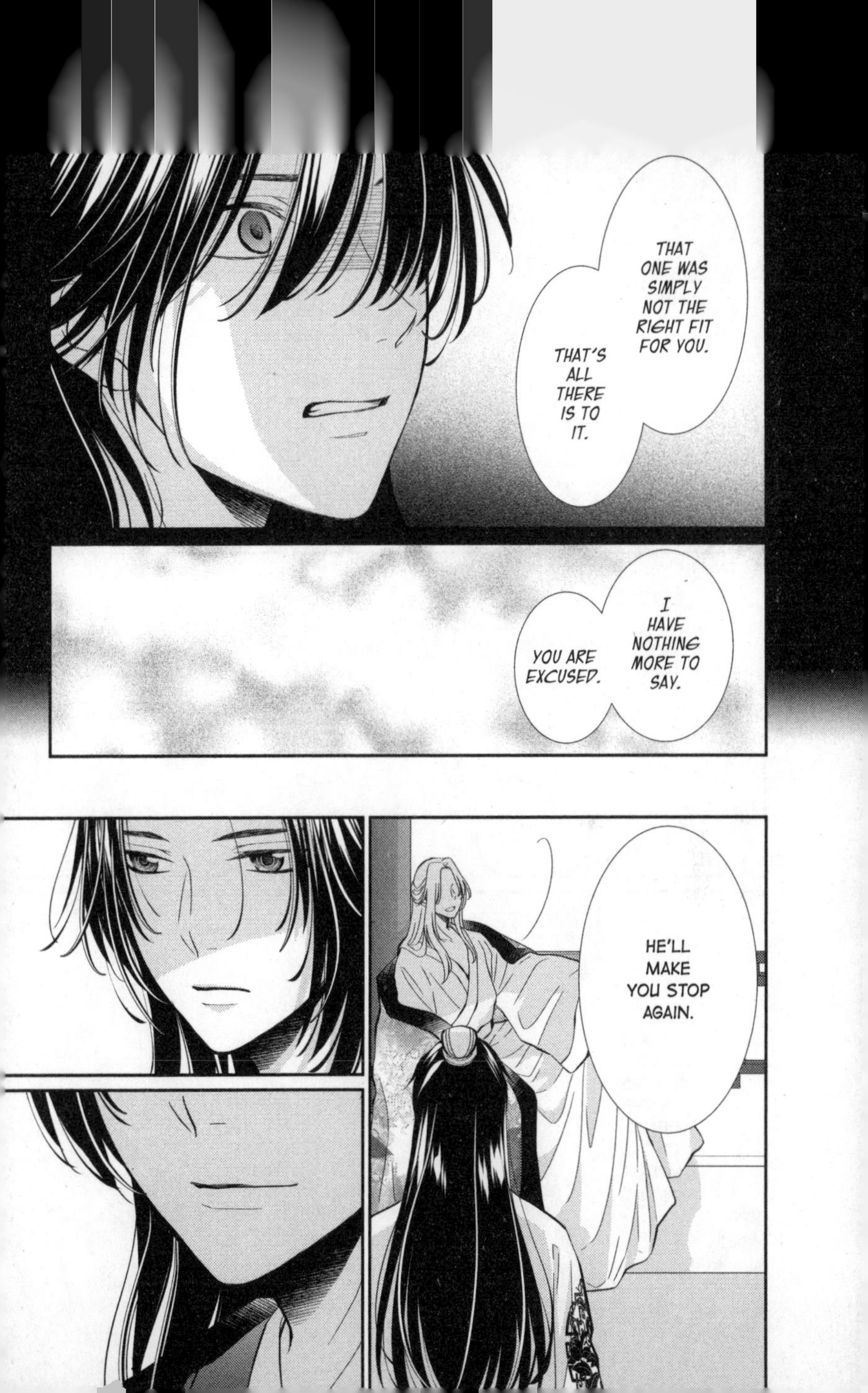
THAT ONE WAS SIMPLY NOT THE RIGHT FIT FOR YOU.
THAT'S ALL THERE IS TO IT.
I HAVE NOTHING MORE TO SAY.
YOU ARE EXCUSED.
HE'LL MAKE YOU STOP AGAIN.

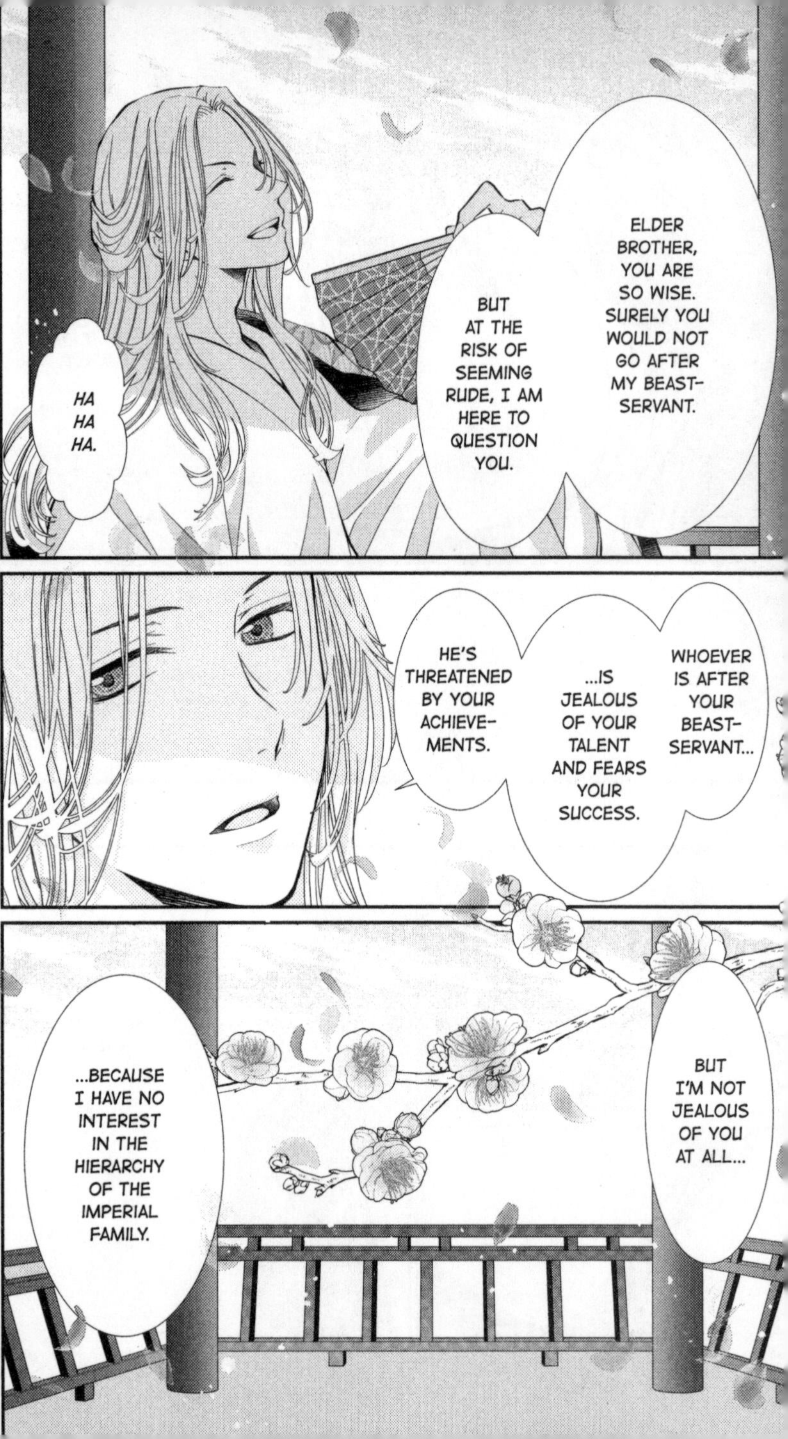
ELDER BROTHER, YOU ARE SO WISE. SURELY YOU WOULD NOT GO AFTER MY BEAST-SERVANT.
BUT AT THE RISK OF SEEMING RUDE, I AM HERE TO QUESTION YOU.
HA HA HA.
WHOEVER IS AFTER YOUR BEAST-SERVANT...
...IS JEALOUS OF YOUR TALENT AND FEARS YOUR SUCCESS.
HE'S THREATENED BY YOUR ACHIEVE-MENTS.
BUT I'M NOT JEALOUS OF YOU AT ALL...
...BECAUSE I HAVE NO INTEREST IN THE HIERARCHY OF THE IMPERIAL FAMILY.

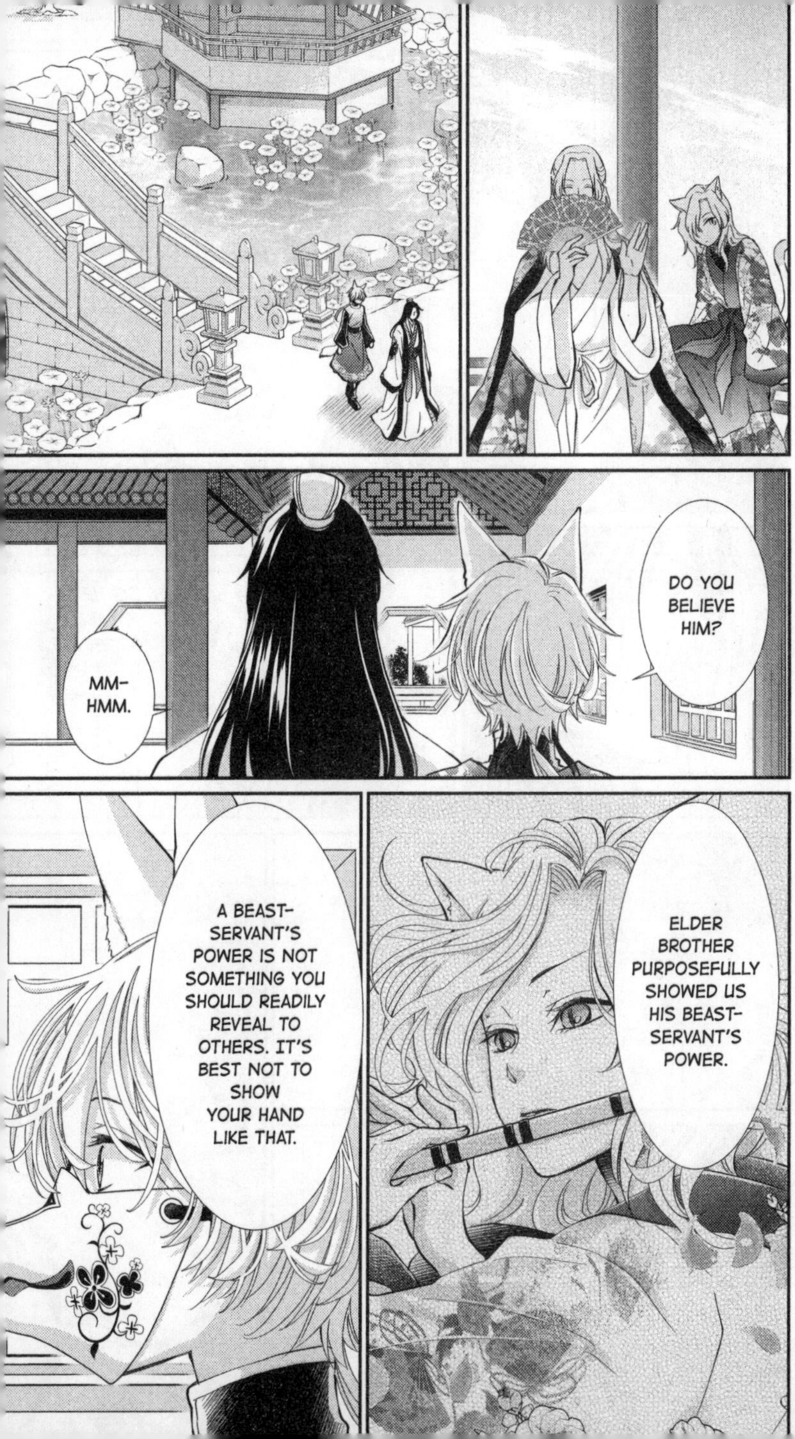
DO YOU BELIEVE HIM?
MM-HMM.
ELDER BROTHER PURPOSEFULLY SHOWED US HIS BEAST-SERVANT'S POWER.
A BEAST-SERVANT'S POWER IS NOT SOMETHING YOU SHOULD READILY REVEAL TO OTHERS. IT'S BEST NOT TO SHOW YOUR HAND LIKE THAT.

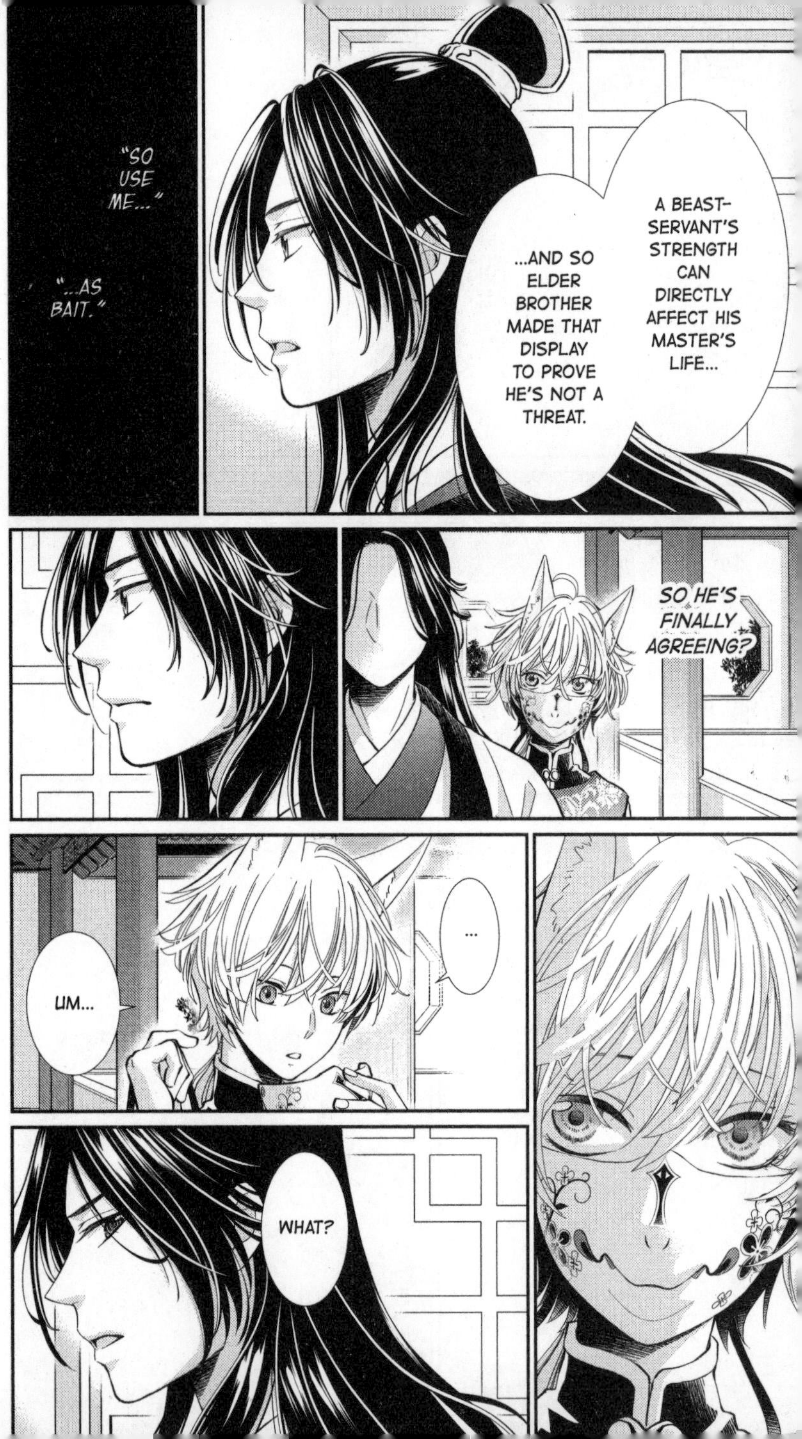
A BEAST-SERVANT'S STRENGTH CAN DIRECTLY AFFECT HIS MASTER'S LIFE...
...AND SO ELDER BROTHER MADE THAT DISPLAY TO PROVE HE'S NOT A THREAT.
"SO USE ME..."
"...AS BAIT."
SO HE'S FINALLY AGREEING?
...
UM...
WHAT?

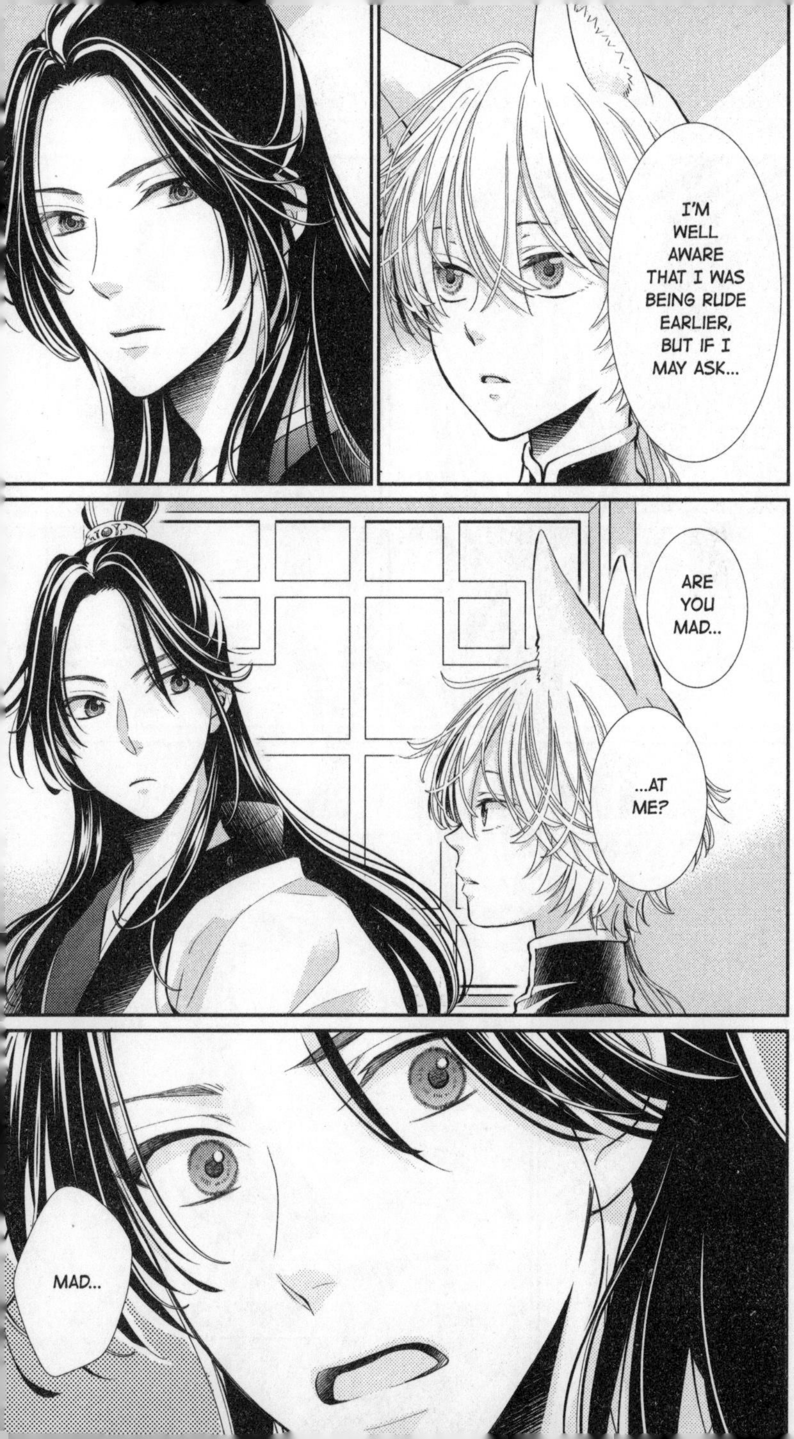
I'M WELL AWARE THAT I WAS BEING RUDE EARLIER, BUT IF I MAY ASK...
ARE YOU MAD...
...AT ME?
MAD...

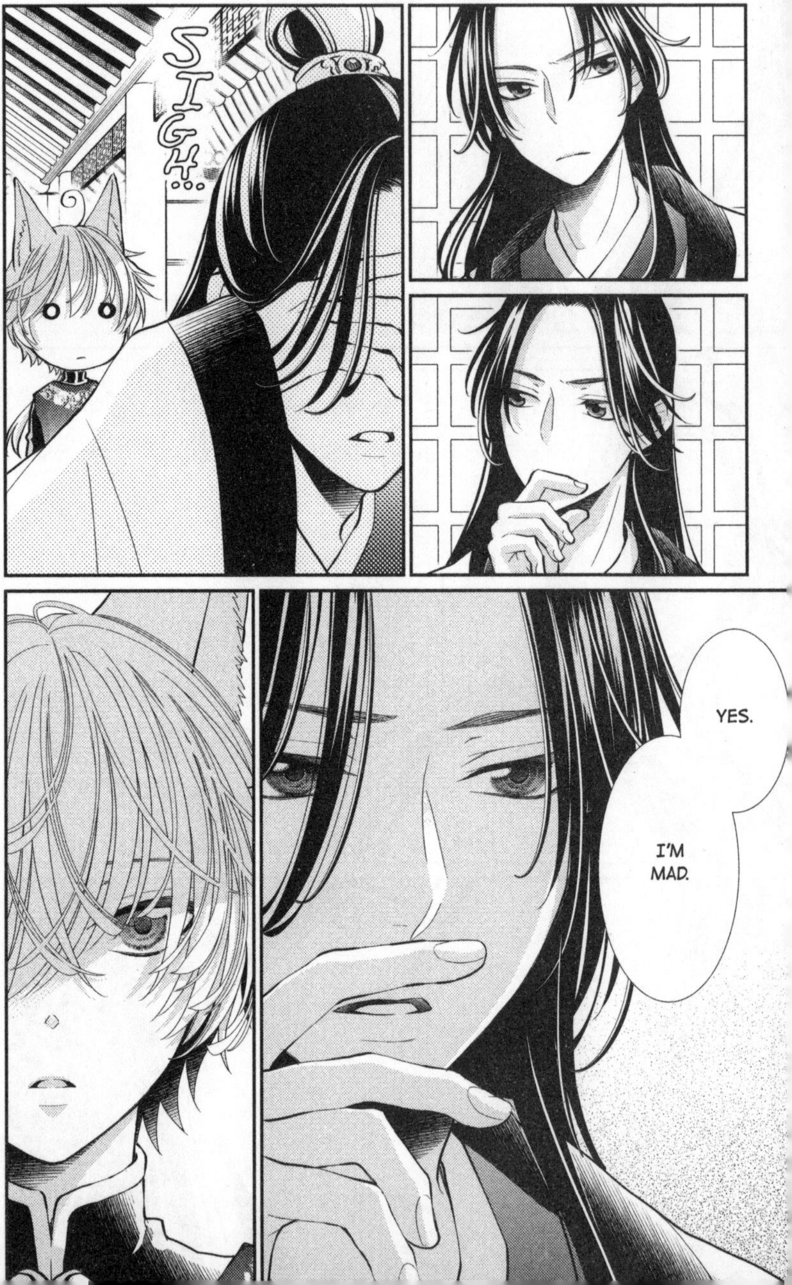
SIGH...
YES.
I'M MAD.

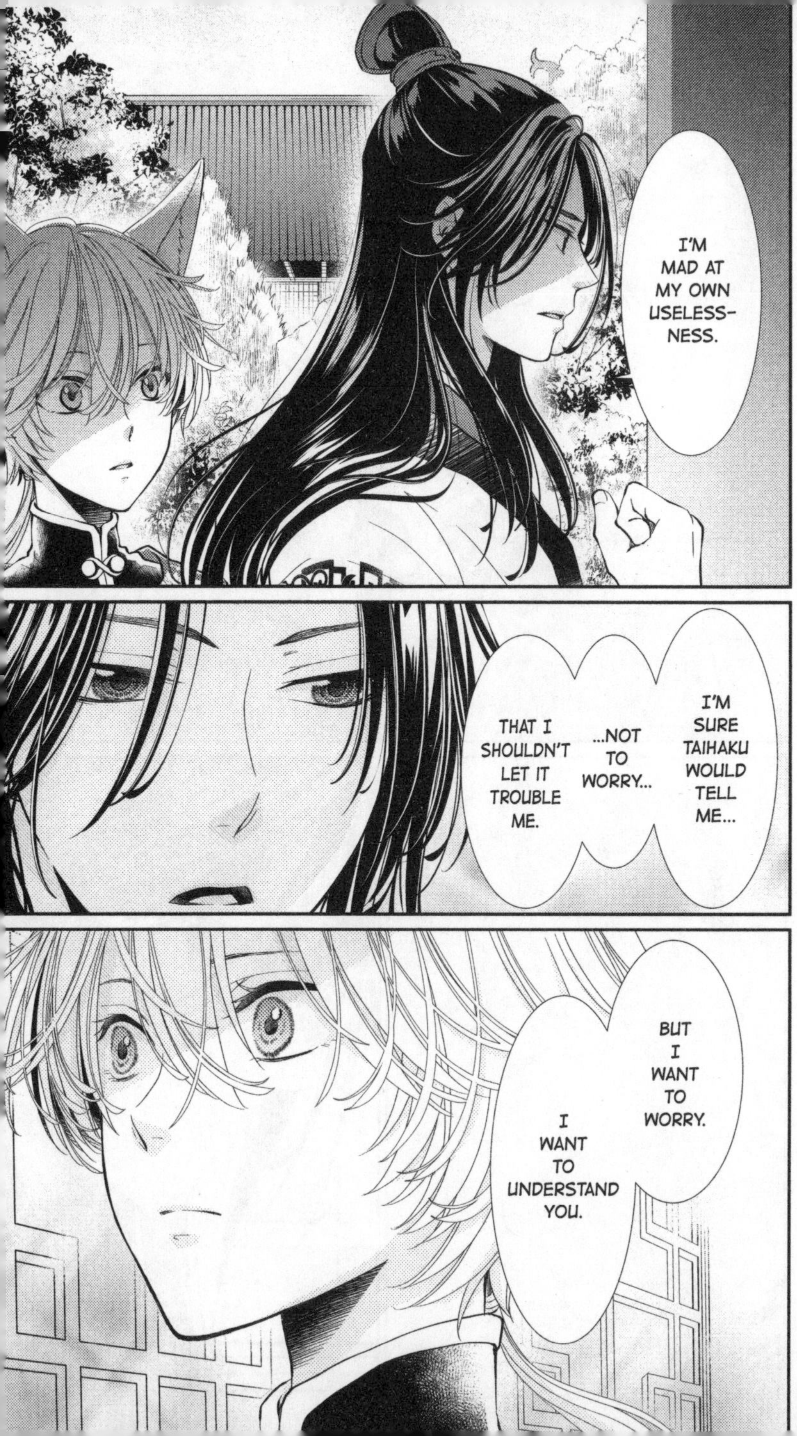
I'M MAD AT MY OWN USELESS-NESS.
I'M SURE TAIHAKU WOULD TELL ME...
...NOT TO WORRY...
THAT I SHOULDN'T LET IT TROUBLE ME.
BUT I WANT TO WORRY.
I WANT TO UNDERSTAND YOU.

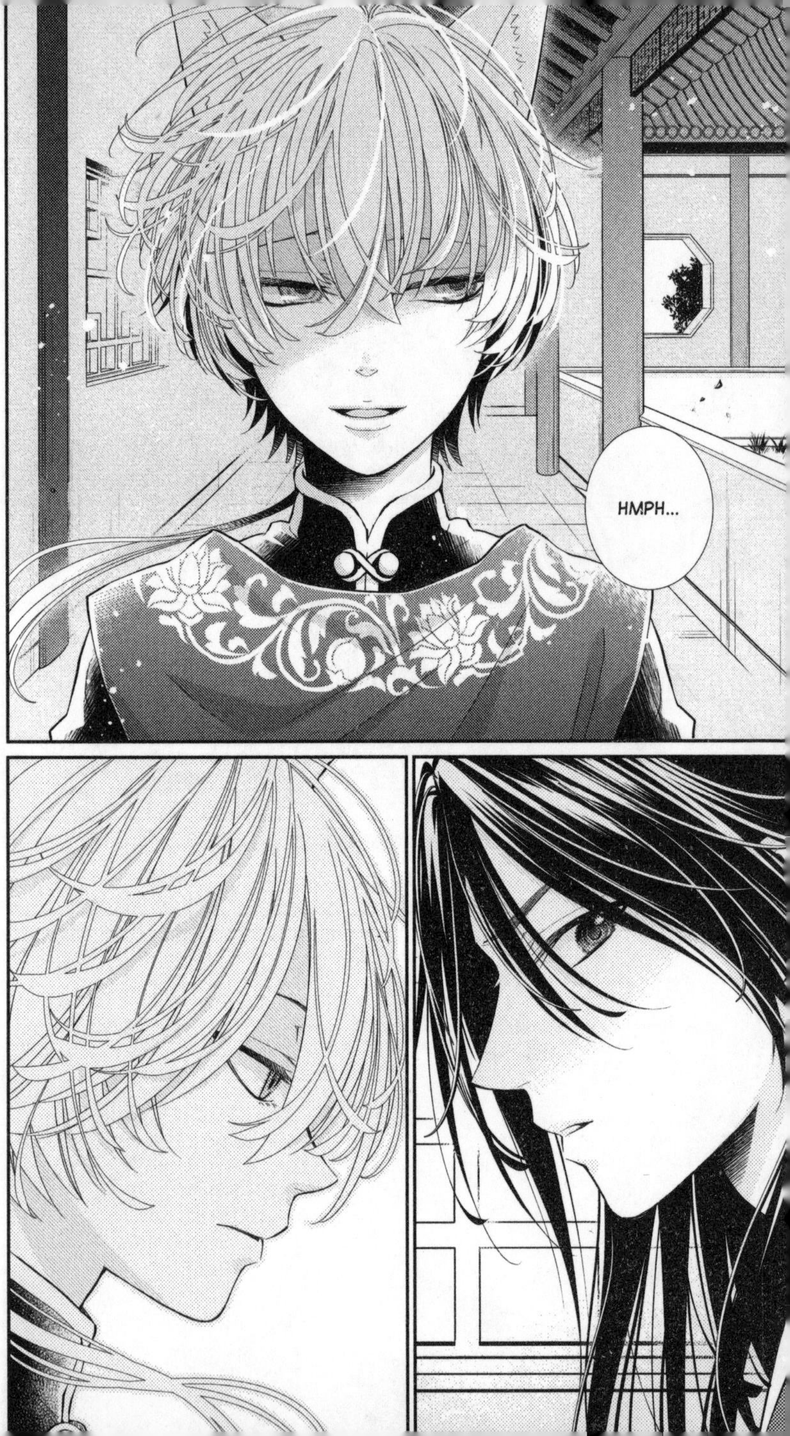
HMPH...

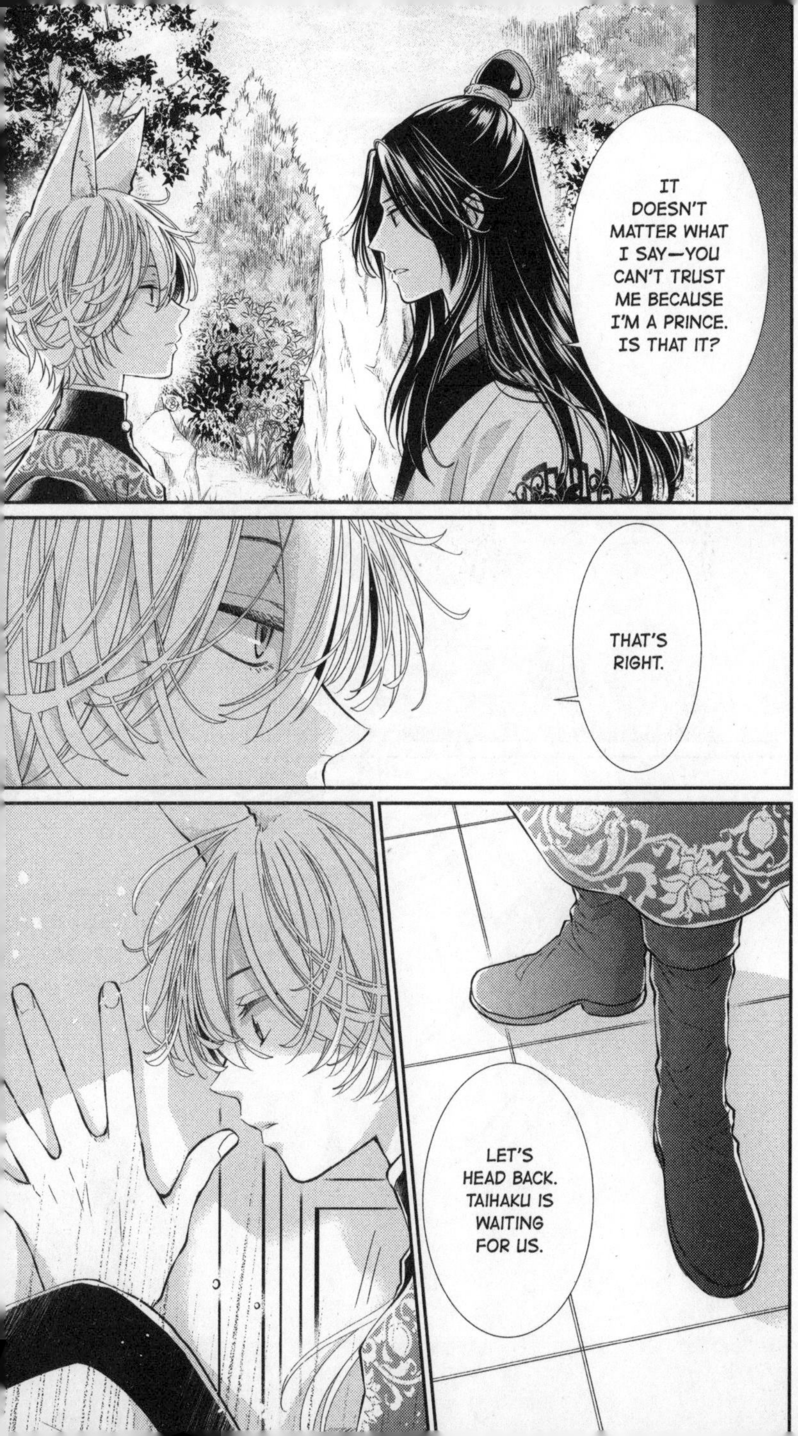
IT DOESN'T MATTER WHAT I SAY—YOU CAN'T TRUST ME BECAUSE I'M A PRINCE. IS THAT IT?
THAT'S RIGHT.
LET'S HEAD BACK. TAIHAKU IS WAITING FOR US.

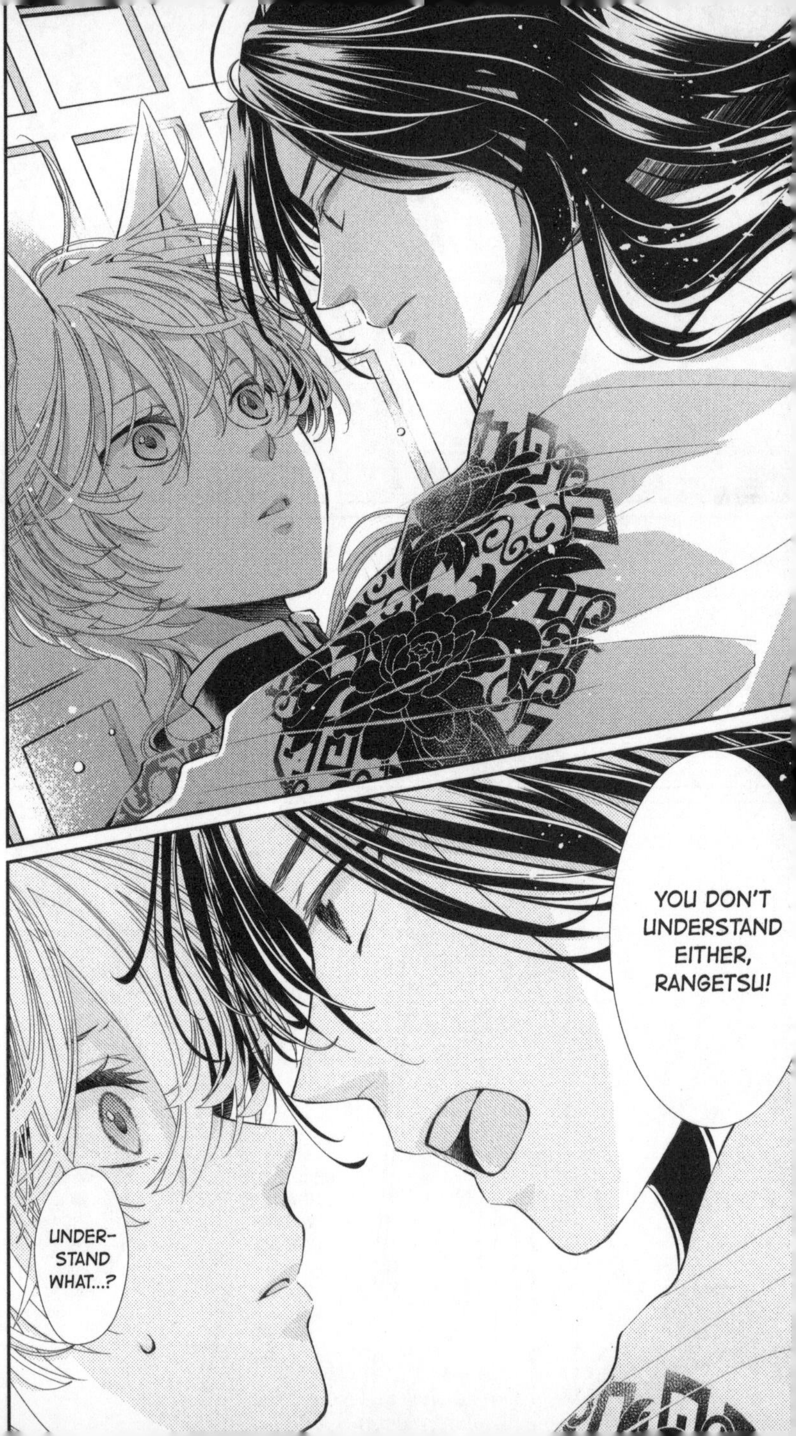
YOU DON'T UNDERSTAND EITHER, RANGETSU!
UNDER-STAND WHAT...?

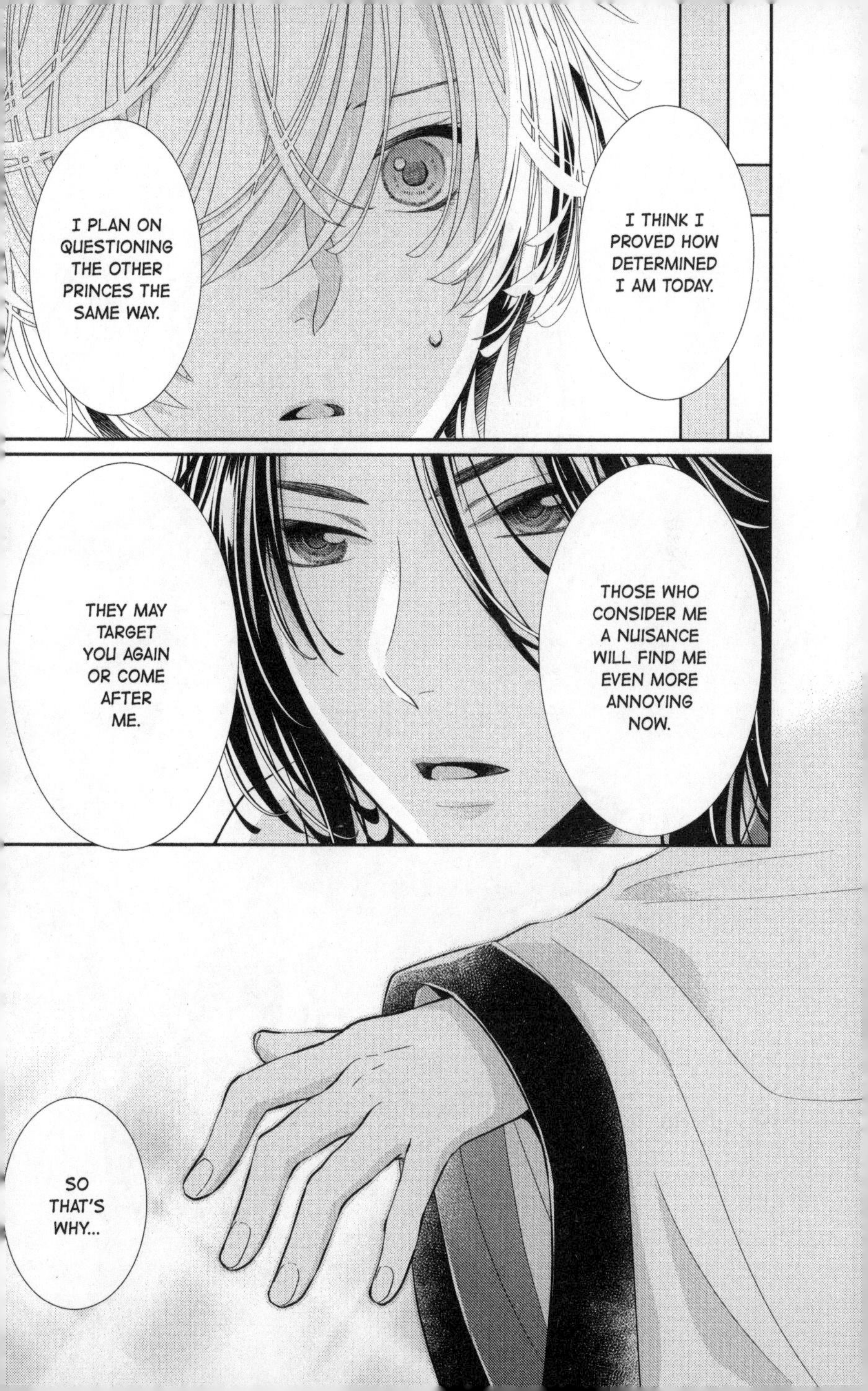
I THINK I PROVED HOW DETERMINED I AM TODAY.
I PLAN ON QUESTIONING THE OTHER PRINCES THE SAME WAY.
THOSE WHO CONSIDER ME A NUISANCE WILL FIND ME EVEN MORE ANNOYING NOW.
THEY MAY TARGET YOU AGAIN OR COME AFTER ME.
SO THAT'S WHY...

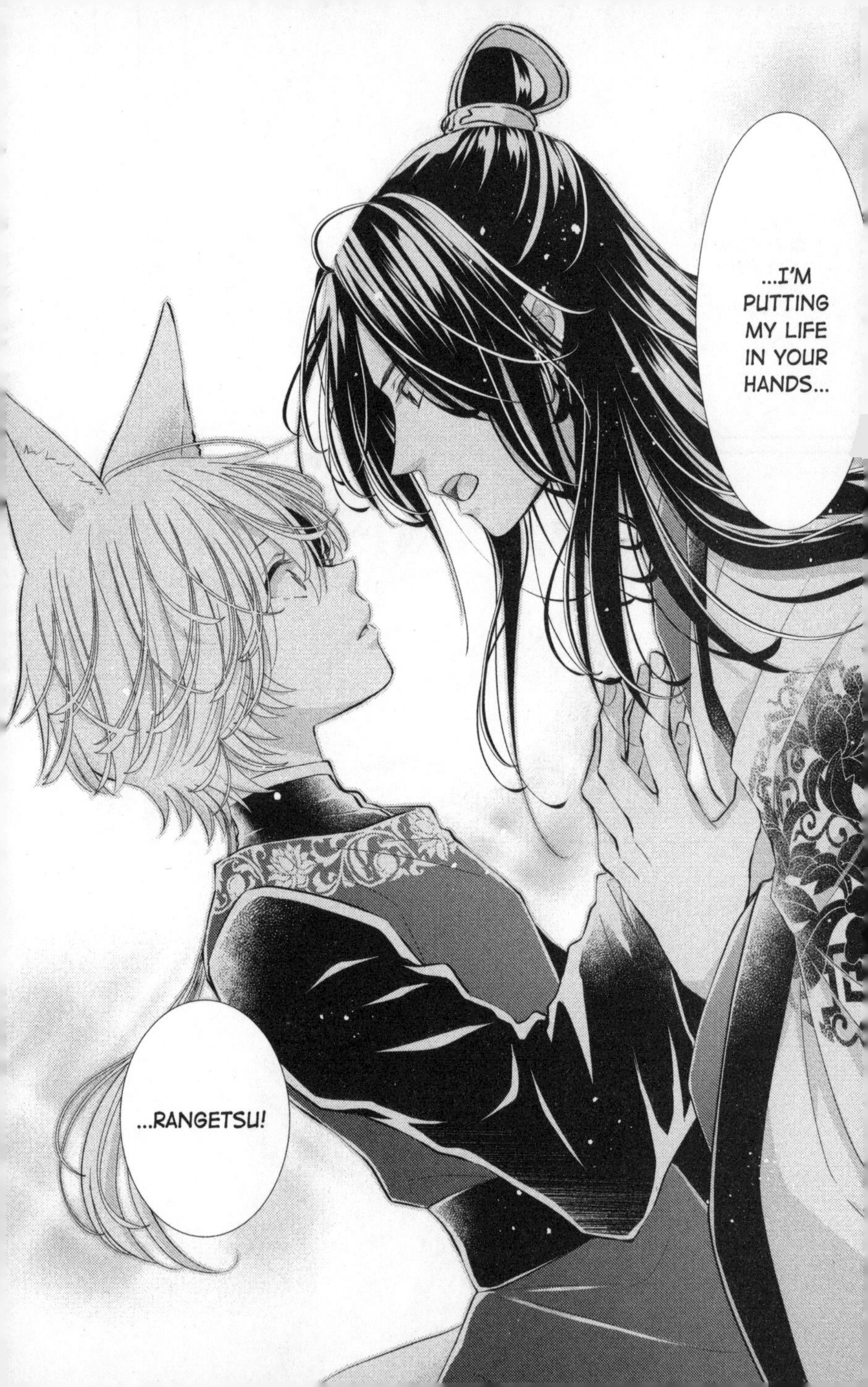
...I'M PUTTING MY LIFE IN YOUR HANDS...
...RANGETSU!

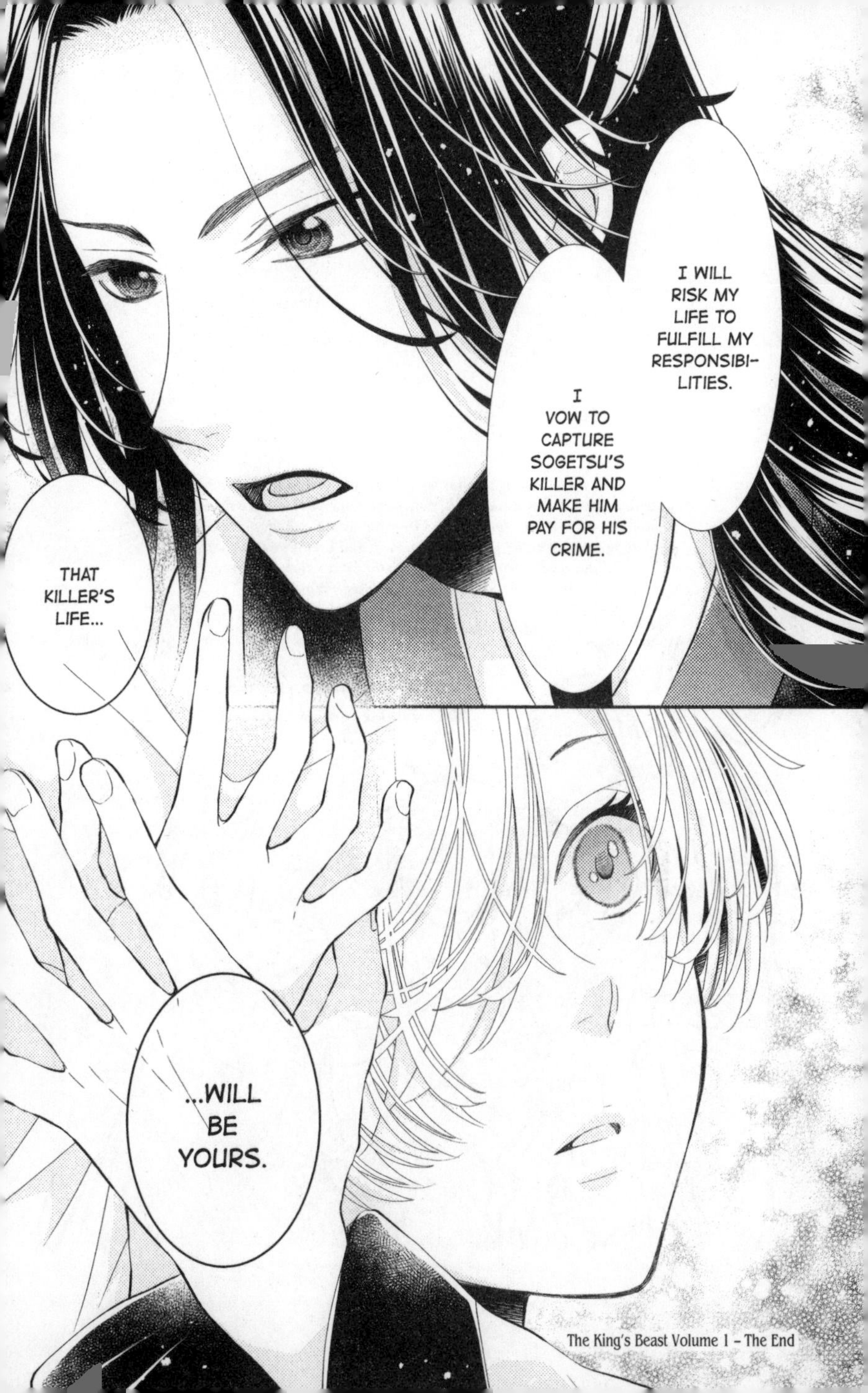
I WILL RISK MY LIFE TO FULFILL MY RESPONSIBI-LITIES.
I VOW TO CAPTURE SOGETSU'S KILLER AND MAKE HIM PAY FOR HIS CRIME.
THAT KILLER'S LIFE...
...WILL BE YOURS.
The King's Beast Volume 1 – The End

I wrote a special bonus chapter for *The Water Dragon's Bride*, which has already concluded. Although some people have asked me to continue the story, for the time being this ending will stand. I've recently started a Twitter account, and I sometimes upload doodles and illustrations of *The Water Dragon's Bride* there, so if you get a chance, please check it out. 😊

https://twitter.com/reitoma777

### The Water Dragon's Bride
All 11 volumes are on sale now!

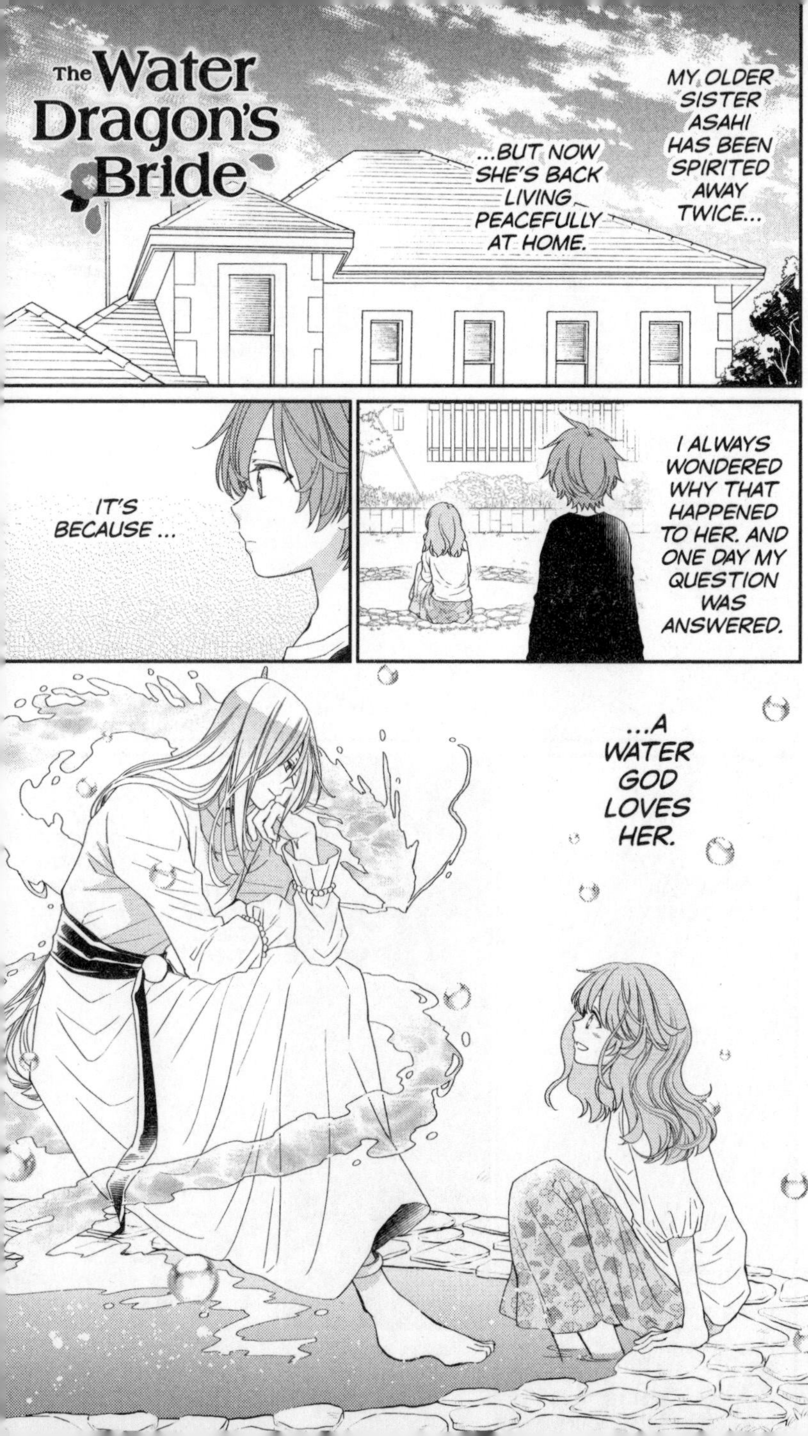
The Water Dragon's Bride
MY OLDER SISTER ASAHI HAS BEEN SPIRITED AWAY TWICE...
...BUT NOW SHE'S BACK LIVING PEACEFULLY AT HOME.
I ALWAYS WONDERED WHY THAT HAPPENED TO HER. AND ONE DAY MY QUESTION WAS ANSWERED.
IT'S BECAUSE ...
...A WATER GOD LOVES HER.

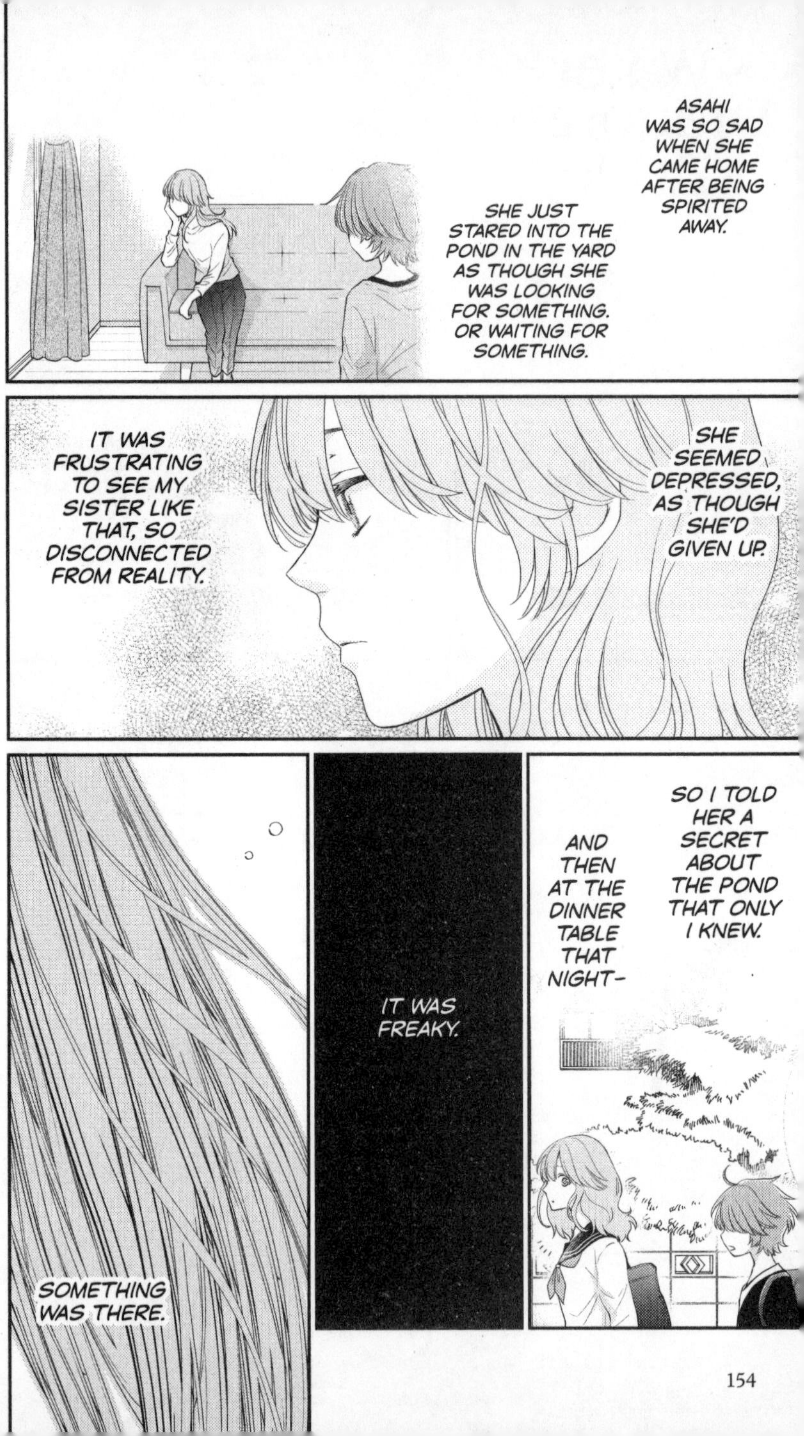
ASAHI WAS SO SAD WHEN SHE CAME HOME AFTER BEING SPIRITED AWAY.
SHE JUST STARED INTO THE POND IN THE YARD AS THOUGH SHE WAS LOOKING FOR SOMETHING. OR WAITING FOR SOMETHING.
SHE SEEMED DEPRESSED, AS THOUGH SHE'D GIVEN UP.
IT WAS FRUSTRATING TO SEE MY SISTER LIKE THAT, SO DISCONNECTED FROM REALITY.
SO I TOLD HER A SECRET ABOUT THE POND THAT ONLY I KNEW.
AND THEN AT THE DINNER TABLE THAT NIGHT-
IT WAS FREAKY.
SOMETHING WAS THERE.

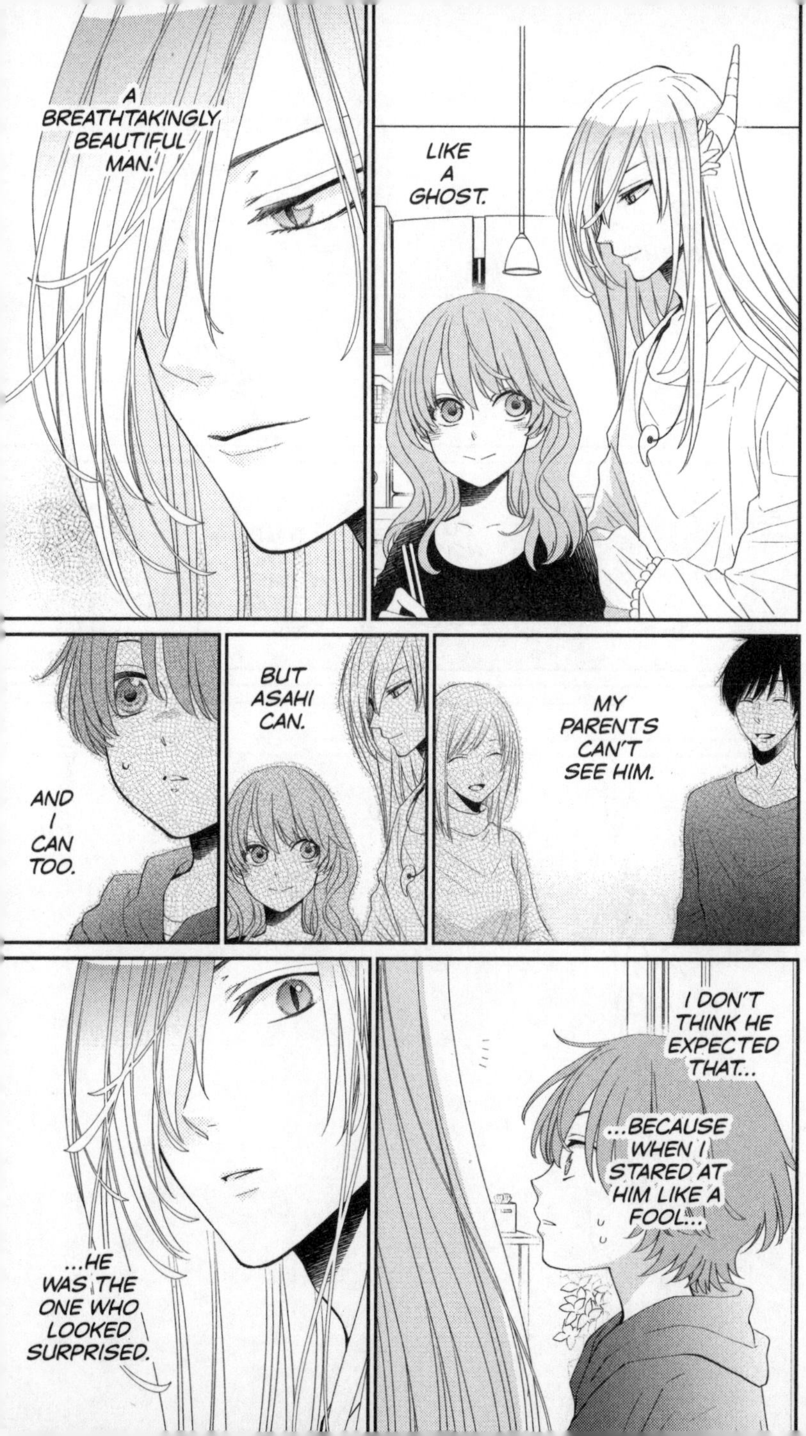
LIKE A GHOST.
A BREATHTAKINGLY BEAUTIFUL MAN.
MY PARENTS CAN'T SEE HIM.
BUT ASAHI CAN.
AND I CAN TOO.
I DON'T THINK HE EXPECTED THAT...
...BECAUSE WHEN I STARED AT HIM LIKE A FOOL...
...HE WAS THE ONE WHO LOOKED SURPRISED.

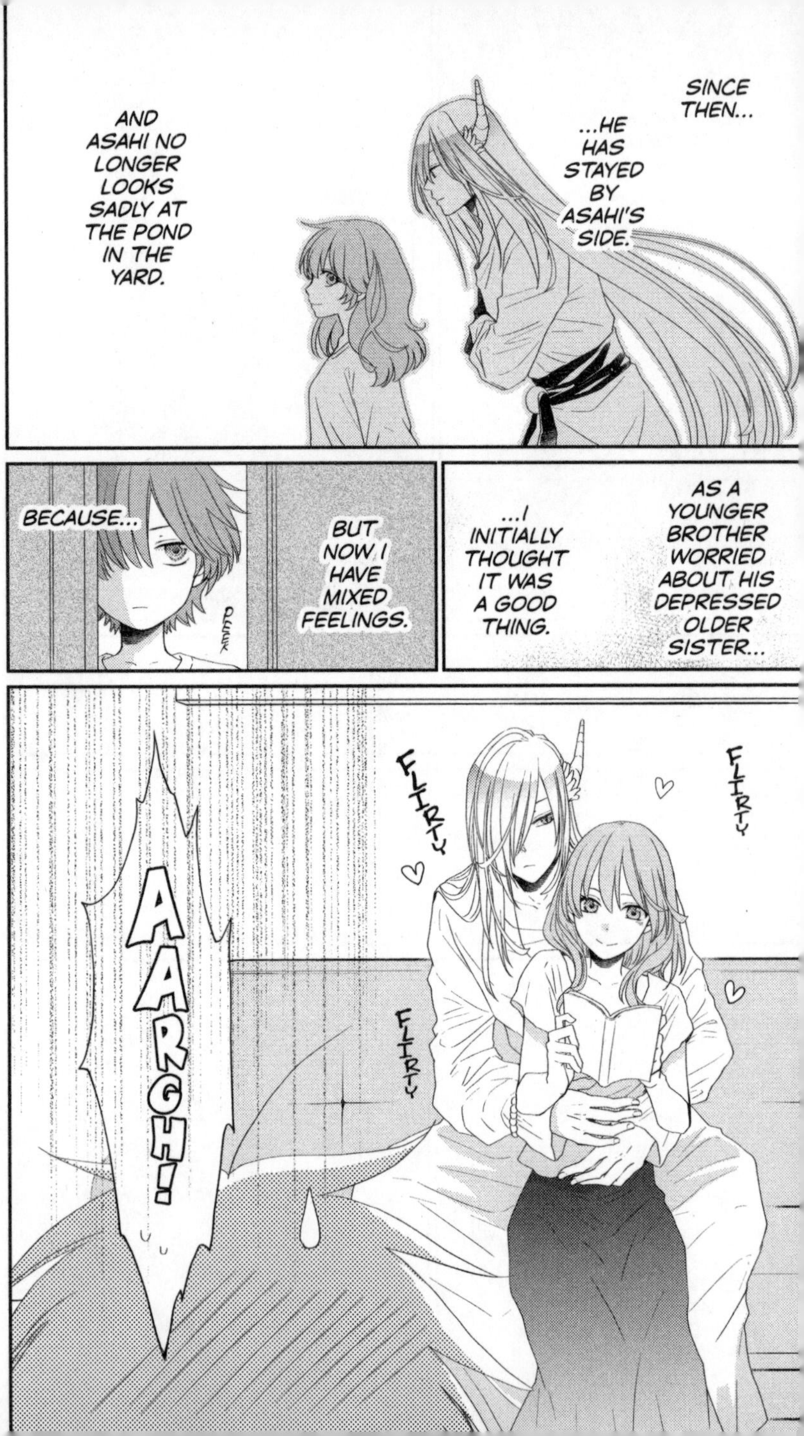
SINCE THEN...
...HE HAS STAYED BY ASAHI'S SIDE.
AND ASAHI NO LONGER LOOKS SADLY AT THE POND IN THE YARD.
AS A YOUNGER BROTHER WORRIED ABOUT HIS DEPRESSED OLDER SISTER...
...I INITIALLY THOUGHT IT WAS A GOOD THING.
BUT NOW I HAVE MIXED FEELINGS.
BECAUSE...
PEEK
FLIRTY
FLIRTY
FLIRTY
AAARGH!

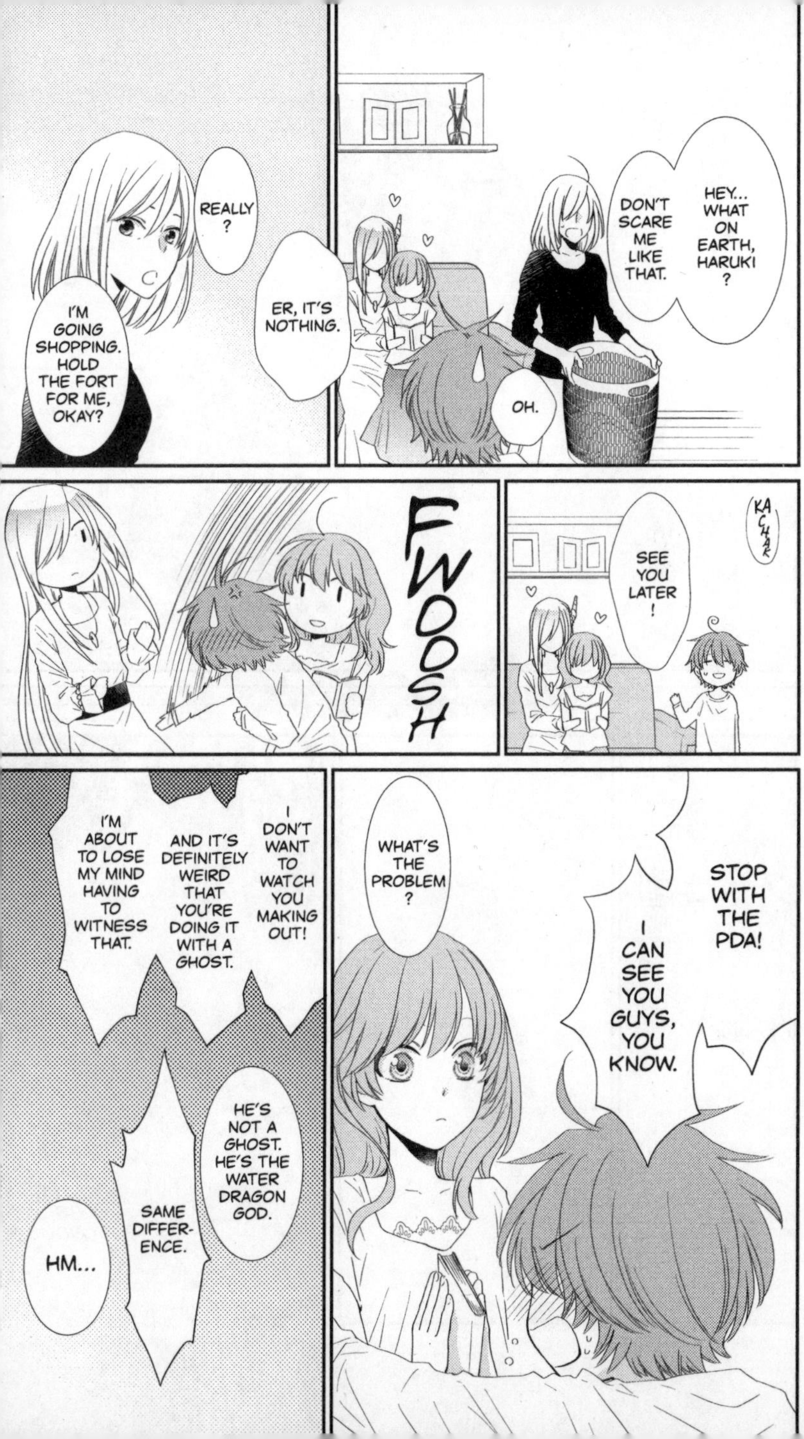
HEY... WHAT ON EARTH, HARUKI?
DON'T SCARE ME LIKE THAT.
OH.
ER, IT'S NOTHING.
REALLY?
I'M GOING SHOPPING. HOLD THE FORT FOR ME, OKAY?
KACHAK
SEE YOU LATER!
FWOOSH
STOP WITH THE PDA!
I CAN SEE YOU GUYS, YOU KNOW.
WHAT'S THE PROBLEM?
I DON'T WANT TO WATCH YOU MAKING OUT!
AND IT'S DEFINITELY WEIRD THAT YOU'RE DOING IT WITH A GHOST.
I'M ABOUT TO LOSE MY MIND HAVING TO WITNESS THAT.
HE'S NOT A GHOST. HE'S THE WATER DRAGON GOD.
SAME DIFFERENCE.
HM...

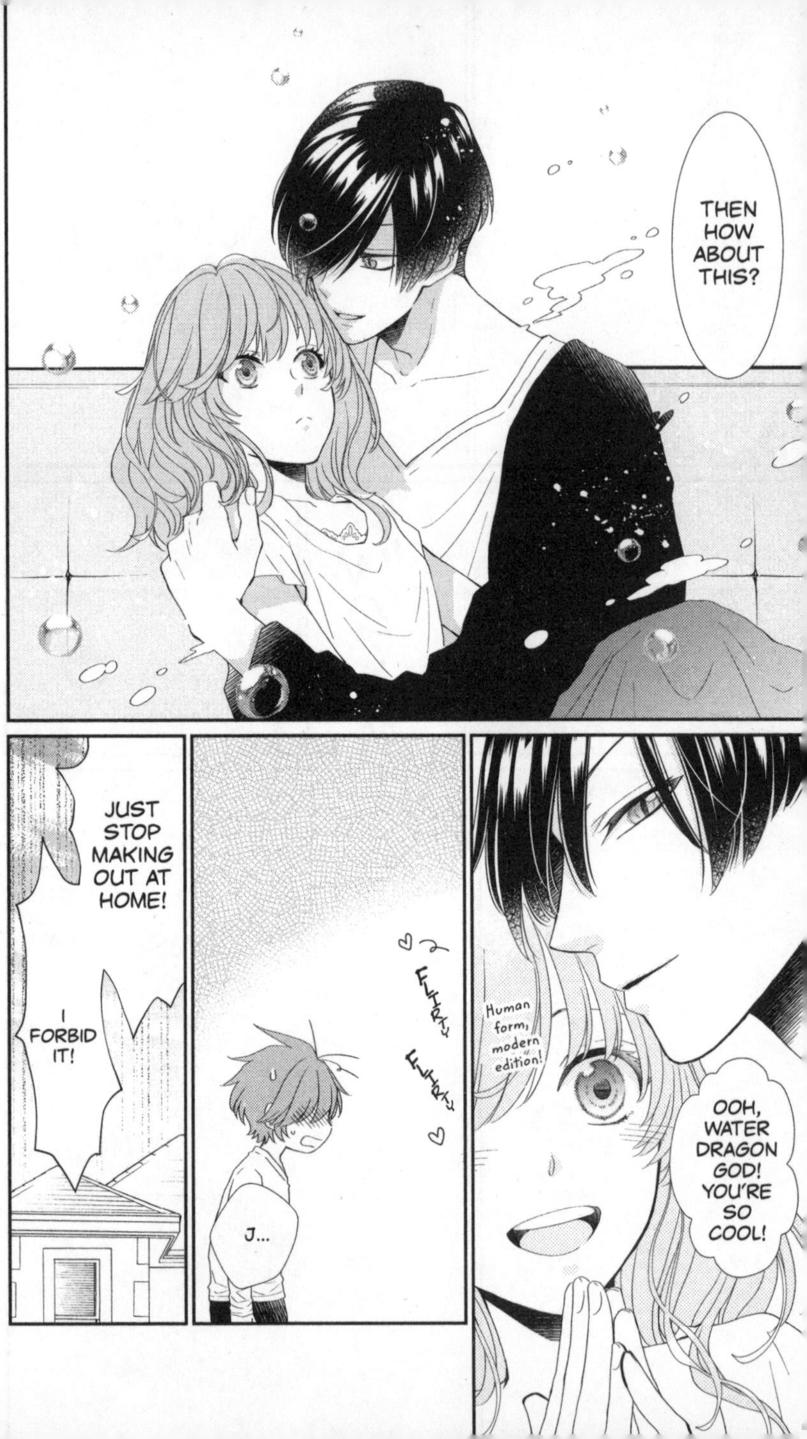
THEN HOW ABOUT THIS?
OOH, WATER DRAGON GOD! YOU'RE SO COOL!
Human form, modern edition!
FLIRT
FLIRT
J...
JUST STOP MAKING OUT AT HOME!
I FORBID IT!

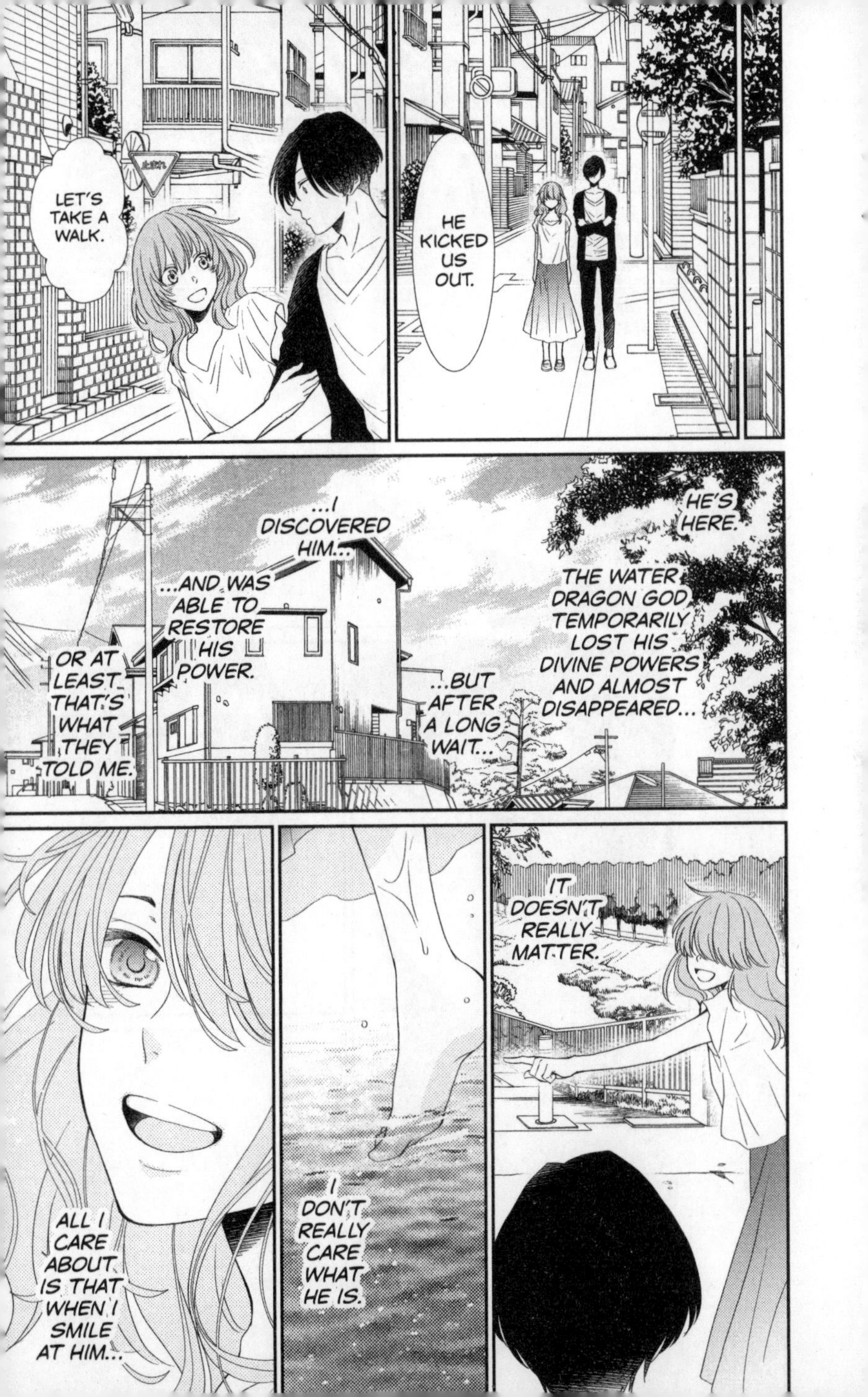
HE KICKED US OUT.
LET'S TAKE A WALK.
HE'S HERE.
THE WATER DRAGON GOD TEMPORARILY LOST HIS DIVINE POWERS AND ALMOST DISAPPEARED...
...BUT AFTER A LONG WAIT...
...I DISCOVERED HIM...
...AND WAS ABLE TO RESTORE HIS POWER.
OR AT LEAST THAT'S WHAT THEY TOLD ME.
IT DOESN'T REALLY MATTER.
I DON'T REALLY CARE WHAT HE IS.
ALL I CARE ABOUT IS THAT WHEN I SMILE AT HIM...

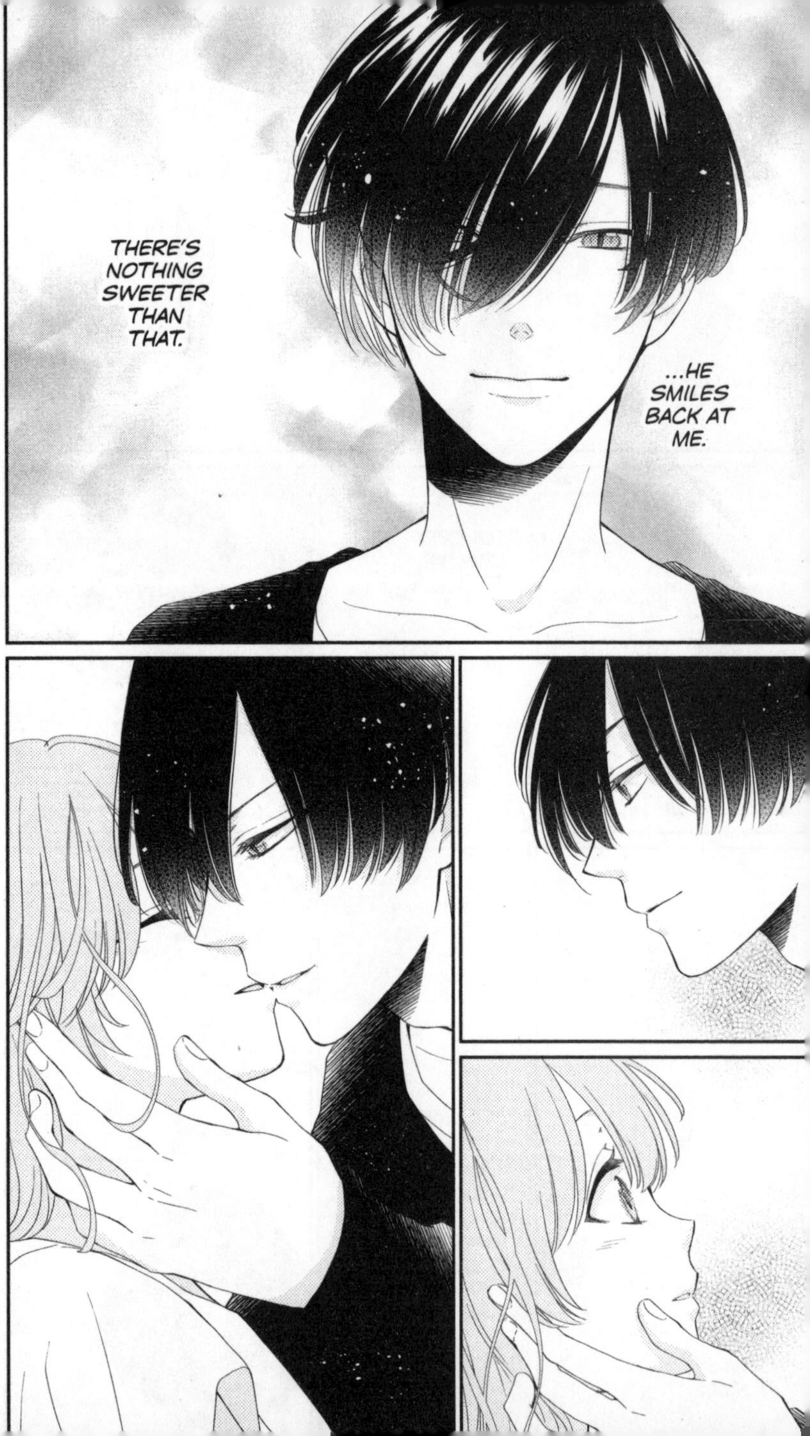
...HE SMILES BACK AT ME.
THERE'S NOTHING SWEETER THAN THAT.

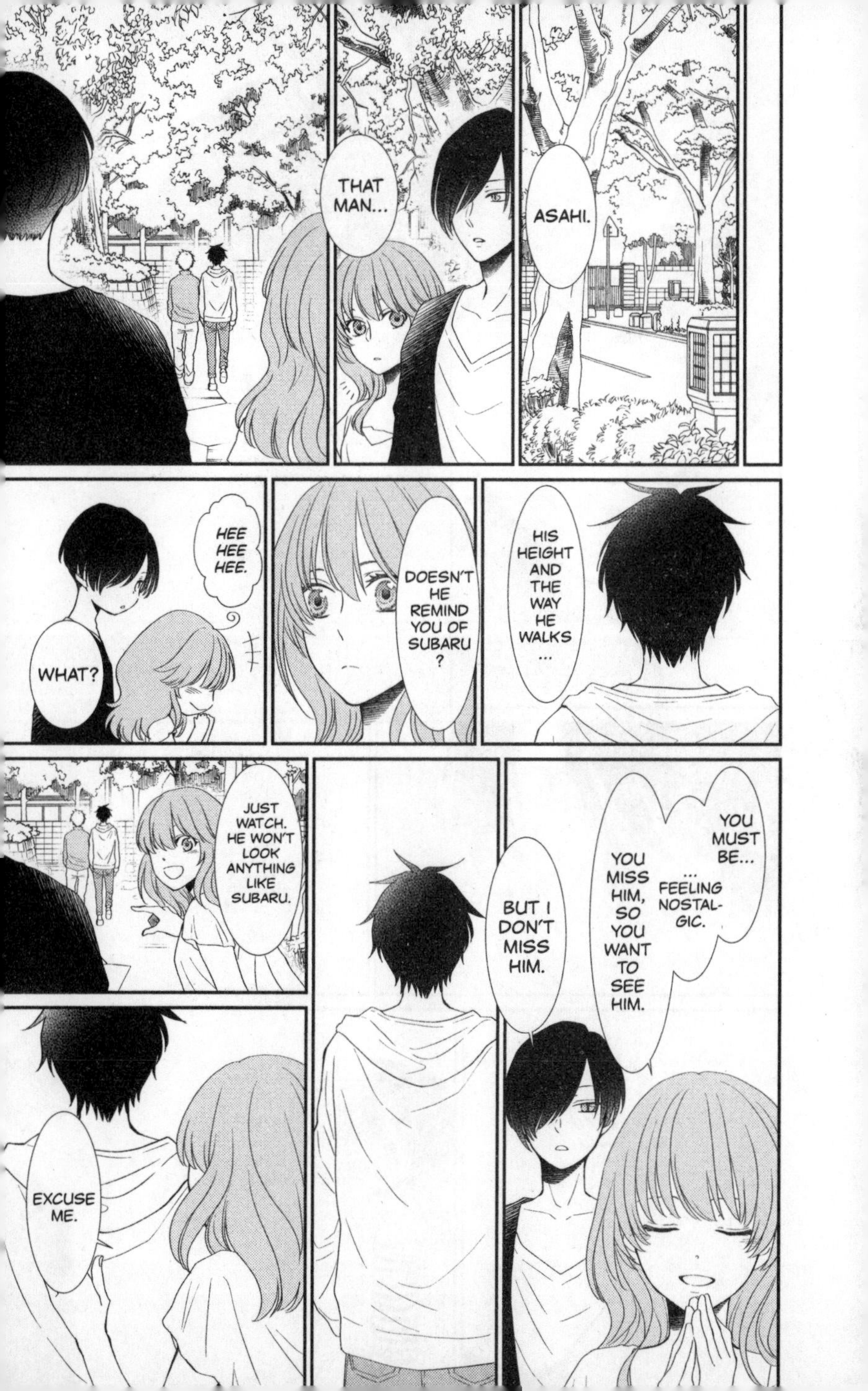
ASAHI.
THAT MAN...
HIS HEIGHT AND THE WAY HE WALKS ...
DOESN'T HE REMIND YOU OF SUBARU?
HEE HEE HEE.
WHAT?
YOU MUST BE... ...FEELING NOSTALGIC.
YOU MISS HIM, SO YOU WANT TO SEE HIM.
BUT I DON'T MISS HIM.
JUST WATCH. HE WON'T LOOK ANYTHING LIKE SUBARU.
EXCUSE ME.

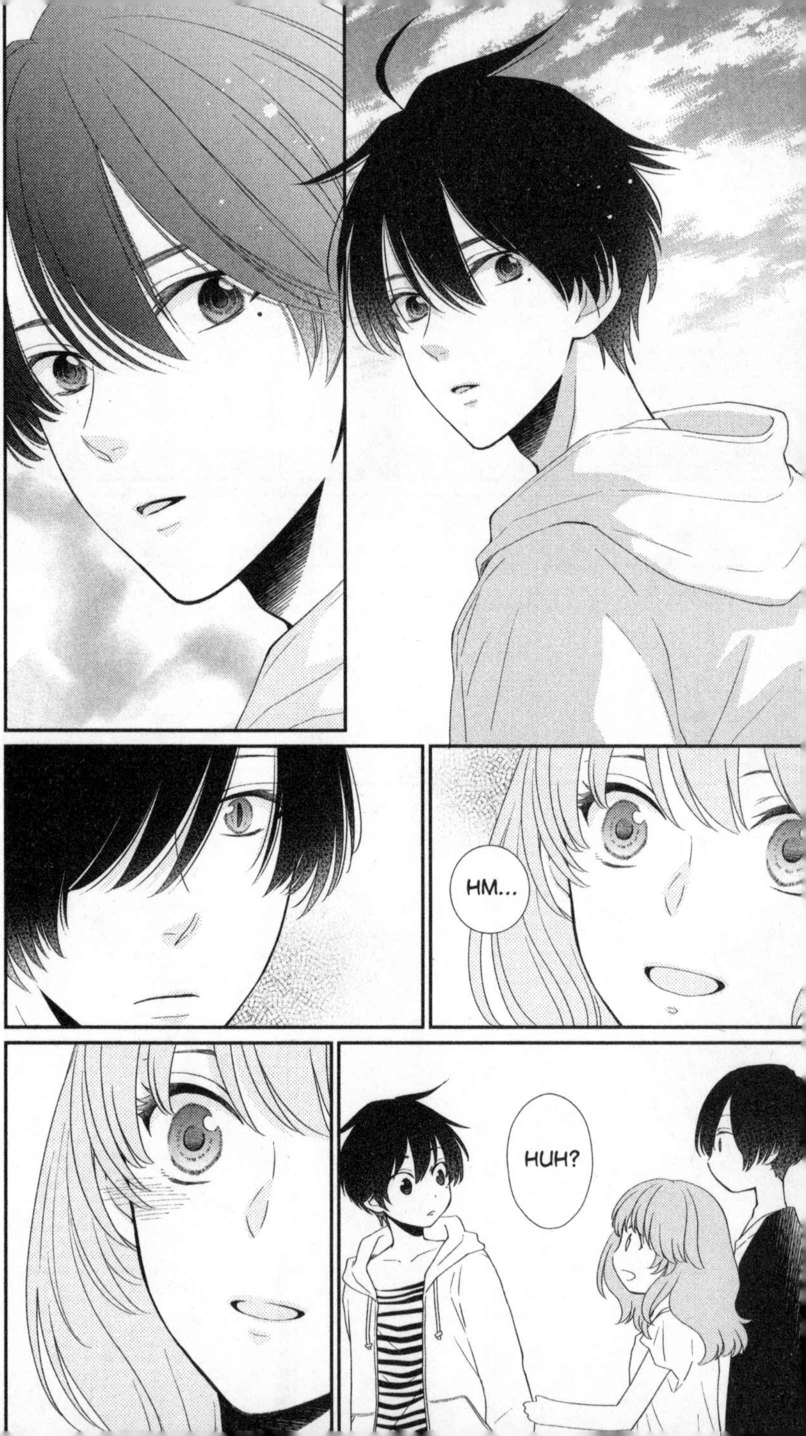
HM...
HUH?

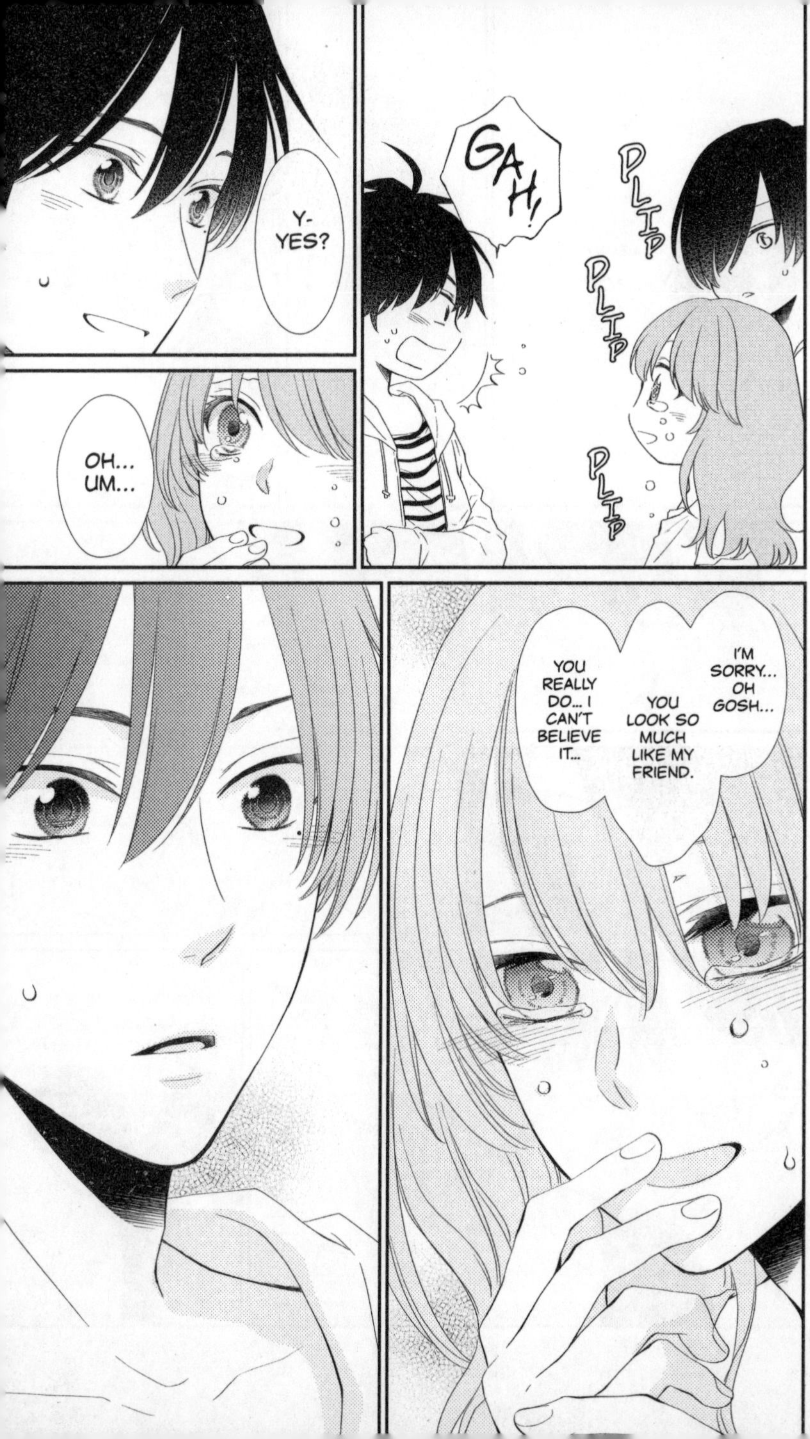
GAH!
PLIP
PLIP
PLIP
Y-YES?
OH... UM...
I'M SORRY... OH GOSH...
YOU LOOK SO MUCH LIKE MY FRIEND.
YOU REALLY DO... I CAN'T BELIEVE IT...

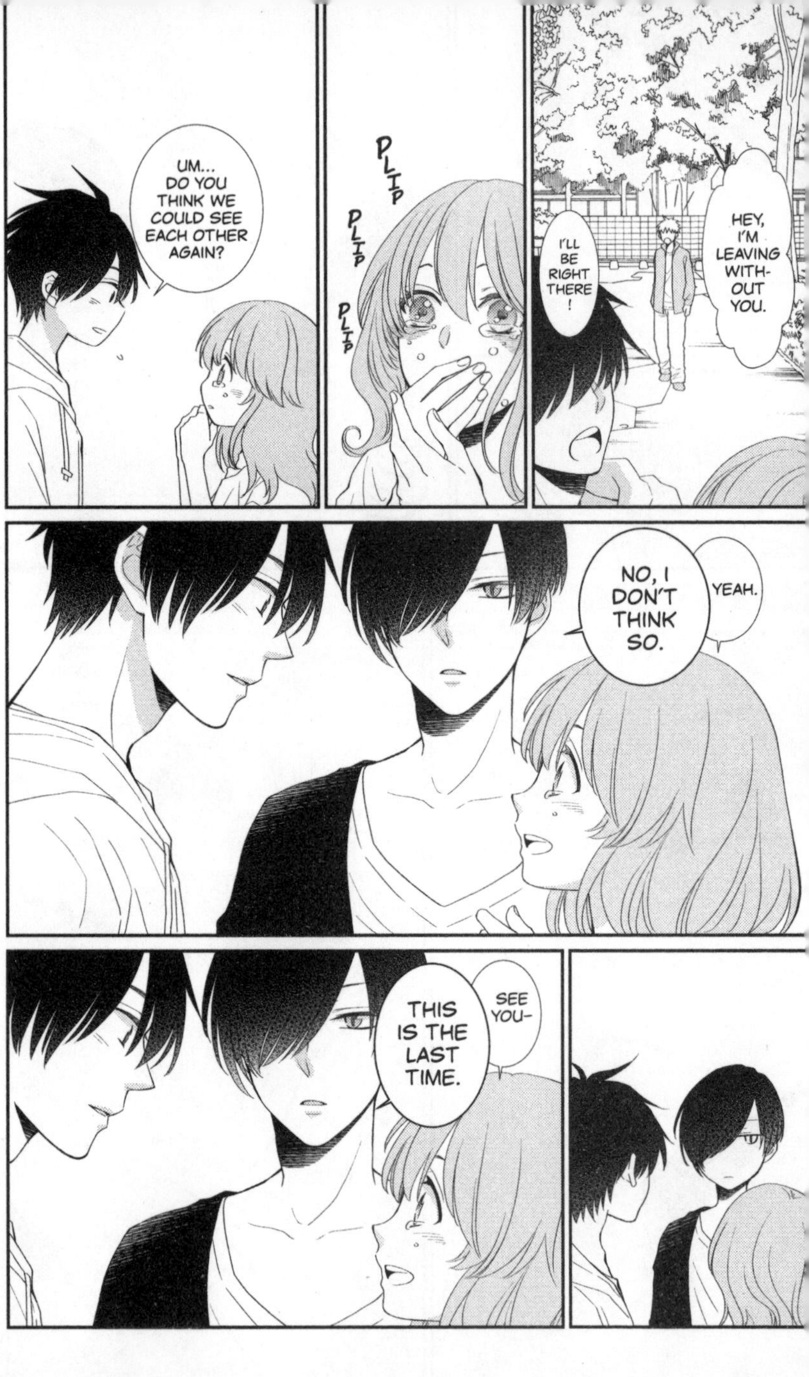
HEY, I'M LEAVING WITH-OUT YOU.
I'LL BE RIGHT THERE!
PLIP
PLIP
PLIP
UM... DO YOU THINK WE COULD SEE EACH OTHER AGAIN?
YEAH.
NO, I DON'T THINK SO.
SEE YOU-
THIS IS THE LAST TIME.

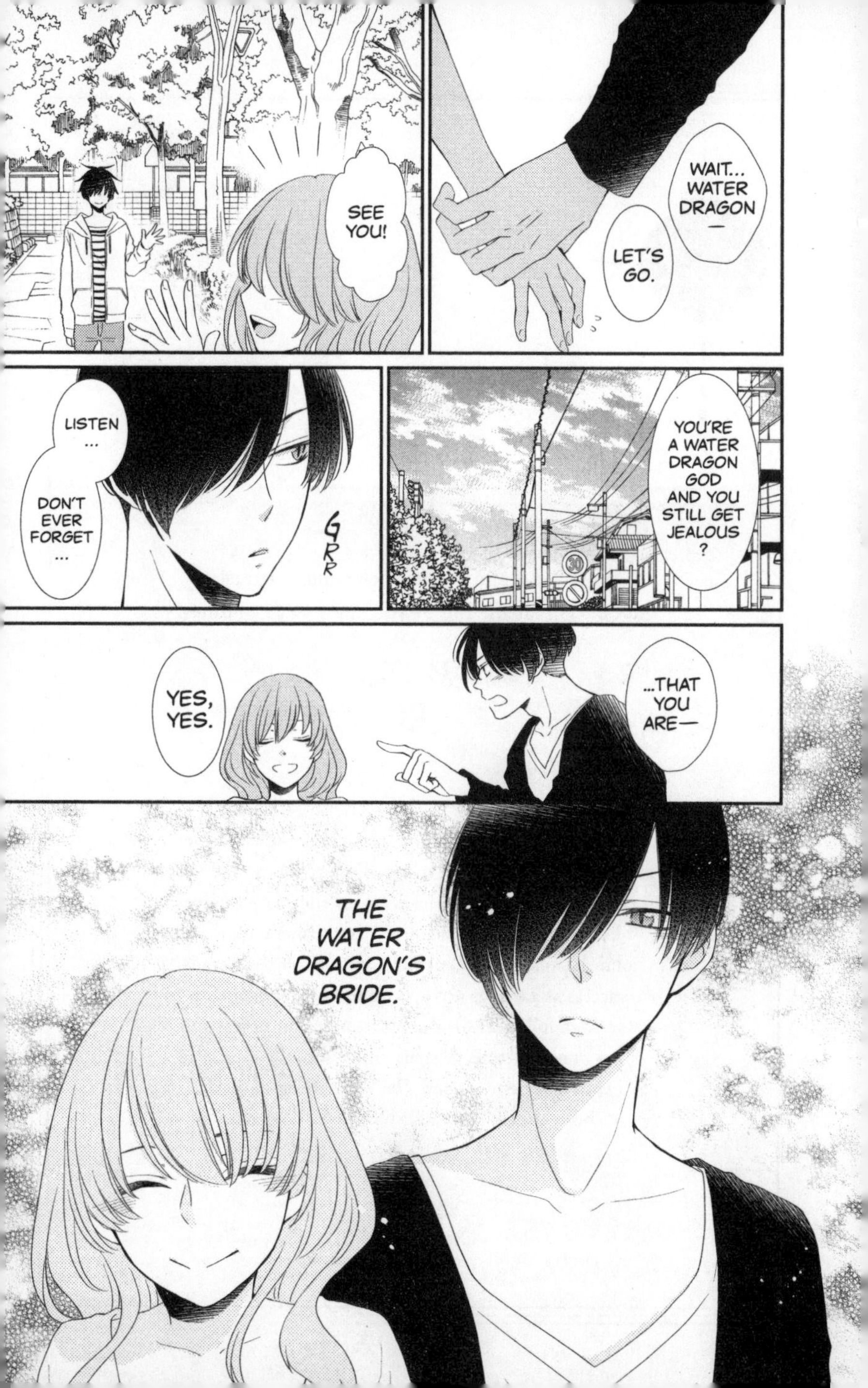
WAIT... WATER DRAGON—
LET'S GO.
SEE YOU!
YOU'RE A WATER DRAGON GOD AND YOU STILL GET JEALOUS?
LISTEN...
DON'T EVER FORGET...
GRR
...THAT YOU ARE—
YES, YES.
THE WATER DRAGON'S BRIDE.

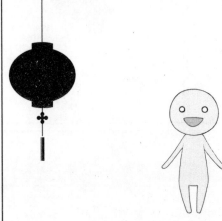

Volumes 1 and 2 have been simultaneously released in Japan. I hope you enjoy both volumes.

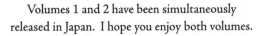

Rei Toma has been drawing since childhood, and she created her first complete manga for a graduation project in design school. When she drew the short story manga "Help Me, Dentist," it attracted a publisher's attention and she made her debut right away. After she found success as a manga artist, acclaim in other art fields started to follow as she did illustrations for novels and video game character designs. She is also the creator of *Dawn of the Arcana* and *The Water Dragon's Bride*, both available in English from VIZ Media.

# THE KING'S Beast

1

SHOJO BEAT EDITION

STORY AND ART BY **Rei Toma**

ENGLISH TRANSLATION & ADAPTATION **JN Productions**
TOUCH-UP ART & LETTERING **Monaliza De Asis**
DESIGN **Joy Zhang**
EDITOR **Pancha Diaz**

OU NO KEMONO Vol. 1
by Rei TOMA
© 2019 Rei TOMA
All rights reserved.
Original Japanese edition published by SHOGAKUKAN.
English translation rights in the United States of America,
Canada, the United Kingdom, Ireland, Australia and New
Zealand arranged with SHOGAKUKAN.

Original Cover Design: Hibiki CHIKADA (fireworks. vc)

Printed in Italy

Published by VIZ Media, LLC
P.O. Box 77010
San Francisco, CA 94107

10 9 8 7 6 5 4 3 2
First printing, February 2021
Second printing, June 2021

**VIZ** MEDIA
viz.com

**Shojo Beat**
shojobeat.com

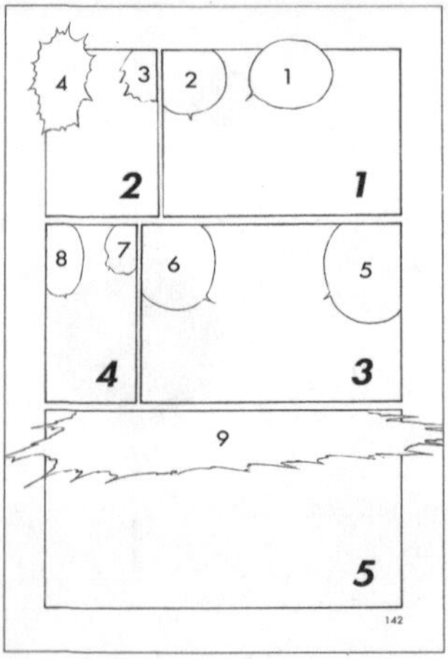

# THIS IS THE LAST PAGE.

**THE KING'S BEAST** has been printed in the original Japanese format to preserve the orientation of the artwork.

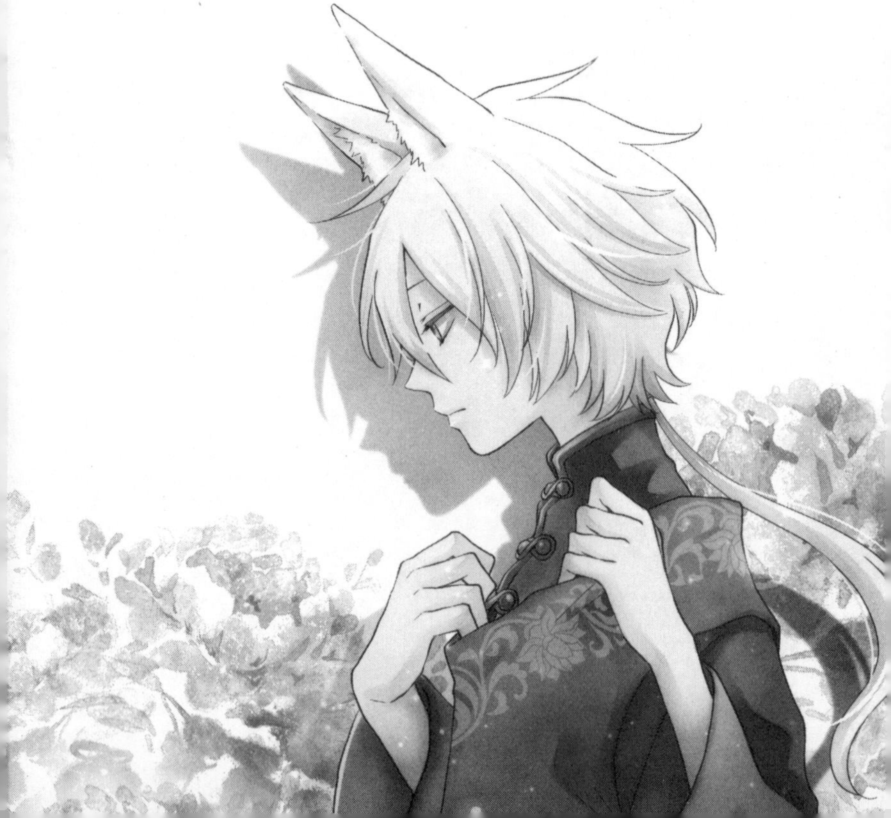